2 <u>48</u>

The Rest of Your Life

The Rest of Your Life

LEO CHERNE

Executive Secretary
THE RESEARCH INSTITUTE OF AMERICA

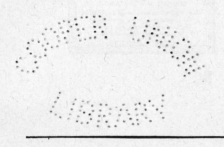

DOUBLEDAY, DORAN AND COMPANY, INC.

Garden City   1944   New York

THIS BOOK IS
STANDARD LENGTH.
COMPLETE AND UNABRIDGED,
MANUFACTURED UNDER WARTIME CONDITIONS
IN CONFORMITY WITH ALL GOVERNMENT
REGULATIONS CONTROLLING THE USE
OF PAPER AND OTHER MATERIALS

TO

Gail

with the deep hope
that the rest of her life will be linked
to the possibilities, not chained
to the probabilities.

Acknowledgments

THE AUTHOR wishes to thank the following authors, magazines, and publishers for their permission to use the material indicated:

The American Press—for the article "Thirty-Seven Reasons Why Country Publishers Like 'Big Business.'"

Columbia Broadcasting System, Inc.—for a quotation from a broadcast by Edward R. Murrow, December 3, 1943.

Fortune—for quotations from several issues.

Miss Amy Greif—for her poem on the postwar world, reprinted from *The Saturday Evening Post*.

Harper's Magazine—for a selection from "What Business Thinks About Postwar America," by C. Hartley Grattan.

Henry Holt and Company, Inc.—for a selection from *Here Is Your War*, by Ernie Pyle, copyright, 1943, by Henry Holt and Company, Inc.

Alfred A. Knopf, Inc.—for a selection from "Youth," from *The Dream Keeper*, by Langston Hughes, copyright, 1932, by Alfred A. Knopf, Inc.

The Macmillan Company—for a quotation from "The Second Coming," from *Collected Poems* of William Butler Yeats.

National Bureau of Economic Research, Inc.—for a quotation from *Wartime "Prosperity" and the Future*, by Wesley C. Mitchell.

W. W. Norton & Company, Inc.—for several quotations from *Beyond Clinical Frontiers*, by Edward Adam Strecker.

The Saturday Review of Literature—for a quotation from an article by David L. Cohn.

Charles Scribner's Sons—for a quotation from *The Man Inside*, by Victor Francis Calverton.

The Viking Press, Inc.—for a quotation from *The Unfinished Task*, copyright, 1942, by Lewis Corey.

Yank—for a quotation.

Preface

We have tomorrow
Bright before us
Like a flame.
Yesterday
A night-gone thing,
A sun-down name.
And dawn-today
Broad arch above
    the road we
    came.
    From "Youth" by
      LANGSTON HUGHES

Mere anarchy is loosened
  upon the world,
The blood-dimmed tide
  is loosed, and everywhere
The ceremony of innocence
  is drowned;
The best lack all conviction,
  while the worst
Are full of passionate
  intensity.
    WILLIAM BUTLER YEATS

THE REST OF YOUR LIFE was shaped yesterday and the day before that. Many of the most fundamental social, economic, and political changes have already taken place—changes in your community, your government, your way of earning a living, your thinking and acting. And of those that are still to come, many are already visible. Maybe you're not aware of them. But if that's so, perhaps it's your fault; don't consider it evidence that things are the same as they were last week. Change is constant, even in the most quiet times. And it is constantly resisted and denied. Like heaven, the "good old days" are devoutly sought by many and achieved by few.

In quiet times the future is shaped so calmly and so slowly that it takes a social seismograph to detect the tremors subtly shifting the ground under your feet. But in periods of explosion the white heat of change is rivaled only by the intensity with which we try to deny it.

No power operates more forcefully or more feverishly for sudden change than war. Out of every major war on this planet have come new ways of living, but few wars will have been more productive of these alterations than World War II. Alterations in *your* life.

"The struggle in which we are engaged," says Wendell Willkie, "has imposed on all of us a number of extraordinary duties. One of the most important of these is a duty toward the future. The nature of the victory that we gain depends greatly on our ability to look ahead clearly."

Of course there are risks involved in following the thread of change through the unrecorded months and years ahead. It would be foolish to assume that there are no unknown quantities in the scales. There are many alternatives ahead. There are many corners in shadow or in complete darkness. But they too will follow the contours of the die that was shaped yesterday.

There are many things about tomorrow that we can't foresee. But even these rest on facts which are already in existence. Take this example. We've already learned that technological improvement—the increased efficiency of our machines and skills—can assure us the same amount of goods we turned out in 1940 even if we were to use one fifth less labor than we used before the war.

This we know, but we don't know the effect of that fact: whether we will have 20 per cent more goods, whether we will all work eight hours less a week, or whether in addition to those unemployed in 1940 one out of every five of us will be out of a job. These are the alternatives ahead, and they all rest on the foundation stone of the present—the technological progress we've achieved in the war.

But that's not the whole story. We are not left baffled before this three-forked road. There are other forces—social and political—which already point to one of the three choices. We can begin to weigh the pressures in operation which will push us in the direction of unemployment.

One of the hazards involved in prognosis—the handicap the would-be prophet always faces—is the conflict between desire and expectation. You will find little here beyond what the author anticipates. The hardships that he sees ahead are not conditions he would like to see. In fact, his own future satisfaction will be all the greater if he has erred on the blacker side.

Precisely because this book involves no advocacy, it makes no attempt to suggest solutions for the problems that peace will bring. Which of the alternatives will be followed is for you to decide. But the probabilities have value because they show the alternative choices that are yet to be made. In the United States, at least, those choices can still be made by democratic decision. To that extent substantial portions of the rest of your life will be shaped by you. At the same time you might just as well recognize that the decisions you will make are partly the result of the forces which have molded you. How you will act under the new pressures created by the war itself is subject to prediction. That's why it's possible—along broad lines in most cases, in specific detail in others—to indicate how you are likely to determine your life, and live.

This exploration of the future has been an awesome and exciting undertaking. It is not accidental, of course, that the writer's preoccupation with the days ahead flows so naturally from the work of the organization with which he is associated—the Research Institute of America. Without the ship, charts, and compass provided by RIA the exploratory voyage could not have been undertaken. For patient and painstaking research Aaron Levenstein and Eli Cantor deserve much thanks. For their criticism and help Dr. Salomon Flink, Mae Churchill, Beatrice Feldman, Charles Siegel, Leo Barnes, Alberta Saletan, Harold Wurzel, and Florence Duffy have fully earned this meager acknowledgment. Nor can I assess the endless discussion and debates with Carl Hovgard, Leon Henderson, and William J. Casey. To all of them—a toast to the future!

Contents

Contents

IV

Your Life Tomorrow

I

War's End

CHAPTER I

Inventory—Armistice Day

IT'S ONE THING to come home after a generation of neglect, wind, and weather has sapped the vitality from the beams, the roof, and the porch. It's another to have lived through the rot and ruin. The folks on Tobacco Road in the off-road corners of Georgia aren't particularly sorry for themselves. They're not really aware of what happened to them. The decay swept over them gradually, like a tide imperceptibly rising.

War is like that. At least it is for those of you in America who will have lived through it. Its change and devastation, its imprint and effect are, in all but the most immediate aspects, as subtle as they are profound.

Suppose now that it's the day after Armistice. The world is new —brand new—and old as all hell.

Except for some physical differences, things will seem pretty much the same to the casual observer. Even the physical changes will have seeped into the consciousness of most people, so that the only thing that really looks different will be the photographs of yesterday—like looking at a picture of a girl who means a lot to you, in the hair style and dress she wore ten years ago.

To get the first glimpse of the rest of your life takes a sort of omniscience, a view from some towering pinnacle. To see it at all means being in many places and knowing many things and, most important of all, being able to compare it with what was before.

As for you personally, perhaps you have a job, when five years before you didn't. Perhaps you lost a son a year back and everything else dims into less meaningful distance.

3

On this first day after Armistice two keys to the future will already be available. The first and most important will be that the war will have solved no basic problems. As a matter of fact, it will have made a good many of them more complicated.

Most of the major domestic and international problems will still be sitting on your doorstep. The war itself will prove to have been merely an explosive expression of some of them. To expect otherwise is like expecting that pneumonia will have cured the physical debility that brought it on. You're lucky to be as well off after the siege is over. So, too, with the war. Look for this thread to run through most of the events which will develop days or years after war's end.

The second clue is one that has been staring us in the face for quite a while, but it's been difficult for us to see it up close. We can describe it as a growing gap between attitude and action. This gap is the difference between what we believe and what we do. And more often than not there's a real conflict between the two. We've just gone through a classic case. We wanted peace and made war. That goes for most Germans, too, or their Fuehrer wouldn't have had to promise peace quite so often or vigorously.

Then just before that we wanted jobs and shut the factories that made them. We wanted food, so we paid people not to grow any. Watch this gap between attitude and action. It's the second key which will open many doors into the future.

Here, roughly, is the way those two keys will work. The first one, the knowledge that we must look back to find the problems of the future, will enable us to locate many inevitable developments which we might otherwise miss. For example, take the new plastic and aluminum "teardrop" automobiles. The ads say they're coming. But why didn't we have them before the war? Because automotive designers and engineers didn't know how to make them? Or because they didn't think you'd want them? No. There were a number of other factors, which for some reason we call problems, that made them inadvisable. Well, unless we find that the war has somehow or other solved those problems or broken the barriers, what reason is there to expect the floating teardrop any sooner?

As a matter of fact, if you accept this first key, you will begin to be different yourself. You used to be one of that great group of men who every generation or so were shocked, hurt, and angered that the preceding war was not *the* last. It said it was. That was at least one of its purposes. It has always been. And you have always been surprised that it wasn't.

Now use that key of yours and you become one of the small band of people who are surprised at the rest of the people. You see no reason why this war should make the next one less probable. "History repeats itself," foolish men have said with seeming wisdom. Of course it does—unless something has been done about the combined elements which produced history the first time.

So the first key makes us face the future in the perverse position of Lot's wife. We must look backward, but it had better be with eyes completely open. It would be so easy to start out by assuming that nothing has changed and that the events ahead are carbon copies of those from which we have emerged. Actually, almost everything will have changed except the basic problems, the fundamental difficulties, frictions, and conflicts.

For example, you will still have to eat. Nothing in war, except death, will have altered that. But the quantity of food being produced will be different. So will its availability. It is the combination of these two components—the static need and the changed scene in which it must be satisfied—that will begin to shape the week end after next.

The first key, then, opens up many of the facts to you. But it doesn't always tell you what will happen when you throw them together. Nitric acid, sulphuric acid, glycerine—these three separately are real enough, but the explosive reality emerges suddenly when they're combined. Therein lies the value of the second key, the one that cautions us to look for conflict between attitude and action. That conflict is the chemistry which determines how the elements will behave. The rat in a maze hits his head against an unyielding trap door because he was led to believe he would find food. The conflict between what he believes and the fruitlessness of his action drives the rat mad. Nations too.

Here, looking out of your window, this day after Armistice,

there is nothing new that is visible. But if you strain your eyes, you may see those two million people who crossed the Rockies in America's latest great migration westward, the war boom of 1940–43, the thousands of new factories, mills, mines, shipyards, and warehouses that have expanded the nation's ability to produce by more than 30 per cent in less than four years. Maybe you will see the greatest miracle of all, that under the challenge of war we have raised our output to one and a half times what we made before.

Every economist worth his salt was sure in pre-Pearl Harbor days that if America were ever to turn out the material and munitions required by modern war, we would have to strip our civilian life down to the bone. All kinds of new phrases were invented to describe our expected state of deprivation: "Guns or Butter," "No Business As Usual," "Bedrock Economy." We were told it was a choice between war goods and civilian goods. But America's machines laughed at the tabulators and turned out both.

To be sure, it's been years since the new automobile, rather than "Greetings from the President," brought crowds into New York's Grand Central Palace. These have been years of no vacuum cleaners, furniture hard to find, all the consumer durables tougher and tougher to get. Yet America kept on turning out civilian goods and services at a greater rate than in the best peacetime year we have ever known. On top of all this we superimposed a whole new gigantic industrial nation called "war economy." After supplying our unprecedented and still unsatisfied demand for things to buy and enjoy, we turned out more war goods, more planes, tanks, shells, G.I. shoes and blouses, ships, and rocket guns than the total of civilian goods we had ever produced in any year.

No wonder the onetime boss of the nation's civilian supply, Leon Henderson, moaned that our real problem was not the high cost of living so much as the cost of high living. No wonder that Germany's economic boss in World War I found America in World War II "beyond belief."

Just cataloguing some of the physical changes gives a portion of the road map to tomorrow much clearer shape. Here you find that since 1939 we have increased our output of that miracle light metal, magnesium, one hundred times. Include the industrial labyrinths that synthesize man-made rubber—and turn out more than our total natural rubber consumption before the war. And add the four syphilitics, all of whose symptoms disappeared after an eight-day muscular injection of penicillin. They're additional assets we have gained. But don't forget the debits. The names of two million American boys also cry out to be listed—in red ink—this day after Armistice. That's how many casualties our military leaders expect before war's shadow recedes from American shores. And don't forget to include the changes in the relationship between the sexes compelled by many things besides the mathematical change in their numerical strength.

The physical inventory is vital, and we shall find it necessary to examine it in detail. The effects may not be entirely visible but they are immediate. In these physical things war will have produced permanent and immutable change. It would be callous and futile to urge on a bereaved family that the absence of a son or sweetheart or husband makes no fundamental difference to the future. Certainly it could not be true when multiplied by anticipated thousands. The effect of our battle losses will extend in many directions. The effect on our mores, on literature, on just living, will be immediate. On the other hand, pointing in a happier direction, is the fact that the medical profession will have learned in Army hospitals to save many more lives than were lost in the war.

The physical effects will remain with us in another sense. The shattered walls of European and Asiatic cities will painfully intrude on our will to forget. Then, too, the changed economic and industrial character of substantial parts of the world will leave us a legacy that we won't be able to reject. Germany will have been defeated, but the German reorganization of European enterprise will evade the sword's point. Japan will have been squeezed back into her three islands, but the thousands of opium-crazed Orientals may continue to look toward the shadow of the setting sun.

Of such miscellaneous stuff is this day after Armistice made. Plus nine million American men in uniform waiting for discharge papers. Plus the thousands of small businesses that closed their doors a year ago for the last time. Plus the uncounted war contracts suspended in a state called "termination," waiting for money, or something or anything.

Before the war, if fifty million of you could have found paying jobs, they'd hang out the flags and stretch the garage walls to make room for another car. Only forty-six million Americans were working in 1940, with about eight and one half million unemployed. But in 1944 fifty-five million had jobs and there was no unemployment. That's part of inventory too. And so are the billions of dollars in cold cash you and the other hundred thirty million of you have saved up. That's all inventory from which we're going to manufacture the future. And so are the Russian armies camped on German soil—and yesterday's editorial in the Chicago *Tribune* telling them where they can go.

Inventory too? The party line-up in the new Congress, and President ——, and unemployment ahead, and . . . ?

CHAPTER II

"The Army Makes Men"

THE FUTURE OF AMERICA is locked in your mind. The combination of what you'll think and what you'll do will make history. The *conflict* between what you'll think and what you'll do will make that history violent. The numerous long threads of that story are still to be intertwined. It could hardly be otherwise when there are so many of you with varied attitudes, diverse personalities, individual demands on your society. Perhaps the most important will be the pressures on the future applied by the twelve million veterans of World War II.

To understand those pressures you must see them against the background of the thought and action that will comprise the warp and woof of the American fabric. Some patterns of thought will so generally characterize the nation that almost all economic and social groups will be stamped with them. Others will distinguish different groups—the businessman, the labor-union member, the unemployed, the farmer, the Southerner, the suburbanite, the ex-serviceman, the middle-class man, the America-Firster.

In addition, like an intellectual Supreme Court, or, more appropriately, a Congress of Ideas, you will have the distinctive and dominating thought of America's leaders. In this discordant assembly you will find Cotton Ed Smith and Raymond Gram Swing, Norman Thomas and Senator Vandenberg, Wendell Willkie and Thomas Dewey, Father Coughlin and Rabbi Wise, Tom Girdler and Earl Browder, Franklin Roosevelt and Burton Wheeler, spouse Eleanor and Claire Luce, Pegler and Lippmann, Grafton and Sokolsky.

9

Mix them together and you have a powerful fuel to feed America's furnaces of action—the radio, the press, the movies, Congress, the American Legion, the Grange, the CIO and the AFL, the Federal Council of Churches of Christ in America, and the Catholic Church. Pour a little of that fuel over the Klan or the Woman's Christian Temperance Union, the American Labor Party and the National Association of Manufacturers, or just the Kiwanis Club of Peoria.

The combination of fuel and furnace makes the fire of action.

An indignant lady wrote to a radio commentator who, as she saw it, had imbibed too freely of the milk of human kindness: "Listen! How about the millions in India, Mexico, Canada, and South America; surly there are enough men from the under privaleged to fight this war without taking the flower of our manhood. Our war was with Japan. I have a son with 1 yr. Cornell—4 yrs. princeton and 2 yrs. Harvad now a *private*." (Emphasis and spelling hers.) America!

A leading American industrialist, keyman of an important war agency: "Nations have spent decades preparing plans for the conversion of a peacetime economy to a wartime economy. So far as I know, nobody has seriously undertaken the preparation of plans for the opposite process—converting a wartime economy back to peacetime economy . . . I sincerely believe that if we tackle this problem of postwar demobilization of industry and manpower with all the energy we are now devoting to the opposite process, we can build an economy and a standard of living the like of which the world has never dreamed of. We can, in that process, lay the groundwork for an industrial system that will have as its only limits the limits of available manpower for production. This system would be based on a price structure designed to reach a vast reservoir of potential consumers that have in the past only been able to afford the basic necessities of life." America!

On the Senate floor a Southern statesman rises to his full height and addresses his complaint to the Commander in Chief of the United States: "I have been here with . . . five Presidents and the thing we have got . . . I enjoyed being a Senator until this miserable thing came along—I mean this miserable party. . . ." America!

A large, barefooted Negress in flowing white tunic stands on one corner of a busy New York intersection as the winter winds and the indifferent crowds pass by. "And we shall pay again and again for our sin and our forgetfulness of the True One." America!

It has always been so—but not all of it. New rivulets of thought are becoming part of the nation's stream of consciousness. Some old springs have run dry. The war itself has shaken up the mind, and the patterns change as in a jostled kaleidoscope. Many of the fundamental American ideas hang on, some strengthened, some weakened, some destined to flare up with a last-minute brightness, some buried deep, seemingly ignored but constantly guiding action unconscious of its source.

Defining the American idea has continued to enchant and challenge essayists, poets, mystics, politicians, and after-dinner speakers for generations. It will for generations to come. One factor alone guarantees it as a permanent preoccupation—the American idea is always changing. Attitudes are constantly molded by the altering contours of environment. No sooner do you put your finger accurately on the core than the core moves, shrinks, spreads, or breaks in two.

What has the war done to your mind? Does the boy pilot in the stratosphere reach earth again with the same aspirations? To your way of thinking, what should America do about the world, and sin and sex, and Jews, and private business, and health insurance and jobs, and Negroes and the poll tax, and elections, and Russia and radicals, and Hollywood? How safe is democracy in your hands?

The sharpest change in the American way of thinking will come from the more than twelve million men whose ways of living have been abruptly and profoundly transformed. The monotonous continuity of the same uniform, the fact of the uniform itself, the bark of the sergeant, the authority of a shavetail, the competition for a marksmanship medal—these do things to a young mind. They'd do things to anybody's mind. So would the apparently endless training and waiting and orders and canceled leaves and clean-ups and inspection.

On some within the group the whine of shells, the listening to the dread silence, the watching and turning away from death will leave an ineradicable imprint. The undivided latrines, the walls of rotogravured girls simulating life, the lonesome dependence on letters, the day-in, day-out sameness of the talk, with its three repeated themes—girls, rank, and furloughs. Attitudes for a lifetime will flow from this maelstrom of jangled interests.

Clotted blood, grime, and stinking perspiration actually prove to be the least impressive of the mind-makers. More "mind" will have been made in the bleak, humorless monotony of Iceland, a muddy stretch of camp in New Jersey, a colorless barracks in Idaho, and the humanless, sandy Pacific islands that only the goony birds can call home.

There is a brew here that will simmer for many a year.

In these pages the mind of the ex-serviceman is considered first. In all things he will deserve first call on your attention and consideration when he gets back. Even if that were not so, his numbers alone would make it possible for him to wrest attention from the nation. In later chapters we shall see what happens to the environment and inner being of the men and women who stayed home. Taken together, the serviceman reunited with his civilian brothers and sisters will make up the composite of tomorrow's America.

The doughboy of World War II will be a new man when he comes back to Main Street, Forty-second Street, the poolroom, the cow pasture. He'll be living with you for a long time. You'll hear a lot about him, and not a little of it from himself.

Know why a soldier fights and you have an excellent preview of his demands on postwar America. That doesn't guarantee his future conduct. He may be fighting for an extension of democracy or merely its preservation, but his actions in the peacetime community after the war will not necessarily hew to that line. In great part his behavior will be colored by what happens to his demands. He might very easily, for example, plump for an American "boss" because the war didn't produce the beautiful idealistic pattern the radio brought to him on a war-bond program.

The American soldier's participation in this war, no matter how generously his motives are appraised, flows mainly from one fact— it was compelled. In some cases he's worked up an enthusiasm for his job. There were a good number, of course, who enlisted—although some were not many steps ahead of the draft board.

Educated to the ideals of peace, the great majority considered war a dirty job, and, in common with the civilian, the soldier has little taste for it, little hope from it. He differs from his World War I predecessors, who felt a certain emotion of the crusade, who had at least the negative force of hate for the enemy. The Pacific troops have caught some of this. Those in the European theater little.

This war started amid the jokes about the last one. G.I. Joe greets the new recruits as they enter the camp with, "Hello, suckers." And he means part of it. His first wish is to get out, get home, get back. His longing is not for the things he didn't have, but for the things he hasn't got—the girl friend, the flivver, the hot dogs, a coke, the girl friend, the boys on the corner, sleeping late, Sunday dinner, the girl friend.

Edward Streeter, the author of the World War I humor sensation, *Dere Mabel,* in a serious moment said, "History is written as much by the reaction of individuals to the impact of relatively trivial things as it is by the leaders."

It's not of tariffs, boundaries, world courts, and international currency that Joe's been thinking. An occasional intellectual set-to in a dull moment at the canteen about "whether there's a way of preventing this from happening again"—yes. But the animation, the light in the eyes, the eagerness and intensity—these G.I. Joe saves for other things.

The Army Special Service section conducted a contest in which the soldier was asked to describe what he was fighting for. The contest was open to all branches of the service. Among the few hundred contestants who submitted their entries, you would expect a higher percentage of the articulate, the literate, the idealistic, the far- and social-sighted. There were some, like the lieutenant in the Engineers, who said: "I want a better government when I return home. I fight for that and I will fight for it when I return."

And there was the private who had previously published short stories: "I fight," he said, "for the future, for the victories, for the world that is to be created from the chaotic remnants of bombed-out civilization. I fight for truth and justice, humanity and wisdom, gentleness and mercy, righteousness and humility." That boy has a fight on his hands.

But more typical in this second great American Army was the shavetail in a bomber who fights "for week ends at the beach or ball park, evenings at home and the kids in my lap." And a corporal in the Engineers, in words that echo from camp to camp: "I'm fighting to get this damned war over and come home."

To "come home" has many meanings to many boys. To one hospital worker: "Because I like riding along Ocean Parkway with Alma perched on my bike's handle bars like a little canary." Or the private whiling away the time in a replacement center, waiting for the next move: "For my girl—that's why I'm fighting."

A corporal: "I fight because our democracies failed to live up to democracy."

An Army doctor hit the jackpot. His fight will satisfy all: "I fight to keep America America."

Maybe the radio writers and wartime dramatists had their serviceman right when, amid the hail of shells, every fox hole had a doctor of philosophy who stood up and announced with sudden inspiration, "This is the last bastion of liberty." But the reporters and observers at the fronts and in the camps won't agree. The average serviceman doesn't talk like Thomas Jefferson. As a matter of fact, the boy with the gun prefers not to talk about war *or* peace, or at least not except as they directly affect him—peace meaning what *he'll* do when he's out. If he's pressed about the deeper implication, then it comes out something like Sergeant Martin's synthesis of the serviceman's hope: "Well, I'm not exactly sure, but I think that the world should be tied a lot closer together so that everybody knows what everybody else is doing. Maybe something like the United States of the World."

It's not surprising that he avoids grappling with those basic realities. Only under prodding do they come out into the open, and then with understandable embarrassment. The inarticulate aspirations are a long cry from the nervous soldier who volunteers to everyone at the camp: "I'm supposed to have a baby this week."

There's something both ominous and reassuring in the soldier's near-indifference to the larger questions. The ominous note was struck late in 1943 and again in 1944 when the bipartisan, War-Department-approved provisions for uniform and automatic voting privileges for the servicemen were rejected by both Houses of Congress. In retrospect it will be hard to believe that this could have been accomplished in a mid-war election year without assuring political suicide. More ominous still was the indifference of the average soldier. Nor did the President's demand for the legislation precipitate any popular ground swell.

The beneficial harbinger for the future that flows from this myopia is less tangible but equally real. The higher the soldier's hopes and aspirations, the greater will be the disillusionment experienced by the returning veteran. The boy who saw some kind of United States of the World in the offing is due for a buffeting. Not quite yet, soldier.

Important studies have been made of the emotional, intellectual, and spiritual transition through which G.I. Joe passes from his induction to his discharge. He went in without any enthusiasm. He may even have tried to talk his draft board into a deferment. He griped when he got in and he's been griping ever since. But no matter how reluctantly he took his oath, he had a certain amount of faith in the purposefulness of the job—if only to justify the years he will be devoting to it. He had a clumsily hidden pride in the new uniform itself, even while he sang, "Sam, you made the pants too long." His adjustment to military life gave him an unexpected courage, an inner lift. Once in the Army, "It is the best goddamn Army in the world."

Here and there an occasional Army official who was incompetent and sometimes dishonest turned up. Some of the procedures in training were not well planned, nor were they always administered with the intelligence that the recruit expected. Unexplained or unreasonable actions injected their acid. The seeming perfection didn't hold up.

Then comes the discovery that you can frequently get around the rules. The fellow who can't, the sucker, the poor sap, is forever immortalized in the famous *Yank* cartoon character, "Sad Sack."

When the first awe gives way to a hard-boiled contemptuousness, when officers are brought down to size, and more frequently below accurate size, gold-bricking becomes the practice. Dodging responsibility, and doing it cleverly, appears almost synonymous with being "on the ball." Of course there are exceptions in the attitudes of every soldier, especially where the responsibility has an immediately visible relationship to life and death, to the fight itself. But the evolution from the wide-eyed greenhorn to the old-timer's cynicism comes inevitably to most men, carrying with it basic implications for the years ahead.

The process actually takes a long time and becomes acute only with prolonged service. It is aggravated by the inescapable inequalities of sacrifice required by war. There is injustice in geography itself. The home-hungry soldier in the Solomons eats soul when the fading illusions no longer nourish. Years of war and extended absence from home make for a staleness of faith, a dwindling of generosity. Exhaustion sets in quickly. The effort to find ease, to "get away" from things, increases. For the next decade we are accumulating an overdose of apathy, callousness, and lassitude in this decline of the spirit. If the world is rotten, let it rot. The philosophy of "take what you can whenever and wherever you can" will gain new recruits.

This feeling is exaggerated by the essentially isolated life the soldier and sailor lead. The small units in which they are mobilized live intimately. They live a new, one-sexed existence. The town is strange and frequently unfriendly. The USO may dispel boredom, but it doesn't destroy the unity, the lonely character, the separateness of the group.

As for you, the civilian, face the fact that as the war progresses the boys in uniform will like you less and less. Their envy and resentment—and sometimes even contempt—for you will carry well beyond the Armistice. How commensurate is your sacrifice? Why don't you live the same kind of existence? Why should you continue to ride on Ocean Parkway with Alma on the handle bars like a canary?

But the more profound influences on the future are the less frequently identified differences between the soldier and his civilian counterpart. Suffering discomfort, the soldier resents the fact that life at home has continued in large part to be what it has always been. He knows it well, or he wouldn't long so bitterly to return to it. The distinctions between his authoritarian military life and democratic home-town existence arouse an understandable jealousy and pain—like the kid compelled by his mother to leave the party at nine o'clock who learns that ice cream and cookies were passed out at ten. It may be unreasonable that he should resent the children who were permitted to remain, but he will.

A new clannishness is in the making, and it will last a long time. It begins with a growing suspicion of those who fought with words or war bonds or even lathes. The noncombatants are considered scornfully as a bunch of middle-aged matrons watching a football game. But the breach between the civilian and the soldier is widened most by the constant awareness of the difference between mufti and uniform. The apparent simplicity of the military life, its regimentation, will leave a lasting impression. More specifically, it will block a smooth readjustment to the ways of the normal community. The stamp of the Army will never be completely removed. Soldiers live in a dictatorship and, whether they like it or not, they get accustomed to its ways. Objectives are made simple. A minimum of decisions is left open to the men. Uniformity, right down to the lacing of their boots, is made an inherent part of their beings. They are given one clear and worthy aim, defined by regulations. In battle itself, life narrows down to its simplest end—survival.

Naturally they want to leave all this behind as soon as possible. The universal dream is of the day when it's over. But the old needs are replaced by new ones formed away from home, and these will not be completely satisfied by the efforts to return to the old prewar patterns. Increasingly, the ways of civilian life will become inadequate.

When it's all over, the veteran's attitude will be: The war was won by the soldier. It was not won by the people, but in spite of them. Living with them, re-entering their community, will involve irritations.

During the war a growing distaste for labor will have developed in substantial segments of the military. Part of that growing antipathy is explained by the slanted coverage given to the strikes that did occur. Part is explained by the inability to tolerate any work stoppage at a time when life and death were at stake. Part is explained by the disparity between the apparent scales of pay—fifty bucks a month as against fifty, sixty, one hundred a week.

Some people will find it hard to understand why strong animosity should be directed at the striker and very little directed at the war profiteer. When you have excited the sense of deprivation in a man you have touched off a wild and bitter emotion. To the serviceman, labor has been the depriving force. A strike is the direct stoppage of guns or food or something he needs. Furthermore, it's his old job and his old wages that are being enjoyed by the civilian. The profiteer, on the other hand, is taking nothing from him. "The son of a bitch is just smart, that's all." August Claessens, the veteran soapbox orator and student of mob psychology, warns the would-be political speaker not to dwell in detail on the riotous luxury of the rich. The street-corner crowd will drool at the mouth, not rise in protest. Only the belief that someone else has "yours" will rouse to action.

The serviceman's concern will be with those he directly connects with his deprivation. Every little story that tends to show how *other* groups are taking what should be his will be accepted hungrily. The resentment that flows from circumstantial injustice will grow. On his home-coming, disillusion, tension, restlessness, and anxiety will measure the width of the gap between what he hopes to find and the realities. True, he longs to return, but he already feels, without realizing it, a dislike for and a suspicion of what he wants. He isn't aware of the changes that have already taken their toll of his original personality. Sure, he entered military life without many of the illusions of the last war, but when he returns he will find that he acquired new illusions, that he built up new idealized pictures in his mind about everything under the sun.

Home will not be what he thought it was. He will not be what he thought he was. The crust of dissatisfactions that formed while he was in uniform will not peel off when he puts on his Sunday best. Then comes the anomaly—disillusion where, so far as he knew, there was no preceding illusion.

Sociologists fear the effects of disillusionment. They believe it will exist with soldier and civilian alike. But it's the man in uniform who should stir your real anxiety for tomorrow. His disappointments will be greater, more emotionally disturbing, and he will be less equipped to adjust himself to the new reality—the actual world for which he had been longing.

Ernie Pyle really got to know his boys in khaki. With foreboding about what he called the "Aftermath," he says:

"The men over here have changed. They are too close to themselves to sense the change, perhaps. And I am too close to them to grasp it fully. But since I am older and a little apart, I have been able to notice it more. . . . A year is a long time to be away from home. . . . At first homesickness can almost kill a man. But time takes care of that. It isn't normal to moon in the past forever. Home gradually grows less vivid; the separation from it less agonizing. There finally comes a day—not suddenly but gradually, as a sunset-touched cloud changes its color—when a man is living almost wholly wherever he is. His life has caught up with his body, and his days become full war days, instead of American days simply transplanted to Africa. . . . Our men can't make this change from normal civilians into warriors and remain the same people. . . ."

Pyle is writing of the men at the front. They live *"almost wholly"* wherever they are. The margin that is left for living elsewhere is likely to be subconscious, and therefore all the more subtle and dangerous. Even the man behind the lines, the fellow who was never sent abroad, can't remain the same person—if only for the deep psychological shock of learning to kill. Whether he ever uses that knowledge, killing has been sanctioned. When they gave G.I. Joe a gun they didn't mean to and couldn't help it, but they pointed it at the rest of your life. Fortunately, the mechanics of military education tend to dilute this effect. "Learning to kill" is not that at all in many cases. First you shoot at inanimate targets, then you shoot at soldiers or tanks painted on cardboards. When the targets become human—mostly at long-range distances—many a soldier insists that he doesn't feel the difference. "The only change," says one, "is that they shoot at you. This gives you a queer feeling which grows the longer you're at the front."

The moralities of peace will lose their vigor. The ex-serviceman will not return to them quickly. Even within his own immediate outfit he will have learned to re-evaluate the men around him. He judges them by what they can do, and the standards in a military environment frequently violate the normal civilian codes. Whether it's the night before "with that babe," the day before "with that heinie," or right in front of your nose "with the sergeant," the new tests by which a man's a man leave ineradicable soulprints.

How much respect for property can the returning servicemen have when with each day in the Army money came to mean less to them? Even Army property will have dropped in value with the necessity to expend thousands on practice, to abandon equipment that can't be carried, to burn munitions that can't be moved. And their own money too. Both the crap game and the avidly sought hour's pleasure devalue Joe's currency more effectively than home-front inflation. The average foreigner has the impression that American soldiers throw their money away. He's right. Again, as Ernie Pyle puts it: "At the front there just isn't time to be economical. Also, in war areas where things are scarce and red tape still rears its delaying head, a man learns to get what he needs simply by 'requisitioning.' It isn't stealing, it's the only way to acquire certain things. The stress of war puts old virtues in a changed light. We shall have to relearn a simple fundamental or two when things get back to normal. But what's wrong with a small case of 'requisitioning' when murder is the classic goal?"

Yes, the vices are taken lightly. Moral horror can't come easily after the experience of war. As for ethical distinctions—well, the boys discovered how small the margin is between good and bad, between being polite and playing rough. Of many changes the men in uniform are not yet aware, but about playing rough they already know plenty. Let the serviceman speak for himself. Sergeant Ray Duncan asked in an article in *Yank*, "Whatever Became of the Old-Fashioned Uppercut?" And here in Sergeant Duncan's words is the reason for his question:

I had the misfortune, a few hours ago, to step on a corporal's shoe in a chow line. It was after our class in judo and hand-to-hand combat. The corporal had just shined his shoes.

He lifted one foot knee high. With a vicious scrape he brought it down against my shin, and at the bottom of the stroke he stamped hard against my instep. As I doubled over in pain he smashed the bridge of my nose with the heel of his hand. Then he went to work on my kidneys with both feet as I lay on my face.

A couple of my buddies rescued me by kneeing the base of the corporal's spine. I'm resting comfortably now—almost through spitting blood—but the incident set me to thinking.

After this war a whole generation of Americans will be trained in judo and hand-to-hand combat. What will that mean to our way of life?

Come with me to the Riff-Raff Room, a cozy little cocktail bar. It is Saturday night and the war has been over for three weeks. Seated at the bar are a former marine sergeant and his former girl.

GIRL: I'm so happy you're back. Isn't it wonderful here?

FORMER MARINE: This place is too noisy. That piano player. I'd like to break his fingers, one by one—like this. (The girl screams in pain, and a former paratrooper and an artilleryman, just discharged, rush to her aid.)

FORMER PARATROOPER (to former marine): Take it easy, Mac; yer breakin' the fingers of the girl.

He deftly dislocates the marine's shoulder and snaps his collarbone in two places. The artilleryman sinks two extended fingers into the marine's abdominal wall. Then they go to work with their feet. Several others join in the melee, and the sound of breaking bones and ripping tissue drowns out everything but the tinkle of the piano. The piano player is banging out "It's Murder, He Says."

The former marine drags himself to the piano and throws an elbow lock on the musician with his one good arm. Then with his teeth he methodically breaks the ten fingers, counting each one aloud.

Last time I was on furlough I happened to ask my little brother what he'd been reading. "What are all the kids reading?" he cried, drawing from his pocket a worn copy of *Kill or Be Killed, a Manual of Dirty Fighting*.

If this trend continues, the American home of the future might easily be something like this:

MOTHER: Jimmy! You've been fighting again! (She anxiously feels the frail little body of her son, who has just come home from kindergarten.)

SON: Aw gee, Mom, I have not! Why?

MOTHER: Your eye—someone's been gouging it again. Your left arm is bent the wrong way. What is it, wrenched socket or fracture? Tell Mommy, honey. Why are you bent to one side? Abdominal wall again?

FATHER (looking up from the evening paper): Stop nagging the child, Miriam. Boys will be boys, you know. Come here, Son, and let me set that arm. (There is a knock at the door, and Mr. Robinson, the next-door neighbor, enters. He points at little Jimmy.)

MR. ROBINSON: That young hoodlum has been fighting my Wilbur again. My boy will be a nervous wreck if your son doesn't stop splitting his kidneys.

FATHER: Either you apologize for calling my son a hoodlum, or I'll crush your spinal base.

MR. ROBINSON: You and who else? (They circle around each other, crouched low and growling. Mother draws a stiletto from her bosom. Jimmy's eyes are fixed on the visitor's groin. Father lashes out suddenly with a well-placed kick. Mr. Robinson turns white and weakly attempts a right to the jaw.)

FATHER: Why, you dirty——. (He seizes the fist and twists until the wrist snaps. He jabs his fingers into his neighbor's neck, and all struggling ceases. Jimmy kicks to the groin, then rushes to hug his father around the knees.)

SON: Gee, Pop, you're swell! I told that old Wilbur my pop could kill his pop!

"To me it's a very funny piece," comments a lieutenant, "but at the same time not a little frightening because true in its exaggerated fashion." And then the lieutenant, perhaps without realizing it, goes on to prove how true the exaggeration really is. Here's his letter:

In the fighting part of the Army, the virtues are cockiness, arrogance, force. It's particularly apparent down here with the paratroopers. An article would describe them as the lean, bronzed, toughened, fighting heroes of the American Army (which they are), but in the individual it takes the form of "I can kick the living —— out of any —— son of a —— who thinks he's as good as I am." The attitude is encouraged by the Army, naturally, on the theory that pride in personal toughness and pride in the best goddam organization in the —— Army is the thing that makes the fighting man. I'm sure it's great in war, but it resulted in H., our current technical adviser, having to stop three fights on the bus coming back from C—— last night. And it's going to be great in that ideal postwar world where humanity is going to settle down to an endless delightful life of constant copulation among the countries. With ten million fighting men trained to the school of force and twice as many kids growing up in adulation of their heroes (look at the comic strips!), what chance is there for a world of understanding between peoples?

Now that the home and church are dead, the only hope for the future of the world is in the bed. A symphony has come on the radio and I'm getting dirty remarks from my confreres. So I'd better quit.

Viva la bed,
C.

Physically, the Army and Navy boys are healthier, more alert, more mature than when they received their induction notice. Every evidence indicates that they're better in these respects than the 1917 veterans. Morale, in terms of living together and operating as a fighting unit, is high. In the months before Pearl Harbor, when the slogan "Over the Hill in October" spread from camp to camp, spirit and the will to continue was pretty low in many places; but no longer, except in individual and isolated units where "dumb command" has exacted a price in spirit.

Even in the first year after Pearl Harbor, when the Army still had a lot to learn about being an army, one of the best indications —the suicide rate—showed the size of the achievement. Not only was it far lower than the comparable figure for boys of the same age in civilian life, but it was actually one fifth of the suicide rate in the Army during the peacetime years of 1935 to 1939.

The physical change and improvement is the most noticeable. Mother sees it quickly when Joe's home on furlough. She doesn't see most of the other changes, though. The letters seem to be from the same boy except that he has a better grip on himself. "Joe's more a man" is a phrase that echoes from home to home across the country. And he is. He certainly can take better care of himself. He's less uncertain. Particularly when he's back on leave. He feels his strength as he observes the softness of the noncombatant environment.

There are those to whom war will have given the ability to assume responsibility. The chap who hadn't quite found himself may lift his head high as a result of his sergeant status. He will have a new pride. For many, battalion life will have sharpened the ability to live co-operatively, to share the work, the problems, the needs, the confidence of the group. Will these characteristics last when the environment which gave them birth and also sustains them no longer exists? There is this maturity, but for postwar life it can be described at most as potential. The challenge of the years after the war will be to harness these attributes to the needs of an entirely different kind of community and way of living.

Some will have ripened in a more subtle growth of the spirit. A few of the boys will develop an appreciation of beauty that was never acute before. Some men, when confronted with death, see many facets of living that were beyond their previous vision. The shackles, the limitations of daily living, when thrown off, release the poet, the artist. Otherwise a poem like that of R.C.A.F. pilot John G. McGee, now dead, might never have been written:

> *Oh! I have slipped the surly bonds of Earth*
> *And danced the skies on laughter-silvered wings;*
> *Sunward I've climbed, and joined the tumbling mirth*
> *Of sun-split clouds, and done a hundred things*
> *You have not dreamed of—wheeled and soared and swung*
> *High in the sunlit silence. Hov'ring there,*
> *I've chased the shouting wind along, and flung*
> *My eager craft through footless halls of air—*
> *Up, up the long, delirious burning blue*
> *I've topped the wind-swept heights with easy grace,*
> *Where never lark or even eagle flew—*
> *And, while with silent, lifting mind I've trod*
> *The high untrespassed sanctity of space,*
> *Put out my hand and touched the face of God.*

Others have learned to see beauty in things that repelled before the war. Ten years after the war we will wonder how it was possible for correspondents to write some of the things they did. Yet it was possible, and their words are stirring and sensitive, even though they describe the aerial bombings of inhabited cities. One illustration is the raid on Berlin in which forty-one of our bombers were lost. Only two of the correspondents who flew with the raiders returned to their base. These few words are from a broadcast by one of those two, Ed Murrow of the Columbia Broadcasting System:

The flak looked like a cigarette lighter in a dark room—one that won't light. Sparks but no flame. The sparks crackling just above the level of the cloud tops . . .

Dead ahead there was a whole chain of red flares looking like stop lights . . . Again we could see those little bubbles of colored lead. . . . The clouds were gone, and the sticks of incendiaries from the preceding wave made the place look like a badly laid out city with the street lights on. The small incendiaries were going down like a fistful of white rice thrown on a piece of black velvet. The cookies—the 4,000-pound high explosives—were bursting below like great sunflowers gone mad.

I looked down on the white fires; the white fires had turned red. They were beginning to merge and spread, just like butter does on a hot plate. But this time all those patches of white on black had turned yellow and started to flow together. . . .

I looked to the port beam at the target area. There was a red, sullen, obscene glare. The fires seemed to have found each other—and we were heading home . . .

Berlin was a kind of orchestrated hell, a terrible symphony of light and flame.

But, make no mistake about it, where one man captured agony and destruction in terms of great descriptive beauty, others were seared by the light of those "sunflowers gone mad." Ed Murrow said it in the same broadcast:

"It isn't a pleasant kind of warfare—the men doing it speak of it as a job. The job isn't pleasant; it's terribly tiring. Men die in the skies while others are roasted alive in their cellars."

In the course of that job and thousands of other jobs that are war, the veneer of civilization will be rubbed off some of the boys and rubbed thin on many others.

Whether on the battlefield, in a camp bunk, lying under the stars alone or in a cheap hotel bed with company, the boys have been confronted with new problems by the war. And they couldn't meet their new needs and desires with the usual behavior. The old attitudes just didn't fit the situation. But the old attitudes hang on—as a matter of fact, they burn a little brighter. You see it in the looking back home. You see it in the songs they sing. The conflict between the new actions and the old attitudes—conflict that will occur again and again on so many levels of future life—leaves the seed which will sprout tomorrow.

The old attitude hangs on—and then victory. The bells and the sirens will bring exhilaration, and after that—waiting. When the bells are silent and the waiting becomes a way of life, the anticlimax will bring with it the inevitable tension and restlessness.

G.I. Joe, more than anyone else, will long for stability and order. He will look desperately for something that will make things what they used to be—more accurately, what they seemed to have been. But even when he finds some things unchanged he will find that they are no longer adequate, because he will have changed. Either way, life can't be the same.

G.I. Joe will believe in the traditional democratic ideals of popular decision in an atmosphere of tolerance. But his emotions are near the surface, and he will feel a strong sense of differentness from the rest of the community. His temper will be aroused without his realizing why—and more easily than it has ever been. Because he wants security so much, he will be more intensely aware of his insecurity.

For years he will have griped about Army pay. Only with the peace will he suddenly realize that Army pay provided a security that no longer exists for him. Congressman Patman, assisted by the War and Navy departments and the Veterans' Administration, estimated that the lowest-paid Army private received the equivalent of $1,700 a year, as follows:

Soldier's cash income at $50 a month, $600; food, figured at $1.50 a day, $574.50; barrack shelter ($10 monthly), $120; equipment and replacement, $170; medical, dental, and hospital care, $100; saved on life insurance, $63.40; saved on cigarettes, $10.95; saved on laundry, $32.50; saved on postage and barber charges, $28.65.

He'll look back with nostalgia at the seven cents he paid for American cigarettes overseas. He'll recall the protection he received against civil liabilities such as income tax, lawsuits, insurance-premium payments, instalments on the mortgage. Now they will be doubly annoying since they were suspended only until six months after the war and the indebtedness will have accumulated.

Reality will begin to close in. The last fling will not end with the war. Many of the boys will feel a great urge for an escape from reality, an escape from routine.

Psychologists say that the veterans of this war will cling to the ideals of individual initiative, endurance, self-reliance, and courage. But the specialists add that, tortured by their insecurity, they will at the same time have an exaggerated desire for someone to lean on. This conflict the psychoanalyst attributes to the normal need for parental love and protection, but that's one need that will be buried deep in the boy's unconscious. The mature, war-made self will reject it as a sign of weakness. And, because of that conflict, in an effort to protect himself against his own concealed soft dependency, he will rush more violently into the race of peacetime life.

The clash between the need for action and the redoubled seeking of ease will hamper the serviceman's readjustment. War brought him a great deal of deprivation; it also brought him a sense of power. He found himself capable of completely and quickly destroying old institutions. His new sense of power, plus his impatience with existing institutions, plus his longing for what isn't, will result in action. And the action will not necessarily be in harmony with the democratic ideals for which he was fighting.

The Army is neither aristocratic, with the virtues of aristocracy, nor democratic, with the virtues of democracy, nor professional, with the knowledge and ethics of the technician. The hierarchy of rank in control and direction will have developed both a respect for authority and a rebellion against it.

After the war you will find the serviceman frequently calling for more authoritative leadership. At the same time you will find him occasionally intolerant and contemptuous of authority.

War has provided a hard and bumpy mattress on which soft and impressionable bodies have been lying for a long time. The dents and ridges in his back will not smooth out just because G.I. Joe wants so badly to come home and sleep again in a soft bed.

He wants like all hell to come home. When he finally does come home he'll find that everyone walks too slow.

CHAPTER III

So Nice To Come Home To

DEMOBILIZATION IS A LONG BUSINESS. It will be a heartbreaking and an unfair business. There will be rancor and irritation, fed by the fears and complexities involved in almost every phase of unwinding war.

We don't really have to untangle ourselves—ever. We could just go on fighting World War II—and a third after this one. Ridiculous? Don't dismiss the idea. It's really the only sure way to avoid the agony that masquerades politely in the word "demobilization."

That would have been Hitler's way had he won. But it won't be the American way. At any rate, not at first. Nine million men and women in uniform will be itching to get out. "Homeward ho!" will be the strongest social pressure facing the nation, and the momentum will start with the end of the European war in 1944.

It's ironic that the whole concept of "demobilization" is something the military would prefer to ignore until the last possible moment. Going home and plans for going home interfere with war, and war will be continuing even when the homeward trek is under way. How America will continue to mobilize for the Pacific war while demobilizing the European war is one of the trump cards in Japan's well-worn deck. The need for a martial spirit after partial peace will be one of the strongest brakes on the release of men from the services. Modern war is in many respects indivisible, and our individual fears will serve only to emphasize this fact.

If the desire homeward will be the strongest social pressure, the hope jobward will be the next strongest force. No assurances of employment, no enactment of job priorities will adequately reassure the chafing serviceman that it will not again be "first come, first employed." He has already seen the stock market dip with every military advance he made and knows the "Armistice jitters" of folks back home. He has already heard the endless misgivings about the ability of the swollen war economy to remain distended under the more polite pressures of peace. Not least of all is his memory of the years since the first "normalcy." The acrid recollection of bread lines and work lines will not have been dispelled by five years of war.

Yes, he knows America will be so nice to come home to, but he's afraid he'd better hustle home first if it's to be nice for *him*.

For the dead, no home-coming. For them demobilization will already have come. Of two million anticipated casualties, up to five hundred thousand are catalogued in the estimates as fatalities. Actually we have been doing much better than the estimates. Our casualties may well be one of the few respects in which the war itself will be dwarfed by our expectations. The number of lives saved by medical science and the number of American lives saved by military tactics are almost incredible.

Given the breaks in the invasion, the end of European war may even find us with fewer casualties than were suffered by our first 'A.E.F., an army one third the size, at war only half the length of time. By November 1943 our casualty record showed that in twenty-two months of war, with more than ten million mobilized, we suffered casualties of less than 1 per cent of our armed forces as compared with 6 per cent of the 4,355,000 men mobilized during the nineteen months of World War I. This showing is so good—in this war as in the last—largely because our Allies have been doing the dying and bleeding for us. Compare our World War I casualties of 6 per cent with the 52 per cent our Allies suffered and the 67 per cent of the enemy.

The comparison may be even more dramatic and startling at the end of World War II. So far the European pyre has been fed mostly with Russian bones. And the Nazis have been paying with their dead and the dead of the countries they have occupied. Even the European invasion may not have added enough American casualties to exceed the estimates.

Where death is concerned, war will continue to strike us hard after partial peace has come. American casualties in the South Pacific and the Orient, as the tide backs up on Japan, may even outrun our European losses.

But perhaps as many as a million wounded, the accumulation of four years at war, will be coming home. For them, as a matter of fact, the economic road back will be comparatively the smoothest, the least disturbed by the question of employment and the fear of insecurity. The more apparent the disability, the more spontaneous and extended will be the organized response of the community.

Help for the disabled will steadily improve. There'll be no dramatic innovations in public consciousness. But the experiences of the war's early days will not be frequently repeated. It was then that a member of the Massachusetts Governor's Council appealed to the public, disclosing that fifteen hundred Massachusetts boys had been released from the armed forces as "insane" and had been shunted back to their families without any provision for their medical care. It will be better than that—much better. The wounded will depend on the mercy of government; the healthy, on the mercy of God—and the economic wisdom of man.

To the widows and orphans, death will bring certainty in several ways. Not pleasant, but at least more concrete than the future for the families of the living. Take pensions, for example. The wives and children of the war dead already know the minimum income for the rest of their lives. Congress has already provided monthly pensions for the widows—$38 if under fifty years of age, $45 if over, with $10 or more for each child, depending on age. There is a modest provision for dependent parents. Add to this the payments coming to the families of those servicemen who took out anywhere from $1000 to $10,000 of the life insurance that was made available, and you have another $5.75 to $57.50 a month for twenty years. They don't know what the money will be worth, but they do know what the minimum amount will be.

Chances are that subsequent Congresses will hike these amounts. The heroic war dead will provide excellent political timber for many a tomorrow's campaign. The silent are always spoken for.

It is for the living that the question marks are reserved. Like the

ever-recurring "How soon home?" Theoretically, if it were not for
continuing military need, everybody could be back in mufti as soon
as ships could carry them. But actually, even if peace occurred
universally with harmony and without recurring threats, demobilization would take longer than the difficulties of transportation alone
would require.

The magnitude of our shipping capacity will be matched by the
great size and wide distribution of our armies. The speed of our
planes and ships will apparently be balanced by the extended shipping needs of continuing war in the Orient. Calculations are that
each returning soldier will require a ton of shipping capacity—a tall
order. But never in history has so much shipping space been available as we will have at the moment of war's end. Shipping will not
delay the soldiers' re-embarkation.

For one thing, the fact is too often overlooked that half of our
uniformed men, at the end of the war with Germany, may be right
here in the United States. Besides, every ship needed to bring American boys back to this country is a ship which must make the opposite run in order to bring war and rehabilitation supplies to the
same ports. A loaded ship traveling home goes no slower than if
it were empty. And above all there will be the unbelievable swarm
of merchant fleets launched from our mushrooming shipways and
made more effective by the absence of the enemy submarine. The
demise of the U-boat will automatically mean almost a doubling
of our shipping capacity.

At the end of the war with Germany the shipping space of the
United Nations is expected to be well over forty million tons. Plans
have even been discussed to build a fifty-million-ton Merchant
Marine for the United States alone. Take the lowest possible figure,
assign just one third of the homebound space to returning soldiers,
work on the conservative basis of one ton per soldier, and the entire
American overseas force in Europe could be repatriated in a few
months. It's encouraging, in this connection, to recall that in 1919,
when our shipping facilities were only one fourth as large as they
will be at this war's end, more than 330,000 Americans were returned in the peak month.

But that one month was seven months after the Armistice. This time, when we will really be equipped to ship home, it isn't likely that we'll be doing as well proportionately, though we'll still be doing well.

If shipping won't be the bottleneck, what will be? There are many factors that must inevitably stall the process of demobilization. The difficulty of half-peace, half-war is just one. In modern coalition war, release of military manpower must take into account the interests and wishes of our allies. American demobilization cannot be more proportionately rapid than England's. Boys don't like the fellow who leaves the game before the last pitch. In the European war theater there will be good reason for sticking around. The extent of our physical expenditure, in comparison with that of others on the same team, may make our haste unseemly.

Besides, the last ball will not have been tossed, even when the contest has been called. Wilson learned that at Versailles. The peace table, more this time than ever, will be the final phase of war rather than the first phase of peace. And the runner on base, whose play is in question, does well to keep his foot on the bag while arguing. Germany, Japan, and Italy profited for years by presenting the world with the *fait accompli*. They sealed their bargains only after they had taken delivery. The post-Armistice disposition of Europe and Africa will require substantial troops, not so much for "policing," as is commonly supposed, as for "protection" or "bargaining."

There will be more involved than controversies over boundaries. Outwardly the excitement may look like a quarrel over territorial limitations. Actually the substantial interest of the sophisticated participants will be "What's to happen *within* the boundaries?" Political, as well as geographical, questions will call for military weights to be left standing on the European scales after the war. Weights? It's your boys we're talking about. And the political questions will determine how long they are left standing.

The political questions will have military overtones. The first year after the end of the war against Germany will forcibly demonstrate what the "longhairs" meant when they rejected the word *war* and insisted on *revolution* to describe the conflict. The end of German hostilities will serve only to throw into graphic relief the "unpeace" of Europe. And it will be quickly apparent that the territorial disputes are secondary to the political and economic realignments. As a matter of fact, there will be a continuing conflict on two separate levels—geographic integrity and political alignment.

With Russia there will be both geographic and ideological considerations. In Poland and the Baltic States the question is almost certain to be solved by the "I got it, sue me" method. Russia's interest, as well as that of England and the United States, in the internal struggle in Yugoslavia is of the political variety. Dividing Mihailovich's Chetniks and Tito's Partisans were a number of the same conflicts which have divided the world into warring camps. The France of tomorrow will be less tormented by the specific allegiance of Alsace to the state than by who the state is. The important question to the grandsons of Mazzini will be the political constitution of the state rather than the geographical constitution of their country.

In this upheaval of ideas and allegiance, in this geologic shift and settling of ideologies, troops are a lever producing or halting motion.

It is true, as competent European observers admit, that the unparalleled *potentiel de guerre* demonstrated by the United States in this war will make her wishes respected for the next decade. The peace is more likely to be kept if the United States clearly leaves the impression that she will act if it is not kept. But once the American forces have been brought home, any unscrupulous adventurer in world politics will feel fairly safe in taking political chances, relying on American reluctance to mobilize again. So at least for the period of greatest transition, the settling of what appears to be permanent identifications and structures, America's withdrawal of troops will be far from complete.

There is an additional domestic political factor which will magnify this likelihood. Postwar American attitudes will not only operate to speed the return of the men, but, even more important, to disarm most of them on their return. So long as they remain in a foreign theater they remain an instrument of foreign policy, a vehicle of international persuasion. Brought home, the troops will add their own voices to that of the community in resistance to any further international moves which could conceivably involve the use of the military. Therefore don't expect too many of the men now overseas to return immediately with the pacification of Germany. Bluntly, no more will be returned than the American people themselves compel. The speed with which the men return will depend on the outcome of the conflict between the foreign policy of the American people and their personal desires.

The clash between individual desires and national policy will serve in still another way to defer the home-coming. There will be no more certain political demise for those in the saddle than to demobilize the Army of the United States only to mobilize its members into the army of the unemployed. The political and economic leaders have put themselves on the spot with their luscious promises and lavish visions of a brave old world. Demobilization day is the delivery date. You can hardly blame the maker of the promissory note if he tries to postpone the due date while he's hunting up the cash.

Two domestic factors pressing in this direction will be the uncertainty pervading our national economic and industrial environment and the inadequacy and incompleteness of the plans for the serviceman's return, his retraining, and re-employment. We have yet to discuss the ever-recurring question that hides behind the word "employment." When we do, you will find ample reason for not rushing the soldier's return or terminating his military pay. It's easier to take a man out of a job and put him in military service than it is to take him out of military service and put him in a job. This is not to imply that there will be no re-employment program; it is merely to emphasize a reason—which will not frankly be offered —for some of the delay in the postwar demobilization of troops, wherever located.

Failure to complete plans for demobilization at an early date will flow from rather heartbreaking causes. There will be a fairly universal desire to be generous to the home-coming troops. But there will also be so much anxiety in the separate political camps to acquire the kudos for giving favorable treatment to the new war veteran that they will serve to block each other and stalemate effective action.

Many of the beneficial and even less controversial aspects of postwar programs will remain in pigeonholes until the echoes of the last campaign shouts of 1944 have been muted and the new Congress sworn in at the beginning of 1945. There will be an ample variety of campaign promises but little action until the political future has been settled. Even then the lunatic fringe will embarrass speedy action with exaggerated demands, as will the native nationalists and fascists with their impossible promises and calculated strategy of dissension.

All this adds up to the probability that the boys won't be back as soon as expected. But they will be back, all except a permanent Army and Navy of some two to two and one half million men. And these, too, will finally be returning to America's shores.

As applied to any individual in uniform, his early return to civvies will depend on a combination of factors. What is his dependency picture back home? What branch of the service is he in? Where is he at the given military moment? How long was he in and how arduous was his service? How's chances for a job back home? How badly does the civilian economy need his skill? How old is he? Age may turn out to be decisive in determining the order of discharge.

Since the end of war will have at least three stages, the speed and nature of the demobilization process must be examined in relation to each of them: German surrender, Japanese surrender, final peace treaty. Peace follows the three. Then the regular Army and Navy —swollen but regular—will comprise the still mobilized American Armed Forces. If a soldier has already "put in" for transfer from the wartime Army of the United States to the United States Army, he's "it." He's the backbone of America's postwar military. Add to this group those who at war's end want the security of the Army and Navy pay roll and then volunteer for additional service, and you have the bulk of America's post-Armistice force. There will be a greater proportion of men staying on as volunteers this time than there was in World War I. Now there is much more fear of unemployment. There is better than an even chance that this group will be amplified by a half million yearly as a result of continuing conscription for a period of peacetime military service. For all of these, the high seas, clean barracks, and an international mobility. For these, no job hunting, no traditional home-coming.

Those who want to come home will present their disturbing petitions. To a certain extent the intensity of their individual irritation will help determine the speed of their return. Fathers, for example, reluctantly accepted by the Army in the first place, will be among the first mustered out. This is particularly true of the greater number of fathers who will never have left the United States.

It should not, however, be assumed that those troops still in American encampments will invariably be the first at the fireside— at least until the curtain has dropped on the war's three stages. There are two reasons that will work against this easiest approach. First, and very much first, is the fact that many of the men still on American soil will have been trained specifically for warfare which is just to begin at the moment when others in arms are ready to relax. It will probably be desirable to mingle fresh troops with the battle-scarred veteran formations shifted to the Pacific theater. Psychological pressures, however illogical from the standpoint of military interests, will be very persuasive, if not completely effective. The men who have mopped up the European end of the Axis will insist on priority in the home-coming as against those most recently inducted. Even before war's end we will hear growing demands for the return of seasoned fighters to American shores while they are replaced or at least spelled by trained troops in reserve on this continent.

As early as November 1943 this attitude had become embedded in the minds of our fighting men. When the service newspaper, *Stars and Stripes*, declared that American soldiers did not want rotation of combat troops, preferring to see Berlin before they came home, a storm of biting letters descended on the editors. As one doughboy wrote:

Who in hell elected you to voice the opinion of the veteran? . . . We have been overseas more than twenty-two months now and have seen six months of combat. I contend that you can't leave combat troops in the line indefinitely and expect the same good work as when they started. . . . When a rear-echelon Johnny says these boys don't want to go home and that they don't need a rest, I think of that old saying, "War has no fury like that of a noncombatant."

This pressure during the European phase of the war will be resisted. In fact, even after German defeat it will not bring too great a response. There is no discount for sentimentality at the exchange of war. Seasoned troops are seasoned troops. The men who survived the hell of Dunkirk turned back Rommel at El Alamein. There is no discharge for performance. At best a system of "rotation" leaves will provide furloughs home for those who have been overseas for an extended period.

The pattern, then, can be outlined. Men not yet overseas when Berlin breaks have a little better chance for a quick return to civilian life. Those with reasonably acute dependency pleas will be among the first home. Men who are needed at home for their specific skills will follow, and with them the few whose return would make jobs for others. Those specifically trained for Asiatic warfare will remain to face the Oriental music.

The draft itself will continue as an operating mechanism even after German collapse. The call for men, however, as transmitted to the local boards, will change in character and number. Reclassification of the few remaining 3-As, the 3-Ds, 4-Fs, and 2-As and Bs will be abruptly halted. Those in 1-A, but not yet inducted, will be sifted to remove fathers and those with limited physical capacity.

Assuming the war ends with Germany before the end of 1944, there will not only be draft retrenchment, but as many as one million men may be rapidly restored to civilian status before the new year gets rolling. Actually, the Army estimates that a minimum of seventy thousand a month will be released or put on the casualty shelf during 1944. After the defeat of Germany the rate will be stepped up.

By the fall of 1945, with the war against Japan then in its most intensive phase, up to four million of America's men—and women—will have finally doffed their uniforms. It is from this point on that continuing discharges remain subject to the fortunes of war in the Pacific. How large will the American land contingent be? Will

China insist on munitions rather than men? Will Russia actively engage Japan in Manchuria? These are the imponderables that postpone the final answer to America's demobilization hopes until 1946.

Assuming that the Japanese war will be largely naval so far as American military participation is concerned, and that the Asiatic land warfare will not require mass American concentrations, it is possible to proceed with a series of projections. By the end of 1945 six million of America's eleven million servicemen will have heard the bugle for the last time. By the end of 1946 the number will have grown to its final demobilization size. Together with the millions discharged before any Armistice, ten to eleven million Americans will be wearing discharge buttons.

Other imponderables will determine the order of release within this demobilized group. The Navy and Marines, for example, can well expect to outserve most branches of the Army. Those units of the Army whose method of warfare has little Asiatic applicability—including some of the Armored Forces—will be among the early eligibles for release. But the character of war will change, and with it the discharge sequence, until the final pattern of the assault upon Japan has been determined. A substantial segment of the Air Forces and Paratroops seems destined for continued participation. The size of our anti-aircraft contingents will be determined by how well Japan's air armada holds up as the war draws to a close.

Military government will continue to hold out its fascinating and civilization-making responsibilities even after the last destroyer has dropped anchor in its American port. The Quartermaster Corps will experience the gradual attrition inevitable with dwindling supply requirements, but hardly in proportion to the over-all forces that will be discharged.

A mixed future awaits the female contingents. Though there will be a continuing but diminishing need for the services rendered by the Wacs, Waves, Spars, Marines, and the rest of the skirted military, their applications to withdraw will be hard to deny. Even by war's end America will not have become fully accustomed to her valuable Amazons.

The most difficult factor that will weigh against thousands of soldiers is their individual irreplaceability in the unit to which they are assigned. Even though acute dependency suggests the wisdom of their return, even though former employers promise the old job back, the fighting efficiency and balance of a military unit cannot always be broken up by sporadic individual withdrawals.

It will be even more difficult for the soldier to accept a decision based on his community's inability, in some cases, to absorb him even where there's no military reason holding up his discharge. A report on demobilization prepared for the President counseled against "local concentrations of ex-servicemen disproportionate to the size of the communities or their employment capacity."

Such will be the pressures against discharge. But war does end— and discharge comes despite all pressures. Except for those honored in the new Flanders Fields and those who seek to remain, discharge, when it finally comes, will bring new problems—pensions to the injured; mustering-out pay to the entire group, Army, Navy, Merchant Marine, etc.; unemployment insurance for those who are thrown into civilian life and don't, after a decent lapse, find jobs. Like the discharge, such measures, too, will be certain. The ultimate amount of money will be haggled over for years to come, but the ink on the initial check will be dry and the cash waiting.

Under the congressional bill passed in January 1944, the overseas veteran who's been in service more than sixty days will get $100 at the time of his discharge—$100 the next month and another $100 a month later. The man who has more than sixty days of domestic service under his belt will receive $100 for two months. Men with less than sixty days of service will get their full payment of $100 when they are discharged. Add to these amounts the regular family allowances which will almost certainly continue during a three-to-six-month period and you have a fairly complete total of what mustering out will bring.

It's very possible that a two- or three-week vacation period at regular Army pay will be thrown in before the monthly mustering-out payments start, though there's some question as to how much of a vacation you can have on regular Army pay.

There's nothing in this entire picture that's even faintly reminiscent of the apple-box days—at least not soon after discharge. For those veterans who run through their allotments before getting work there is the additional near-certainty that unemployment insurance will be paid for something like twenty-six weeks. Here, though, we begin to run into trouble. The allotment's one thing and unemployment insurance another. The allotment or mustering-out pay, or whatever else it will be called, will be given by the federal government. It takes one legislative measure to accomplish and, when accomplished, will apply universally to every ex-serviceman in civilian jeans. But unemployment insurance is a benefit granted by each state. The amounts they give aren't uniform. The length of time for which unemployment benefits are paid varies from state to state. Most important of all, it won't be easy to short-circuit the legislatures in each separate state; they will have to amend their own unemployment-insurance laws. Under the existing setup the ex-serviceman is simply a worker who has been out of employment for a couple of years. No employer has paid tax on his pay. No account has been built up in his name—at least no more than was already chalked up for him on the work he performed before he got his "Greetings from the President."

There will be some resistance to monkeying around with the unemployment-insurance laws when the war's over. We've already had some taste of it. The National Resources Planning Board, before its demise, urged the federal government to decide on uniform benefits for servicemen in all states and then compel the state legislatures to conform their laws to the new federal requirements. You can expect some grumbling, fighting, administrative rivalries. There'll be the opposition typified by the Patterson newspapers: "The NRPB is vague as to where we're to get the money to finance this bliss. . . . The NRPB document is a ground plan for an American state that will closely resemble Fascism."

But this kind of opposition won't present the major barrier. The most serious difficulty will be a purely mechanical one—the fact that forty-eight separate state legislatures have to meet and that many of them meet only once every two years unless they are specially summoned. The war's end will come, at least in part, before the necessary action can be taken by many of the states. By and large, though, this will be one of those instances in which lethargy will not dominate. You can count on the unemployment insurance.

You can be almost equally sure that when Yank Jones finally reaches the age of sixty-five his social security will not have been docked for the two to three years out in service. The government will lumber and grunt, but it will eventually decide that, even though taxes weren't paid on his behalf during these years, he spent the time in useful employment.

No matter how liberal such provisions are, however, no one will be satisfied. This subsidized hiatus between war and peace will not be tolerable to thousands who have long chafed at their economically secure, if personally dangerous, position on the government pay roll. The boys will want to get moving, and the taxpayer will want to unload. But there's no automatic bridge back. There are skills that must be resharpened. There are aptitudes that need shaping, aspirations that demand harnessing. And personality itself must be rerouted into more pacific channels.

The Army has long boasted that it makes men. It does. But for war, not peace. The road back this time will be smoothly paved with government funds, even if occasionally sprinkled with the broken glass of confusion. There is little doubt that large educational opportunities will be made available to men in the services who would like a further immersion in academic life before entering the market place. The potential educational resources will be great; the extent to which such liberal-arts schooling will successfully adapt the learner to his competitive struggle will be considerably more dubious. Where purely technical training is involved, however, the educational program is likely to be very practical. We have always done a better job of teaching a man to run a machine than to run a community.

The war will have provided a substantial incentive to collegiate education. The principle of "When in doubt, school" will move a good number of the men. Even during the war large numbers have been added to the college-trained group. The high-school and college correspondence courses made available to servicemen through the Armed Forces Institute have helped in this direction. How much academic credit the men will receive remains in doubt, but the intellectual value of this most extensive correspondence course in the world is unquestioned. More than 100,000 students in uniform have been bitten by the mail-order education bug. It has even been suggested that these Armed Forces correspondence courses be continued and expanded after the war. Education has also been advanced, even if feebly and with little direction, by the orientation lectures, motion pictures, and the assorted civic activities of the Special Services Command. Language study has gotten a tremendous lift.

Perhaps the most lasting of the impressions will have been left by the Army Specialist Training Program which has provided intensive college training in specialized subjects for more than two hundred thousand soldiers. To be sure, many of these soldier students have been shifted into a course of study dictated by Army requirements rather than by their own inclinations.

A further flow of some portion of Army pay for those continuing their educational activities in the period immediately after the war will do for education what the fund-providing activities of the National Youth Administration did in the depression years. Not least attractive will be the opportunities for men in foreign war theaters to attend foreign universities at Army expense. But the Army will be wary of any scholarships in educational fields in which there is an oversupply.

Additional pressure and encouragement will be supplied by the universities both here and abroad in an effort to sell and swell this group further. Academic credit bonuses will in many instances be awarded for military service, just as if the Army stay represented a regular course in the curriculum. But, by and large, the "students" will be a relatively small group. Many soldiers will want to learn something new and useful. The rub is that we won't know for what to retrain them.

A heavy pressure against the resumption of study for many of the younger men in the services will be their own desire to assume a more mature role in the community. The strongest drive toward the campus will be the community's inability to provide that mature role, its inability to give jobs.

We are brought back to the second basic demand of the man in service. He wants a job. First he wants to get out. Now he's out, and he wants work. He feels a little gloomy about the prospects, but he expects that job. And he's well prepared to be angry if he doesn't get it. He has reason to be.

The plain fact is that jobs will begin to be at a premium in the year of heaviest demobilization, 1945. In a later chapter we'll see why this is likely. At this point that basic environmental fact is anticipated because it's part of the second problem of demobilization.

The same Selective Service Act which separated so many millions of the inductees from their former jobs compels their erstwhile employers to make room for Joe. But there's a catch, an unavoidable one. In many cases the statute will turn out to be mere tongue-in-cheek legislation. If the employer's circumstances have so changed as to make the re-employment unreasonable or impossible, then it's no soap for Joe. So, too, if a physical disability prevents his re-employment. Or even if the desire to get away from it all results in his not applying for his job within forty days after he is mustered out.

Even where the boss hires him back there are certain to be many cases that will irritate already frayed nerves. The employer may be more satisfied with the replacement. His compulsion under the law is to rehire his former inductee at the same pay and status. What's status? Will it really mean the same job? Or will equal salary for similar status suffice?

A real effort will be made well in advance to straighten out such questions before the boys actually get back. Selective Service has a Re-employment Division which is working out the rules. For example: During the war a firm has reorganized its setup for efficiency's sake, and the old job just can't be located in the reshuffle. But Johnny comes marching home, fully competent to take on new duties. Is he going to be left out in the cold because Billy-stay-at-home got there on the scene? The Re-employment Division says, "Nothing doing. If you can afford to take Johnny back and he can do the work, you can't weasel out of rehiring him."

Incidentally, even though they aren't specifically mentioned in the Selective Service Act, the ladies who switched from dresses to khaki skirts or navy blues are being promised the same protection. The boss they left behind will have to welcome them back on the same terms. The same is true for the men who left their desks or workbenches to join up with the Merchant Marine; Congress has already ordered their reinstatement on an equal footing with the boys from the armed services.

But going back to old jobs won't be a fraction of an answer to the whole employment question. Many if not most of the men coming out of service will be dependent on new jobs.

One thing is certain. Much more will be done to put the veterans in appropriate jobs than was done after World War I. The reasons are fairly compelling. First of all, explicit promises have been made. Secondly, induction began after an embarrassing ten-year interlude of unemployment. Thirdly, the boys aren't crazy about the fact that "everybody's been makin' hay while we were gone." Fourth, and most important, is America's sophisticated realization that employment doesn't just come natural—that, instead of being a personal misfortune, joblessness is the result of complicated economic, social, and political factors beyond the victim's control. Most of those who were sure during the thirties that anyone who really wanted a job could have one have passed away to a happier atmosphere.

Certain problems facing the whole community will be aggravated for the ex-soldier. He will be rusty at many an old civilian job, inferior to the more recent recruits. Much of the specialized skill he has received in the Army or Navy will have no peacetime utility. His return will present new personnel problems to his former employer, problems of social as well as industrial adaptation.

On the other hand, the community will lean over backward to favor the ex-serviceman. Public pressure will mount until a greater percentage of available jobs goes to the veterans as against the job-seeking civilians. The job-priority principle, already established before the war in the draft law, will dominate substantial segments of private and public employment as a result of spreading legal, social, and psychological compulsives. The discharge button will pay off. In civil service, official priority will again give the veteran something of an edge over his brother in mufti. The American Legion and the already enlarged Veterans of Foreign Wars will devote a considerable part of their energies not only to finding jobs for servicemen but to indoctrinating the community with the culture of veterans' superiority.

Nevertheless, the veteran will find himself in a competitive environment. And some of the things that will happen in the scramble for jobs won't be nice.

The unions will present a special problem. It won't help any if a serviceman runs up against union restrictions when he tries to enter those skilled occupations for which he may incidentally have been trained during his military service. Nor will high dues or entrance fees enchant him on this job hunt. Most likely, though, these obstacles will be the first to crumble. Aware of how serious veteran hostility can be, unions will in most instances pull down the bars where servicemen are concerned. The unions will undoubtedly organize their own servicemen's organization, since they have substantial numbers of members in military service. Because of their traditional hostility to the Legion and Veterans of Foreign Wars, they will try to corral veteran support sympathetic to labor's organizational and political aspirations.

Even where racial and religious prejudices have traditionally closed the door to employment opportunities for minorities, the returning veteran will initially find a little easier access. But this will be only a brief and limited reprieve from the intolerance which the community is likely to revive with greater bitterness as time goes on.

In short, compared with those who stayed home, the average returning veteran will find himself somewhat less equipped for work but with a better chance of finding it. Not least among the factors strengthening his job-seeking effort will be the official government program.

As we have already noted, the law says that Joe's boss must take him back. And don't for a moment think that Joe hasn't been counting on it. True, he's worried, but it's to his old bench that his mind's eye has been turning. The National Opinion Research Center asked the boys in arms, including those who had never worked, "Do you have a definite job ready for you when you return after the war?" Two out of every three answered, "Yes." Maybe they haven't, but the important thing is that they think they have.

But that many will *not* get their old jobs back. The experience of the first year of war—90 per cent of the servicemen discharged from the Army finding jobs for themselves—will obviously not continue when demobilization steps up and the peace contraction begins. That's part of the reason for the War Department's plan for "Selective Service in reverse," under which the Army would discharge men only as jobs opened up at home. The United States Employment Service offices would be used to bring the jobs and the soldiers together. It is certain that a conscious effort will be made to spray the stream of demobilized men over the country rather than flood individual cities, towns, or villages with more men than they can reabsorb. The purpose will be to avoid disappointing that 67 per cent who expect their old jobs until the size of the disappointment can be whittled down. The results will be less impressive than the purpose.

The big hitch, however, as we've already seen, is that it'll take more force than even the Army has to hold the men for other than military reasons or purposes of national security. When the shooting's over they will want to get away from bugles and back to alarm clocks, away from the top sergeant and back to the girl friend. And their families at home are going to want them back just as fast as boat, plane, train, or bus can bring them. Job or no job—home.

Pressure then will be to dig up the job rather than hold the men back. And Selective Service will really move in reverse—once the boys are out. Every local draft board will have a special re-employment adviser assigned to it. He will be Joe's personal representative and agent in getting back the old job or finding a new one. When Joe comes marching home he won't be left to shift for himself. The same draft board that sent him into the Army will be there waiting to boost him back into civilian life.

There'll be more of a helping hand than just one local draft-board adviser. Backing up the adviser will be a local community committee to work on cases that the local draft board can't handle by itself. And backing up these community committees will be the National Employment Clearing House, either separately organized or operating within the United States Employment Service. If there just aren't enough jobs in one town to take care of the boys who are coming back, the national clearing house will try to find work in another area.

The really solid base on which this voluntary job-seeking mechanism will rest promises some very significant results. Many important national organizations, ranging all the way from the American Farm Bureau Federation through the American Legion, the CIO, and the United States Chamber of Commerce, are banded together in this National Clearing House Committee.

The helping hand won't stop at finding a job. The local draft board is likely to become the central point where the returning serviceman can get all kinds of help on benefits to which he's entitled and even assistance in solving his or his family's personal problems.

The United States Employment Service will be devoting its primary energies to placing ex-servicemen. Almost every fraternal and civic organization will have a hand in enlarging the results in its own special way.

Unlike postwar education for the veteran, which on the whole will be diffuse, the job of channeling the specific skills he acquired in service will be handled with precision and a high degree of effectiveness. These skills, the technical and mechanical training involved, should not be underestimated. They will be more numerous and more efficient than we expect—outstripping our ability and capacity to use them. Finding the peacetime aviation equivalent to delivering two thousand tons of bombs nightly is no pushover. We will not have enough trucks in need of repair to match the number of those equipped to do the work.

But, to the extent that skilled jobs are open, the government will be able to provide men, fresh out of uniform, with the requisite training. Where industry needs men with slightly different skills, smooth results will come from a retraining program, no small part of which will be played by business itself. As a matter of fact, some companies, like General Motors, will set in motion dramatic programs for re-equipping former employees who return disabled or handicapped. Those programs will have to be good. General

Motors alone will have on its hands some eighty thousand demobilized former employees.

Even with all these approaches some of the re-employment problems will remain unsolved. Many soldier heroes and officers will find it difficult to get back to their civilian jobs as file clerks, bookkeepers, gas-station attendants. Many handicapped veterans may find it difficult to get back at all.

The bigger business organizations will be ready in most cases to cope with the problem of the handicapped worker, sometimes a little better prepared for him than for his fully able-bodied comrade. Many injured men will be able to return immediately to their old jobs; others will have to be retrained within the plant for new work. Where a returning soldier is completely disabled, whether temporarily or permanently, the Veterans' Administration will act.

The first specific demobilization arrangements made by Congress were along this line: Not only will the Veterans' Administration provide hospitalization, education, and training for handicapped servicemen, but it will provide subsistence allowances for them and their families. The eighty dollars a month for single men and ninety for those married, with an additional five dollars for each dependent, will hardly be a lavish sum. But, when the serviceman's care and board are thrown in, the amounts won't be insubstantial.

The Veterans' Administration is already well provided with laboratories, nursing and training facilities, hospitals, and experimental equipment. Its activities and preparations are described in detail in the official *Handbook for Service Personnel of World War II*, written in the form of easy-to-read questions and answers. Despite its style, it is hardly recommended reading for the fastidious. For example:

QUESTION: What is one of the most remarkable rehabilitation cases?
ANSWER: The most remarkable rehabilitation case is that of a veteran who came out of the war with the loss of both eyes and both hands. Sightless and handless, he resolved to do something. With mechanical appliances he learned to comb his hair and to operate a typewriter with mechanical attachments. After this preliminary training the government provided a special instructor, and he took up the study of law and became a practicing attorney.

One of the probabilities is that the Veterans' Administration will work out a quota system within industry for the hiring of disabled servicemen able to resume work. Under such a system each of the major industries would be responsible for absorbing a certain number of the rehabilitated.

Companion to the industrial-placement programs will be an agricultural-settlement mechanism. A limited number of qualified servicemen will be set up on small homesteads. But plans in this direction are likely to be more ambitious than the actual results. The trend away from the farm will not have been reversed by the war. Nor will the farm promise greater security or prove more attractive to any great number of the men who came from the cities originally. The planning agencies themselves are worried even by the mere mention of such a proposal—worried lest the farms become a dumping ground for the industrial unemployed.

But the valuable drilling that will be performed by all of these separate mechanisms will finally run up against bedrock: How many jobs will there be? All of the demobilization efforts will be directed toward ferreting out the last possible job and putting Joe on the receiving end of a pay check. But none of the job-placement efforts can make jobs that aren't there. No more than you can get water from the fanciest faucets in your washbasin, if the reservoir is empty.

We'd better look at the reservoir.

II

The Future of Your Job

CHAPTER IV

Rusty Guns and Rancid Butter

WE'D BETTER LOOK AT THE RESERVOIR. Maybe you've been too busy to notice it yourself, but here's what happened. Several thousand new folks suddenly moved into your community, and the city council became worried about a water shortage. So a reservoir-expansion bill was pushed through, doubling the capacity. It was costly; still you needed it. But now that those newcomers have pulled up stakes, and your town is settling back to normal, you have more water than you know what to do with.

Well, what's the harm in too much water? None at all, except that there's water-purification equipment you'll never use, recently constructed water mains already rusting. And you'll go on paying high taxes on equipment that gives no value.

Water-department workers will be laid off in rising numbers, without other jobs to go to. You see, your whole town is beginning to feel the depression that came when the new folks left and money moved out with them. Yet would you go on running a twenty-thousand-population water pump to supply ten thousand people? There's even some talk around the barbershop about dismantling the extra equipment and selling it for scrap. Either way, it's a heart-breaking business.

That water-supply system is the productive machinery and job-producing capacity of the country. The problem of that figurative reservoir is the problem of *reconversion*, say the economists. Call it what you like, reconversion is everything involved in getting back to peace.

Reconversion sounds like a conference subject for business tycoons. But when they convert business they're converting you and your job; they're deciding what you're going to do and what's going to be done to you for most of the rest of your life. Reconversion is the answer America will give to the question: What are we going to do with our hard-earned victory?

It all boils down to the one word that has already plagued us on most of the preceding pages—employment. For two years the physical resources of the nation have provided jobs for just about everybody interested in holding one, competent or not. Capitalism plus war has given full employment.

Reconversion will determine whether capitalism without war can give full employment.

The trouble is we'll have only one crack at reconversion. As war orders are canceled and billion after billion of government money is withdrawn from the national blood stream, the country could just contract—like a tire going flat with the car doing sixty on a dirt road. Deflation is a good description of what happens. You can almost see the millions of men oozed out of industry as the factories shrink. You can see the bankruptcies as bills remain unpaid. That's what happened in 1920 and 1921.

The United States Chamber of Commerce, in urging planning for the same problems this time—the same problems magnified many times over—vouches for the fact that after World War I "inventory losses of many businesses were so staggering that to this day not all companies have recovered from those losses." The magnitude of the problem confronting us this time makes World War I experience look petty. Here's a sample: Rough estimates indicate that if the Glenn L. Martin Company were to continue full operation for just four weeks after the government stops buying bombers, all its 1942 profits would be wiped out. In the case of the Lockheed Company just a little over two weeks of pay-roll payments without business would be enough to erase its 1942 earnings of eleven and a half million dollars. The real loss to you, as you will see in another chapter, is that the slim difference between survival and failure for a company like Lockheed may mean the end of an important promise in postwar housing—and the end of the permanent jobs it could create.

A second possibility is "boom." It may or may not be accom-

panied by a serious inflation. Industry knows that your pockets will
be loaded with cash, your unspent earnings. Remember that a good
part of industry will not have enjoyed your patronage for some
time. In an atmosphere of loose money it's difficult to have such
ardent competition without bidding prices up. All the participants
are sure it won't last; every sale is a fire sale. The merchandising
ethics are more nearly those of a carnival than a reputable establishment. Everybody's trying to sell anything—and fast. Few are
working for the long pull.

That's what happened in World War I. It breezed by so fast it
was even difficult to call it reconversion. The sequence is significant
because of the parallels that may prevail this time. For six months
after the Armistice in 1918, business unwound itself slowly from
the coils of war and waited watchfully for the next fellow to move.
Then, suddenly, the hesitation came to a end. Someone let the stop-
cock go, and for nine hectic months the gusher roared. In the
shortest boom America has ever known prices went on a crazy
uphill hay ride. That didn't do business much good. It was just
cleaning out the shelves. Despite the outward appearance of boom,
the physical output of the nation expanded less than usual—and
that's the test. Dr. Wesley C. Mitchell, dean of America's economists, who has thoroughly analyzed this first postwar experience of
ours, points out that the nation's output of pig iron, for example,
rose by little more than one fourth of what its peacetime average
would normally have been during this boomlet. Steel ingots came
from the furnaces only half as fast as might have been expected;
our passenger-automobile production went up 48 per cent instead
of the normally expected 71 per cent. Only in the case of building construction was there a genuine advance in the creation of
physical goods.

For the first nine months speculation was intense; the great
American gamble was on. But the showdown came. It came quickly
and dramatically. It would be difficult to capture its impact more
completely than did Dr. Mitchell:

Few men who were in business during those exciting years have forgotten the reckoning that came in 1920-21 with its collapse in prices,

epidemic of bankruptcies, wiping out of paper profits, and grievous sufferings among the unemployed.

If American business resumes its wonted way, will it repeat this performance by first slowing down for a few months under the impact of peace, then grasping for the big profits promised by an enormous consumer demand at skyrocketing prices, thus bring upon itself staggering losses, and delay its resumption of efficient operations for three years after the close of World War II? If the performance is repeated, the popular appeal of over-all economic planning by government will be enormously strengthened, and the nation may decide to try that bold experiment, not immediately after the war, but a few years later.

There's a third way of reconverting—determining in advance the problems that will come with war's end and deciding how those problems will be met before they occur. No, it doesn't even sound easy. Nor is there any real precedent for many of the problems which this time will herald, accompany, and follow the white dove. It doesn't even sound easy the way government economist Mordecai Ezekiel puts it: "If all the major industries should simultaneously operate at low prices, increased wages, and substantially full production, they could both keep all workers fully employed and at the same time pay out and maintain a volume of buying power large enough to make markets for all they could produce."

Yes, it's true. If every factory would employ enough people, paid sufficient wages to buy up what every factory turned out, peace would be wonderful.

The basic problem is wrapped up in the question: "How can we be both peaceful *and* prosperous?" There will be a lot of double talk about technical and financial problems, legal and fiscal issues. Of course many of these phases of returning to peace do present difficulties, and they will be examined in these pages. Underlying all of them, however, is the concern over maintaining our employment and income.

As a people, we've seen our own strength, our production potential, for the first time. By and large, we like the results of a situation which calls for the services of all our manpower and resources, even though we don't like the situation itself. But we're not sure that war is the only cure for the old disease of unemployment, excess capacity, and the other forms of wasted resources which we accepted fatalistically during ten years of depression. Since then we have tasted full employment—even overemployment —and we like it. Can we go on enjoying it?

Part of the answer depends on the size of our present larder and our ability to keep renewing it. Before the war we didn't seem to be able to put to work everything we had. After the war . . .

Well, you will start the rest of your peacetime life in a nation capable of turning out more than one and a half times as much goods as it ever bought in the best peacetime year. The Twentieth Century Fund reaches the dramatic conclusion that for the first time in this nation's history industry will be "physically equipped to give every family in the country what we know in the United States as a middle-class standard of living."

Industrial-plant expansion in this country since the Fall of France in 1940 is almost incredible. In just the first two years the federal government put more money into building new plants than the entire private investment in plants from 1929 to 1940.

Additional amounts were poured into other kinds of construction. There are bitter reconversion problems involved in the more than twenty-five billion dollars' worth of war housing, military and naval establishments of all kinds, utilities, and a vast assortment of physical appendages to war. These, too, are part of the nation when war ends—and part of the reconversion job.

It's not merely that the nation's physical strength has been expanded; in many ways it's been basically altered. We're turning out seven and a half times as much aluminum as we did before the war, and a nation whose diet has been steel begins to ponder the far-reaching consequences of this expansion. When we find our output of magnesium leaping a hundred times, when we find we can extract the metal from a source as inexhaustible as the sea, horizons begin to expand. The ferment of the future may well be in the air. Here, too, there has been enormous expansion. At war's end one plant alone will be turning out almost twice as many planes in one year as the whole nation turned out in the two generations since Kitty Hawk. As for ships, don't stop to count them.

Even the land has groaned under the weight of war and changed its customary yields. Millions of acres and millions of men have been converted to the extraordinary demands of agriculture at war.

America will enter the peace with an industrial establishment, the magnitude of which defies description.

To most people, unemployment in the face of such job-producing machinery will be incredible and certainly unacceptable. The nation will find it hard to swallow two bitter pills: (1) Much of the shiny new factories and equipment isn't worth a darn in peacetime. (2) Most important, the lack of productive facilities was not the cause of prewar unemployment.

To search for a method of finding a peacetime use for *all* our production facilities, including the expanded plant and equipment, is to hit your head against a stone wall. Yet if we want to total the number of job seekers who will be lined up outside the employment agencies we must first know what part of the industrial community will receive a death sentence at war's end.

Part of our future trouble is the fact that the war will have been comparatively easy for us. If we had been forced to cut our output of civilian goods sharply, if we had been compelled to shift our resources radically to the production of weapons, then peace would involve nothing more than bouncing back. In other words, if our choice had really been guns *or* butter, and we had chosen guns, we would just switch back to butter. But except in a few instances that choice was never really necessary.

America's war economy, her apparatus for turning out the products of death, was largely superimposed on a broad and rich civilian base. The truth is that in some cases the civilian base became broader and richer during the war.

America entered the war with idle productive capacity of almost every sort, except for certain imported raw materials like rubber, tin, and some minerals and chemicals. Rapidly the war took up the slack in our excess capacity; fairly rapidly the eight and one half million still unemployed in 1940 were absorbed and a huge military force built up.

But the sharp sacrifices in the essentials of day-to-day living never came. We have managed to turn out fabulous amounts of war goods without seriously dislocating civilian standards of living. We have made few automobiles, tires, and vacuum cleaners. Furniture has been harder to get, radios and electrical equipment more and more difficult to find. But, substantially, the war was not supplied at the cost of civilian goods. It was supplied through a much greater use of existing plant and equipment, a greatly expanded raw material flow, and the addition of a whole new collection of industries constructed specifically for war production.

At the peak of our war effort almost one half of the nation's activity, production, mining, resources, employed manpower, will have been ticketed "on government service." The other half of this colossus, stretched to its full height, will have been producing a civilian output almost as great as America reached in its best year.

But then comes the unwinding. The best customer American business ever had starts pulling in its horns. Even before the end of 1944 much of Uncle Sam's business will be missed. From Washington the notices go out: "Your war contract, GX-22739, is hereby canceled." First the prime contractors, the ones with whom the government did business directly. That's General Motors and Glenn Martin and International Harvester and Endicott Johnson. Immediately they contact the endless thousands of large and small businesses that have been supplying parts, bits and pieces, materials, for prime contracts. Right down the line, to the tiny crossroads nut-and-bolt shop, the message is the same: "Contract canceled. . . . Stop operations." A cold breeze sweeps through America. The breeze becomes a hurricane.

Reconversion is the process of riding the storm. Overnight, over many nights, American business will again become private enterprises looking for private, not government, customers. The functions of private property will again revive, raising the age-old questions that flow from ownership:

"What will I make?"

"How many?"

"Whom will I sell to and how?"

"How do I meet the pay roll?"

"How do I . . . ?"

These, though, are the normal difficulties to which business is accustomed. They are the problems to which executive judgment can be applied. But there will be novel problems, responsive to no individual business adjustment. The word *government* is stamped prominently on most of them. Watch out for the questions that start with "What will the government do about . . . ?"

What will the government do about stimulating expansion? What types of expansion will be discouraged by the government and how? The whole field of continuing material shortages, at least for a short while, will be pre-empted by Washington. But "With what mechanism?" and "For how long?" remain the unsettling questions. A priorities system may be used, so long as there is shortage, to channel key materials first into industries that promise maximum quick employment. Which industries will get first pickings remains to be discussed.

What will the government do about price control? New ceilings will at first have to be fixed on the goods that are coming back into production. You can't start out with the old prices that were charged before the war. Costs of production will be higher: the workers will have been getting better pay; a few materials may still be scarce and cost more; transportation may be more expensive.

If these questions tease you, you're showing the right reaction, because these problems are nothing more than teasers when you consider the other phases of federal policy and action. For example, decisions have to be made on what to do with the billions of dollars' worth of shoes, shirts, ladies' slips (don't forget the Wacs, Spars, and Waves!), canned goods, jeeps, blankets—an endless variety of usable merchandise left in military storehouses. Even the loosest business planning has to take them into account. And solving this problem will be child's play compared to the unloading of that vast industrial empire now in the hands of the government. Would you like to prepare your postwar plans for the marketing of aluminum if you were Alcoa, knowing that the government owns more aluminum capacity than you do and can influence output, market, and price more effectively than any single producer was ever able to do?

Yet you've got to estimate your peacetime price levels. That question alone will complicate and color every decision made by every type and size of establishment. Inflation or deflation: high or low prices? Take your pick or just wait and see.

The "wait and see" of reconversion may yet be the point on which American business will impale itself. "Wait and see" will be the big difference between conversion and reconversion. In war no "wait and see," no fear of the competitor, no uncertainty about the customer. The government absorbs all competition, says what it needs, pays good prices, lays cash on the barrelhead, and is ready for more. In peace the best-laid plans *gang aft agley*, for no more complicated reason than that the customers don't want.

"Wait and see" will dog every step on the road to peace. What materials to use? Shall I safeguard my position in the market by rushing out my old product or prepare my new model and lose time? Shall I dress up the old model so that it looks new? What's my competitor going to do? Shall I scrap the whole idea and move into a new field? Shall I hold back on buying materials—maybe prices will come down? What's my competitor going to do? Shall I run along on low inventories and take a chance on getting stuck without goods? What's my competitor going to do? What does the customer want? Shall I hold on to my extra labor or hand out discharge slips? Will the motorist coast another year or two on the old bus or jalopy while he waits for the new streamlined car?

One observer says that everyone will be wanting the new "super-duper bazooka," with engines or rockets in the rear. The Committee for Economic Development says, "Come out fast with what you've got." But what's my competitor going to do?

Everybody will be tempted to wait. That doesn't mean that everybody will wait. But waiting, wondering, worrying will dominate reconversion, at least in spirit. And spirit is one of the unmeasurables involved in action producing prosperity or depression. Much of the waiting that does occur will be in anticipation of lower prices. The producer waits for the price on materials to fall. The purchaser waits for the price on the product to fall. The employer waits for wages to fall. The laborer waits for the cost of living to fall.

And some of the waiting has a dread circuitousness. The seller waits for some sign that will tell him the size and the taste of the market and give him open sesame to its purse. The buyer waits for a sign of the value and efficiency of the maker's product, and for an assurance that something better is not under the counter. No one wants to be a sucker. So—many wait. And waiting is death to enterprise.

CHAPTER V

One Fourth of a Nation

THERE HAS BEEN BITTER WAILING about the blow that private enterprise received from OPA. Your marrow may have been chilled by the heart-rending cries about how a label on a can of peas destroys the American Way. And the time that professor called American businessmen "profit seekers"—how can free enterprise survive that one?

But—in less than two war years the government has acquired almost one quarter of the industrial machinery and manufacturing capacity of the entire nation. No outcry, no fuss, no moaning at the wailing wall. Quietly, Uncle Sam has become the world's biggest business firm. In little more than twenty-four months the sovereign government of the United States emerged as the leading borrower and lender of money, the greatest buyer of goods, the most gigantic going business concern in all of the world's history.

"They don't like business, they don't understand business," a businessman says, his eyes turned toward Pennsylvania Avenue.

The fact is they *are* business, awfully big business. They like it so well they've taken title to at least one quarter of it. In Uncle Sam's hands are eighteen billion dollars' worth of productive plant and fifty billion dollars' of available merchandise.

Not long after the war is over we will see that the whole argument was like complaining about the pressure of a pebble under your back while being run over by a ten-ton truck. Balking at the tight fit of a price schedule while the government builds a factory potentially competitive to yours!

One fourth of the nation government-owned. Some of it good

for a long time; some of it worthless at war's end. Some of it run by bureaucrats; some of it operated for the people by private business. One fourth of the nation government-owned; providing jobs in the millions; turning out spendable money in the billions. And who knows what to do with those factories, smelters, pipe lines?

That, too, is reconversion. The answer will be influential in determining the number of people in jobs, where they work and who pays them; the kind of society in which you'll live; the direction of the free-enterprise system in America.

Before any of these central questions can even be approached we've got to know what the colossus called Government Plant really is. While some leaders of the business community insist that the most important problem that faces free enterprise is the disposition of these tremendous national properties, the National Industrial Conference Board finds it an exaggerated problem. Most of it, says the Board, is useless in peacetime. If that's actually so, this one fact may be responsible for the greatest effect on the rest of your life. If the vast industrial empire owned by the government is useful only during war, can create jobs only with war, how great may be the temptation for some future American government, wrestling helplessly with unemployment, to solve its difficulties with the same instrument.

Actually it will be difficult to compute the value of the government-constructed plants. In many instances money was no object and was spent like water. But the safest estimates are enough to make anybody who can remember billion-dollar digits hold his breath. A conservative guess is around eighteen billion dollars; some estimates go as high as twenty-five billion. Take rock bottom, and it's still obvious that government production facilities constitute a whole national economy by themselves. Under President Roosevelt's war administration the government has acquired title to more productive capacity than there was total national wealth in the country under Abraham Lincoln's administration.

All in all, lumping government and privately owned production facilities, the nation has more than a seventy-five-billion-dollar total. What we are going to do with the government's share after the Axis runs up the white flag will be headache enough. But that's only part. Uncle Sam has mountains of goods in warehouses, depots, and storerooms. When the conflict is over, the unused war weapons, like planes, jeeps, guns, tanks, will be counted in the many thousands. And an army uses essential civilian articles too, such as blankets, shirts, trucks, radios, soap, canned peaches, ships. Fifty billion dollars' worth of these surplus supplies puts Uncle Sam in business with a whale of an inventory.

But the productive potential represented by government-plant capacity is the permanent fixture in the economic scene. It can't be wished away or used up fast. It can't be dumped in Africa or sold in Army-Navy stores.

There are two factors which magnify the value of that portion of the government property that is usable after the war. It is the most up-to-date, technologically perfect equipment that modern construction, engineering, and science could produce. Yes, the government's got the best. And some of the productive equipment gains added significance when you examine its strategic character. The fact that the United States owns the largest chain of hotels in the world will have little impact on the foundations of our economy. But the war has demonstrated that a whole national economy can be held in line and directed toward national aims by simply controlling key relationships and key commodities. For example, the Controlled Materials Plan, which has been the key instrument in directing American supply and production, revolved around a set of restrictions on only three basic commodities—steel, aluminum, and copper. Limiting the amount of a basic metal which a manufacturer can get reduces automatically the amount of other materials he can put into production.

Jesse Jones, who as head of the Reconstruction Finance Corporation has opened and snapped shut a fat government purse, estimates that the Treasury has spent about twenty-five billion dollars' total during the first three years of war to build war-necessary plants and facilities. Perhaps as much as one third of this was spent for purely military establishments, such as camps and depots. But here's where the trouble starts. How much of the balance, the remaining fifteen to eighteen billion dollars' worth, can be beaten, like the biblical swords, into plowshares? Those who minimize the problem say that *only* five billion dollars' worth can be considered as potential competition in the production of materials or goods for peacetime living. Others insist it will be twice as much.

This much is certain. Some of the plants will be useless when the war is over. Constructed entirely with a view to the production of special war commodities, they will be unable to turn out the kind of goods that a nation at peace can use—so long as it remains at peace. Our powder plants, for instance, have no function in a peaceful world. Even the buildings are useless, since they are located, for reasons of safety, in places where no businessman in his right mind would ordinarily put up a factory. When the need for munitions is over there will be little alternative but to close those plants. So, too, with many of the ammunition plants, shipyards, and factories turning out extremely specialized items for war. Some of the aircraft and ordnance facilities will also prove to be unconvertible.

Actually the argument over the number of plants that can be converted is likely to prove academic. The real question is how many will be converted. If we faced a peacetime emergency that had all the grimness of war, we'd all be surprised at how many of the plants could be turned over to civilian production. Or if America were short of industrial goods, of desperately needed new factories, or had a ready-made market for the goods that these plants could turn out, mountains would move and factory walls would groan. You'd see conversion as miraculous as that which made of America, starting from scratch, the world's greatest arsenal in only two years.

But these conditions will not exist. And the economic environment, political attitudes, and action will make the decision. There will be a fear of glut. It is precisely because American business was afraid of a swollen supply of goods without markets that the United States Government today owns this huge industrial machine. Private business was reluctant to expand its own capacity to produce war goods. An understandable reluctance. In the heyday of 1928 and 1929 America was still producing at 20 per cent less than capacity. It was a simple philosophy: no sense buying a suit five sizes larger when, as it is, the one you're wearing swims on you.

Washington held out every kind of attractive bait to get private companies to build the new plants, but few nibbled. In place of the normal twenty-year period, business was permitted to amortize or wipe off the cost of wartime expansion in five years. Government loans were available almost without strings and in almost any amounts. But business, by and large, was not going to be saddled with useless factory space and feel the pressure for using it when the shooting was over. The war presented two alternatives: either business would build the necessary plants or the government would. Business didn't—the government did. And business is now hoist by its own prudence; it faces a powerful competitor.

For labor, too, the future of government plants is troublesome. Most of the government facilities are operated by private companies on a lease basis, some with and some without purchase option. In other cases a private company functions as the manager. Here labor doesn't deal with government, the owner, but with private enterprise, the manager. When the plants stop working, the private companies will step out. No more negotiations; no more jobs. If the operation reverts to the government, labor runs smack up against Roosevelt's peacetime decision that you can't strike against the government. Don't minimize this labor headache. Rough estimates show that in Cleveland, for example, one fifth of all the industrial workers are on the pay rolls of plants wholly owned by the government. And Cleveland's not unusual.

The most visible effect of the use to which the government-owned plant is put will be in the type of commodities the consumer will be able to buy. The future, according to the engineers, belongs to the light metals. Even before the war some of the automobile designers insisted that the most economical and most efficient car would be one that substituted aluminum for steel. But before the war we had been living in a period of high price and restricted supply of the light white metal. Expanding supply and use and a reduced price are difficult to secure if one company owns almost all the facilities.

But what trust-buster Thurman Arnold could not do with his four-year anti-trust prosecution, his 155 witnesses, his 40,708 pages of testimony, the war has accomplished. No longer is Alcoa king of the roost. More than half of all aluminum-processing facilities are in federal hands. The government's nine bright new plants can turn out more than a billion pounds every year. Throw in the forty-five plants for fabricating the aluminum and the United States will be *the* power in the metal of tomorrow. But there are important "ifs."

If the government continues to turn out aluminum. If Alcoa doesn't turn out to have effective strings attached in the form of patent licenses. If the plants are not sold to Alcoa, scrapped, or gradually permitted to settle into disuse.

The same is true in the case of magnesium. Here again a control exercised over a precious light-weight metal has been broken by the demand of war for a vastly increased supply. After World War I, several companies entered the magnesium market, but it didn't take long for two groups to corner the business—Dow Chemical and American Magnesium. Alcoa stuck its finger in the pie by buying up complete control of the latter, then making a deal which put all production in the hands of Dow. Came the war, and Washington went into the business. Today, by comparison, Dow is an insignificant producer. The United States owns 94 per cent of the nation's magnesium facilities.

The rest of your life will be affected by the alternatives in this one sphere alone. The government has the power to eliminate monopoly in these two key light metals of the future, aluminum and magnesium. Or it can create a new monopoly far larger in size and power.

One billion dollars spent by the government on steel represents a change that will be lived with for a long time. Its three large mills, 120 smaller plants, and additional facilities, added to existing private plants, may amount to only a small slice of America's master material. But the effect will not be small. The government's 10 per cent in steel is more important than at first appears. If, after the war, private steel production were to shrink to its worst depression level and the government were to decide to keep its steel production at capacity, the United States would be turning out about half of the nation's yield. And it is precisely during a depressed period that the pressure of unemployment will be greatest on the government to move every wheel under its command.

Disposing of government-plant capacity is a long-range problem. The ultimate decisions are likely to bear little resemblance to the action that is taken on or around demobilization day. The plants will live through many an administration, many a political philosophy, and many extremes of economic environment. These plants will stand to embarrass and to stimulate, to gather dust and belch smoke, to be inveighed against and prayed to.

The government's capacity to produce metals like steel is more important because of its strategic position rather than its size. Government steel in Texas, Utah, Nevada, and particularly California, opens important new industrial possibilities in the West. The Eastern control of metal may be over. Henry Kaiser and Uncle Sam together may build a new Western industrial empire.

In some cases entire industries are on the inventory recorded by the United States Bureau of the Budget; in other cases, shreds and pieces of many industries. Metals like copper, lead, and zinc are being processed in government plants, but they are quantitatively and proportionately small. Don't scratch off their importance, though. If they remain in government hands they will be commanding yardsticks against which the output and price of private holdings can be measured.

There is a tangled and curious future ahead for many industries as a result of the government's ownership of just one thing—machine tools. Until the war little attention was paid to the machine-tool industry. But when the public mind was haunted by fears of an Axis victory the first defense bottleneck brought everybody up sharp. All eyes were on the machine tool, the root from which production springs, the very parent of production itself. This has been a war of metals, and the backbone of the metalworking industries is the machine tool. And there weren't enough in 1940, and '41, and '42. The government went into the market. When the war is over at least half of the tools working in thousands of separate private plants, large and small, in almost every industry will be government-owned.

One study reports that 70 per cent of the tools in use in 1940 were at least ten years old. The government's tools are almost brand new, with an average productivity about twice that of the prewar machinery-making instruments. Thus, even where the government doesn't own particular plants, it has at least a theoretical control because of its title to these basic tools in use. Don't stretch this one too far, though. The machiavellian possibilities are great, the probabilities small. This is one case where business will quickly exercise its option to buy and scrap the old tools.

The potentialities inherent in other government properties, however, may come to fruition. The government's investment in airplane production is ten times that of the private companies. Free enterprisers are hopeful that the airplane will do for you what the automobile did for the generation after the last war. More cautious observers, though, aren't quite sure that both the government and the private plane industry haven't taken hold of a lion's tail, and no matter what happens somebody is going to get clawed. Both groups are apt to be right—at different times. The immediate future for the airplane will be dwarfed by the size of the industry available to do the job. Before our generation has passed out of the picture the airplane may well be king. There's little certainty, however, that the present plant will be the force that engineers the coronation.

Closely linked with the future of the airplane is high-octane gasoline. Here, too, the demands of war have brought major government activity that will long outlive the war. Unlike the airplane, there is nothing dubious about the future of the high-horsepower gas. Transportation by air or highway will experience the stimulant provided by the twenty petroleum cracking plants owned outright by the government and the thirty financed in part by federal funds.

Traditional means of transportation will feel the elbow of government in its side. Oil from the Gulf coast to the Eastern seaboard will continue to pass through United States-owned pipe lines. Before the final Armistice there will be some thirty-eight hundred miles of such underground tunnels, including the famous Big Inch with a capacity of 300,000 barrels a day.

Transportation brings us to a real headache ahead, even if it's a headache on balloon tires. Jesse Jones's RFC has built synthetic rubber plants that can provide 800,000 tons of synthetic rubber every year. More than fifty such plants will be available after the war to supply one third more than America's largest prewar civilian needs.

The difficulties will be as large as the supply of synthetic rubber but nowhere as flexible as the product itself. What about the normal American imports of natural rubber, once peace has reopened the tradeways of the world? Will we follow the economic nationalism demanded by the existence of the synthetic rubber plants and the jobs they represent? Will the cheaper foreign product be embargoed by tariffs, and will all American industry that needs rubber have to pay the higher price for the more costly artificial product? Or should the government subsidize the price downward until further advances in the manufacturing processes bring about the same result? What about the Dutch East Indies, and Liberia and Brazil?

The consideration of headaches brings back the painful memory of the ships rusting in the Hudson and Delaware rivers after World War I. Are there enough rivers for this war's crop? While the public imagination has been captured by a Henry Kaiser, it is worth remembering that three quarters of the nation's shipbuilding resources are owned by the government. By the time the seas are restored to peaceful travel the Maritime Commission will own a larger merchant fleet than any other three maritime nations combined.

The figures will prove less impressive when it becomes necessary —as it will—to withdraw the hastily built Liberty ships from the oceans. But it is significant that the government turned in mid-war to the manufacture of more durable vessels, the Victory ships, which will continue to sail after the war as the equal of any others.

The shipyards will remain a big item on our national ledger, but as with the ships, the yards must be listed as a liability rather than an asset. Not only is there unlikely to be any reasonable basis on which continued large-scale shipbuilding can be justified, but the government may even move in reverse in order to achieve harmony with other nations. The resurrected maritime nations of the world— France, Holland, Norway, Belgium—will want to join England and the United States and resume their old positions on the high seas. So will Germany and Japan.

The extent, variety, and size of these assorted government holdings are sufficient to assure a long period of postwar indigestion.

The job of reconverting government plants is more than six times the size of the job involved in turning over private plants to peacetime use. New private construction was little more than 15 per cent of total wartime expansion. And most of that consisted of adding a wing or section to a prewar factory. Most of the expansion of private output came about simply through using to the full what was there before.

Actually there are few possibilities available to the government in tackling its reconversion task. And you can bet your boots that all of them will be used. Some of the new capacity can be retained by Washington and operated like TVA. Some can be sold to private industry. (Some government factories will already be in private hands before the war is over.) The government can follow a policy of gradually disposing of this vast accumulation, keeping a lot of it in grease to be unloaded when it will not disturb economic conditions. There's always the possibility of junking entire plants. The one advantage of this is that the buildings won't be there to taunt by their presence.

To anticipate accurately the action that will be taken, two primary realities must be faced. One of them will dominate the period immediately after the war. The other will dominate the entire postwar generation.

America's complexion after the war will bear little resemblance to the New Deal. America's direction during the initial postwar period will be to the right. Government ownership and operation will be unpopular political programs. The day will belong to private enterprise. Political, economic, and social policy, the behavior of government and people, will reflect this trend—until an extended period of mass unemployment.

The second and lingering reality will be the recurring question of jobs. Unemployment is the phobia of this age. The whole issue of reconversion is essentially: How many jobs, how fast, and by what means? The idle shipyard won't disturb the community. Americans are tolerant of waste. A reserve water reservoir doesn't irritate simply because it isn't being used. But watch the cityfolk and their rising ire if an unexpected drought reveals that the reserve reservoir has been neglected and can't be used when needed. So, too, the moldering shipyard will stand out like a sore thumb in a period of work famine.

Because of this concentration on employment, certain war-expanded industries will be singled out for both public attention and government action. We will focus on them not because of their economic utility in peacetime but because of the monumental employment they once gave. Tragically, though, our civilian needs after the war will have little relationship to the employment capacity of the most job-giving industries in wartime. The outstanding illustration will be the aircraft industry, which, together with explosives, accounted for more than one third of our war expansion. Both those activities will be the most difficult to keep going at a fraction of the levels we enjoyed so much.

During the first year after the war the main government emphasis will be on unloading—a regulated unloading that will not upset the business community. The celebrated Baruch-Hancock Report made two things clear—that the government's ownership would contract, but not so hastily or disorderly as to injure business. Even before 1944 the advocates of free enterprise were already beginning to press for a reduction of government holdings. Curiously, the congressional committee concerned with studying national expenditures directed its first shot at the government's real-estate holdings. The disclosures were startling.

One fifth of the nation's land area is vested in the government. It's difficult to realize that our government owns more acreage than the combined areas of Maine, New Hampshire, Vermont, Rhode Island, Massachusetts, Connecticut, Pennsylvania, New York, New Jersey, Delaware, Maryland, West Virginia, Virginia, North Carolina, South Carolina, Georgia, Florida, Ohio, Alabama, Kentucky, and Indiana. Most of this land, of course, has long been in the public domain, but in just the first three years of war the War Department alone acquired land almost equal to the size of the state of South Carolina and larger than West Virginia. Training and maintaining a military organization like the one America kept on continental shores during World War II takes a lot of acreage. Total government land area used for direct war purposes is equal to the combined territory of Connecticut, Delaware, Maryland, Massachusetts, New Hampshire, New Jersey, Rhode Island, Vermont, and half of Maine.

Measured in other terms, the size of the area is only slightly larger than the difficulties it causes. For the state governments the growth in federal landowning will mean serious financial problems. Government acquisition of these properties, by whatever method—purchase or condemnation—results in their elimination as a source of local tax revenue.

The demand after the war will be that the government start selling—and fast. Little by little the government will let go. A factory and its site will be sold together. With a hotel returned to private ownership will pass the earth on which it sits. Farmers will return to till the soil pounded hard by G.I. boots. Land will be made available for the rehabilitation of veterans who want to move back to the earth.

The disposal of much of this real property recently acquired will be a very easy job compared with the intricacies involved in getting rid of the government plant facilities. Industry will be loath to have the government hold on to the aluminum mills, steel plants, plane factories, and so forth. But industry will not be too eager to purchase them for its own use. If private enterprise were willing and able to buy, it could liquidate these government holdings and end its problem. All it would have to do would be to exercise its options to buy. But businessmen are already worried about what they're going to do with their own facilities which have undergone some expansion.

About half the new government plants are owned by the Defense Plant Corporation, a subsidiary of the Reconstruction Finance Corporation. Most of the DPC property will prove easily convertible to peacetime production, unlike the plants built and operated by the Army and Navy. This DPC capacity will be the most desirable of all the government properties from the standpoint of civilian manufacture.

Though owned by the government, most of these holdings are actually being run by the corporations which, after the war, would be competing with the government plants' output. Three fourths of the government steel facilities are now operated by five big corporations, almost 50 per cent under the wing of United States steel. A small group of aircraft and automobile corporations operate the government's aircraft plants. The situation has been summarized by Lewis Corey: "The synthetic-rubber program revolves around the Standard Oil group, the Dow Chemical interests (four plants), the DuPont and Mellon interests, and the big chemical and rubber corporations. The Dow interests (Dow Chemical and Dow Magnesium) operate seven of the new magnesium plants, and five corporations operate most of the balance. Alcoa was highly favored; it gets almost one half of the new aluminum capacity (thirty-three out of seventy-six plants). Some of the earlier contracts outrageously favored Alcoa, and brought protests from the Senate Truman Committee and other sources."

In most cases the private operators have an option to buy the plants they've run. Significantly, such options don't exist in those industries in which the danger of monopoly is greatest, the lightweight metals, synthetic rubber, and the pipe lines.

Having an option, though, and exercising it are two different things. Under the options which exist in the present contracts, knockdown prices have been ruled out. The existing legal clauses hold out no great promise for bargain hunters. But chances are that the government will change its mind when it sees the crowds staying away from its auction block. Either prices will come down or many of the plants will simply rust.

Another hitch is that the present operator must take the whole plant or nothing. The government has thus protected itself against the private company's walking out with the heart of the plant, leaving the government saddled with useless hulks that it could not operate itself or sell to anybody else. But the alternative for years to come would be placards with faded lettering dotting the landscape: "For Sale." That's why Baruch's proposal to break up the plants will gradually replace the original contract arrangements.

One of the biggest barriers may yet prove to be the disadvantage of buying a plant you've run yourself during the war. The workers will be accustomed to the high wages negotiated when Uncle Sam was behind the pay window. Hardheaded business interests may decide in many instances that it is better to cool down the community's expectations before purchase—cool 'em down by not operating the plant.

In still other cases the private operators will decide to buy and continue running the government-owned plant, scrapping their old facilities. Since the government's are more modern, they can frequently produce at lower cost. In steel it's likely that former government-owned mills will be able to capture customers even in an oversupplied market. The contests will be keen. Bitter argument will take place over which should be protected, the privately owned plants facing competition for the first time or the customer's interest in a lower price.

In terms of employment, scrapping the old company properties in favor of plants purchased from the government may reduce the number of employment opportunities. The efficient plant is the technologically superior. The better the machine, the less labor needed for the same volume of output.

Determining who may buy will be a national issue. The fear of monopoly will spring up soon in the months immediately following the war. The dangers of concentration and trusts will be increased if present operators are in a position to pick and choose among the well-planned and highly economic facilities. On the other hand, if government policy is specifically designed to get these plants at bargain prices into the hands of operators not now in the field, the high-cost war producer may well stagger under the competitive blow. He will charge that the government has ill repaid him for his war production. But if the policy is sale to the present operators, cartels may find it desirable to buy up government properties for the sole purpose of retiring them from a competitive market. There is no easy way to sit on this fence.

The consequences are grave. This picture just can't be prettied up. The industrial journal, *Business Week*, concludes:

It'll be no easy job to dispose of the plants without providing a field day for speculators, or without giving some companies unfair advantage over others, or without preventing fullest practical use of the new capacity. And with the control of whole industries at stake, it's a safe assumption that most of the strongest financial and industrial interests in the country will be in there fighting for preferred position.

It is not too difficult to forecast what will happen. Not many months will elapse before the option clauses in the plant contracts are liberalized in favor of the companies. Reduced standards will be fixed for negotiating prices. Still, haggling and jockeying will continue for months, and in many cases years, because both business and government are on the spot.

Before long the talk of selling will take on new color. The government will find itself renewing the leases to the present operators for another few years, playing for time and continued negotiations. Settling price will not be easy. To charge the original cost of the plant, less the amount it has already depreciated, as provided in the options, obviously won't make sense in many cases. After all, cost was pretty much disregarded in the building of the plants.

But one factor could change the whole picture and speed up sale. If inflation were to occur in any large degree, plants which weren't really worth their original cost would suddenly become bargains in terms of the inflated dollar. In that event something new would also be added: not only would the wartime operators be anxious to purchase, but so would speculators buying just for resale, not for production. Businessmen, however, are wise in not banking on this eventuality. Prices may continue upward for a little while, but as for inflation—forget it.

Where continued lease, let alone outright sale, still won't tempt private capital, there is another possibility quite compatible with the private-property system. The government makes a deal with a company to split the profits while the United States keeps the ownership. It will be surprising if some mixed corporations aren't formed in which the ownership is held jointly by the private management and government.

A good part of the property will not be unloaded, despite the bargain prices that will eventually be offered, despite the easy credit and fluid financing, despite the business insistence that the United States disgorge. A large amount will be retained by the Army and Navy. That will be true of property that has no convertible value, its utility being limited essentially to military needs.

Fortunately, one disposal slot is still left. Machinery, tools, factories, public works, and almost every other form of productive wealth have been partially destroyed in many countries. Even before the war is over a good part of Europe will be crying for industrial rehabilitation. Except in the rarest instances, it will be difficult to send entire plants; but a great variety of machine tools, both government-owned and those swapped in by private industry, can be made available for the restoration of Europe's machinery.

Less complex but more drastic in immediate effect is the problem of the estimated fifty billion dollars' worth of every conceivable type of commodity in the hands of the government on Armistice Day. A danger that concerns the business community is the possibility that the government will dump some of these goods on the consumer market, that the fifteen billion dollars' worth of shoes, shirts, blankets, canned goods, etc., will find their way quickly to your neighborhood stores in competition with what otherwise would be newly manufactured goods.

This fear is almost certain to prove ill-founded. Little of the merchandise will be dumped in this country. It will be held and stored and gradually moved into civilian channels. Some of it will be resold to the individual manufacturer who first made the goods, in order to enable him to dispose of his merchandise through his ordinary outlets.

The community, though, has a real interest in what the government does. Whether it dumps the goods or resells to the manufacturers, the number of new jobs available will be affected. Those goods may mean competition with job-giving production of new goods. Distribution abroad, through the channels of the rehabilitation agencies and Lend-Lease, appears to be the only alternative.

One of the first tasks will be finding a place to keep the goods. One of the ticklish situations in reconversion comes from the government property sitting on factory floors in private plants. A sudden end of the war will leave many producers with enormous inventories of finished goods, as well as raw materials, earmarked for war. They will want to get the stuff out of the way as fast as possible. But the knife cuts two ways. Once back in government hands, that inventory represents a threat: it can come back on the market to compete with newly manufactured goods. The variety of articles involved is almost inconceivable: all sorts of textiles, the great assortment of merchandise found in the post exchanges, machine tools, hand tools, building materials, and every kind of raw material. Part of the government's great holdings consists of stock piles of many critical materials—chrome, wool, rope, alcohol, drugs, diamonds, mercury, silk, sugar, rubber, etc.

Much of the loose and movable government property is already scattered to all corners of the earth. One important armament manufacturer, as a matter of fact, sees this as a silver lining in the cloud. In peacetime he makes agricultural equipment—tractors for farms. During wartime much of the same kind of equipment has been devoted to war needs, and a great deal of it is abroad. He has little doubt that the merchandise will remain there and doesn't feel bad about it. He can't think of any better way to encourage foreign countries to buy the rest of his line. The Army has been carrying the sample case for American industry.

One thing on which all the interested parties seem agreed: there is no intention of using the old Army-Navy-store technique as a method of disposing of any real portion of this civilian merchandise. Will Clayton, head of the Surplus War Property Administration, has definitely taken the stand that this time all of the regular channels of distribution will be given a shot at the government's knockdown goods. The trick will be for the government to keep it flowing smoothly and fairly. Part of the accepted strategy is to fight postwar inflation. If the enormous amount of saved-up money in America were to start competing for the limited amount of existing goods at the end of the war, Uncle Sam would have to dump in order to prevent inflation. In many ways the most effective government weapon against an inflation due to a shortage of goods will be this sword hanging over civilian distribution. Our experience after World War I—when the cost of living rose 25 per cent in the year and a half after the Armistice—will not be repeated this time if the Surplus War Property Administration has its way. It has definitely set up the policy of "selling all it can as early as it can"—in fact, even while the war is still going on.

But these are only small phases of the overshadowing problem. America has aged a generation in just the first three years of war and has altered its direction along new paths, some of which have not yet quite been charted.

For instance, in five industries—aircraft manufacture, shipbuilding, synthetic rubber, aluminum, and magnesium—businessmen acting for the government will have accomplished almost a total nationalization, although no one intended it. In other instances government will own a little piece in one place and a big piece in another. In some cases—and it has been suggested that the new aluminum industry be one—business and government may find themselves in actual partnership, divvying the take.

Fortune Magazine is afraid that some big corporations will "sequester and privatize sections of the free market . . . by killing competition, not with better mousetraps, but by a variety of devices learned in the lobby, the locker room, and the jungle." It will take more than business-minded *Fortune's* alarms to alter the probabilities. Monopoly is here to stay. One of the most difficult aspects of demobilizing the government plant will be to sell it in such a way as to increase free competition.

The National Planning Association insists that "industrial and economic patterns of the country for the next generation will be determined largely by the disposition and use of the government-owned war plants." The National Planning Association is right, but the force of history, the pressure of time, the magnitude of the problem, are not likely to permit an alteration of the basic industrial control in America.

So there it stands, this vast industrial machine that private enterprise refused or was unable to build in wartime and will be reluctant to buy in peacetime. Capable of feeding, clothing, housing and employing millions of our population when geared to destruction, these facilities present an important key to tomorrow. Simply left in the hands of the government, they can conceivably become the instruments of a new economic tyranny. Or they may just rot and bother no one—except the people who might have been employed in them.

CHAPTER VI

The Machine That Makes Work

STEP CLOSE TO THE BRAWLS in the streets of Boston in midwinter 1946 and you will hear *the* question. Open the closed doors of the executive board of the Committee for Economic Development and the words will hit you as you enter. Sit with the uneasy councils of the Allied Military Government in occupied Vienna and the refrain will trouble you as it will the military leaders. Move with the underground as it explodes in Hamburg, or with the not-very-free Free German Committee as it operates in Moscow, and you will hear it repeated.

"Will I have a job?"

The world after the war will be dominated by that question and your life after the war will be shaped by the answers to it. Almost every single postwar problem flows from that query. And you will be the one asking it.

In large measure that question, repeated by millions of people in scattered corners of the world, brought us World War II. The war will not have removed the causes that produced it. The basic concern over employment will continue to motivate the authoritarian states, the democratic states, and the object of their affections, the rest of the world.

It's the question which underlies Communism. Communism is an answer to that question. It's the question which underlies Fascism. Fascism is an answer to that question. They may be good or bad answers, but they are answers to, "Will I have a job?"

Unemployment. Infant of the machine. Father of modern war. Grinning ghost at the peace table.

81

If you think this is a new preoccupation with employment and a "brave new world" emerging from this war, look back a moment to World War I. H. G. Wells wrote during the final spasms of that holocaust: "The old order is finished. We are facing the century of the common man."

Sidney Webb, intellectual leader of the British Labor party, wrote in 1917: "The first principle of the new order will be an organized revolt against the inequality of circumstance. . . . By means of the National Minimum (providing full employment under minimum wage standards), sanitation, education, and sustenance can be assured to every willing worker in good and bad times alike."

Editorials in American journals were echoing Woodrow Wilson's "New Freedom," appraising the steps taken "to meet the evils of the old system to which its radical critics had long called attention in vain and which the war had rendered intolerable."

Yes, war renders unemployment intolerable. It always does.

War is a time of uneasy conscience and glib promise. But the easy promises may themselves multiply the employment difficulties America will face. A promise of full employment, accepted at face value by the people, will compound the dangers of whatever joblessness will exist when disillusionment comes. During the first years of war, capitalist enterprise used the language of socialism. It intoxicated itself, misled the nation, and paved the way for a larger postwar hangover than it might otherwise have suffered.

For the first time in its history, private enterprise has pledged full and continuous employment. But full and continuous employment is not a private enterprise promise. It is both a Marxist and a Fascist promise and may yet bring on private enterprise some of the consequences of either system. For enterprise, a more realistic statement of its own potentialities would have been healthier.

The promise was given for understandable reasons. Wasn't enterprise providing full employment in 1942 and 1943? Or was it war that was making jobs, with enterprise merely the employment agency for Mars? Modern war imposes many of the economic attributes of socialism (if not the political characteristics) on the most rugged of capitalist nations. But with peace the attributes change.

So will the promise. As a matter of fact, as the light of Armistice grows brighter, as the problems and realities of peace become more difficult to dodge, the free enterprisers begin to show more caution. By January 1944 representatives of the CED already flatly denied that private enterprise had ever promised full and continuous employment. "Full employment" dropped out of the literature of the Committee for Economic Development to be replaced by "high levels of employment." Eventually it will yield to "satisfactory levels of employment." And that too will remain to embarrass.

How much greener the more distant pastures look. When representative executives were asked whether they expected boom or slump two years after the end of the war, a greater number expected a boom in business generally than expected a boom in their own enterprises. Among the pessimists, more anticipated a slump in their own business than in the economic life of the nation. The optimism fades as the businessman gets closer to the area of intimate knowledge.

The same was true in the case of civilians and soldiers. Sixty-seven per cent of the servicemen, removed from civilian life and problems, expected a definite job on their return. But apparently the general public is more pessimistic about its own future. Only 23 per cent thought there would be enough jobs, while 45 per cent expected some unemployment and 28 per cent anticipated considerable joblessness. Four per cent had no idea.

Who is nearer the truth? The probabilities can be appraised, and part of the process is simple. Simple, not pleasant. It merely involves stating the realities. But there are also many "ifs" about the postwar world. The advance blueprinting of the mechanism and its functioning can't be complete. It's a little like having three stones of different weights, two of which equal the third. There are several ways of placing them on the opposite ends of a scale, but only one way to make them balance.

Factors accentuated by the war increase the possibilities of a period of great spending. There are other factors which will depress the economic life of the nation. The number of jobs after the war will depend on the weight of each set of conditions, how they operate, and at what time their pressure will be felt most intensely.

For example, the huge quantity of savings accumulated during the war years *can* make millions of jobs. But there are questions that must be answered before *can* reads *will*. Will the savings be spent? How much of them? Will the flow be even? At what time after the war will the savings turn into actual demand for goods? Will the spending be so great as to bring about inflation or so little as to allow a deflationary shrinking of prices and production? How much employment *can* one hundred billion dollars of savings give if they are a one-time expenditure? Does the presence of the spendable savings prove much more than that water flows downhill and stays there? To these questions there are surprisingly reliable answers. They are discussed in this and the next chapter.

The inherent features of capitalism have not been fundamentally changed. Its motivations and trends, its strength and weaknesses—they're just about what they were. No change in character. Yet there are differences. More productive capacity has been created. More dollars have been saved and are lying around unspent; more men and women are eligible for peacetime jobs; more plants are capable of turning out more goods; a worker is able to do more work. These are differences—in quantity not kind. But don't misunderstand. The quantitative changes will bring consequences that are deep and far-reaching. The old gray mare is still a horse, though the head is longer, two legs shorter, the tail clipped, the belly more rounded. She remains a horse; we know she eats hay and attracts flies. But she's going to run differently.

The trick everybody will be looking for is a method of organizing our resources so that they will provide employment for practically all who are willing and able to work, with pay at a level that assures an adequate standard of living. Business will say: "Call off the dogs. We can do the job if you respect us, our ability, our property, and dignity. And when we say respect, brother, we mean don't bother us any more than is absolutely necessary."

Others will insist that private business can provide jobs, lots of them, but not enough. Government must pitch in by continuing to make jobs as it did on a puny scale with WPA before the war and on a grand scale with armament during the war. Some few rugged individualists will say bluntly that the free-enterprise system is incompatible with full and continuous employment. To them the survival of the fittest in the competitive structure of free enterprise means a free and available labor market with a certain portion of loose labor vainly asking for jobs and a certain portion of loose machinery looking for work and a certain portion of loose materials begging to be bought.

There is even a small group, headed by a man who ought to know, Dr. Julius Hirsch, Germany's State Secretary of Economics after World War I, who say that not enough *useful* jobs can be provided by either private business or government; that government must therefore accept a permanent new category called "occupation," a kind of work-relief status, to assure a basic standard of living for those who can't be absorbed into profitable private or useful public employment. Basic in this approach to the future is the conviction that the improvement of modern machinery has already ruled out useful employment for an increasing portion of the population.

Labor joins in the debate with, "Cut the hours of work to thirty-five, then thirty, then twenty-five." Some reply, "Not in a private-enterprise system. There's a point beyond which hours should not be reduced merely to make jobs. Another answer must be found to provide work."

All of these are attempts to find a satisfactory level of employment within the framework of our present economic and political setup, the system we've been living with. We're attached to its forms and its symbolic values. Right or wrong, we like them so far. We get so excited in discussing them that we level the epithet "socialist" or "communist" even at some of the stanchest capitalists. The smoke may get in your eyes, but you can be dead sure of one thing: the anti-capitalist will be whistling in the wind in the first years after the war.

We can anticipate some things about the future because we know many things about this system. We know that before the war, even in the good old days, it did not achieve the kind of economic organization that made full use of its resources. There'll be carping at this statement because it sounds like criticism. Carping or not, it's fact. You've already seen the level of unemployment in

1940. You've already seen the sad decade of the thirties in which unemployment assumed the familiar aspect of a chronic disease, something to be lived with until it killed you. And before that, for a number of years, we went through jagged fluctuations in production and employment. America was grateful for the prosperous intervals and baffled when they came to an end.

The last time it took a long while before we accepted the fact that prosperity wasn't just around some corner, but once the lesson was learned our congenital optimism was replaced by a kind of weary sophistication that saw only different levels of depression as real; prosperity was gone forever.

Then suddenly disaster really hit us on a colossal scale in the form of total war, and, paradoxically enough, we're prosperous again. Most people understand neither the forces that push a nation into collapse nor those that raise it to prosperity. In wartime it is clear enough that everybody works because the nation is at war and every hand is needed. Does that mean, then, that we will have a fully functioning economy only at the cost of decent world relations? If that proves to be the case, many will feel that we ought to scrap the whole deal and start from scratch. Without realizing it, others will find themselves moving in the direction of martial prosperity.

If we can figure out what makes this fine thing "prosperity," the nation may be better able to capture it instead of being victimized by its fickleness. Even if that isn't so, we will at least have a better chance of knowing where we're going, understanding why, and measuring the war's effects on the rest of your life.

We tend to think of prosperity in terms made familiar to us in the past. It means plenty of jobs to go round, an abundance of things to buy, and the money with which to buy them. Certain facts are relatively clear. Our economic system is engaged in the production of goods and services. Generally, the higher the level of output, the better off we've been. That output (or most of it) creates income, which you use in many ways.

In 1940 you, the consumer, spent about 30 per cent of your income on perishable items like food, cigarettes, and toilet preparations. Then a nice chunk of your dollar, 40 per cent, went for the numerous services like rent, personal and professional services, taxes, repairs. Another 10 per cent went for items like clothing and accessories—the semi-durables that last, but not too long. And then about 10 per cent paid for durables, such as furniture, which just hang on and on. The rest you saved or put into some kind of investment.

If there's enough money spent, it may not make much immediate difference what it's spent on. War is an example of that. But in the long run there's a fairly delicate relationship between the way we use our dollar and what happens to prosperity. The year 1929 was one of top prosperity, as measured by nearly all the economic thermometers. We produced more, paid out more in individual incomes, employed more people, and paid them more than at any time up to the invasion of Poland. What we have in 1944 is a bigger and better 1929, with the important difference that something tells us in advance it can't last. We know our prosperity arises out of war-production activity, and we are quite certain that it will all be over one of these days. The 1929 prosperity wasn't dependent on war production and it didn't last either.

The changes produced by war will not have been uniform. Whole communities will have been altered, some depopulated. Others will have been needled by new industries and will enjoy intense local activity for some time to come. It is conceivable that the nation as a whole may be healthy while areas like shipyard centers are ghostlike shadows of their war selves.

Round numbers, millions of workers employed or unemployed, frequently become impersonal and meaningless. But, in dealing with your own job prospects, you must think of yourself as a unit in the nation's total. Only a vocational adviser could approach you in more personal terms, weighing your skill, experience, and the job market. Here the answer must be an average. If there is full employment, you will have a job. But if there are ten million unemployed, one out of every six of you will be out of work. Considering the number on the farms and the group of self-employed individuals that won't shrink equally, ten million unemployed is even more likely to mean that one out of every four job seekers would be out of work.

One of every six of you was unsuccessfully looking for a job in 1940, one of the best peacetime years America ever had. All of the machines and factories and service establishments and stores and government agencies were turning out about ninety-seven billion dollars' worth of goods and services. Economists identify this national output as our "gross national product." To get that figure they counted anything you bought or paid for—the new Willys you bought, the suit you had cleaned—plus the stuff that had been made and not yet sold. They included the money the government spent on a battleship, on Boulder Dam, and on feeding the deer in Yellowstone Park. Between that total and the number of you on pay rolls there's an obvious connection.

Ninety-seven billion dollars was the reading on the thermometer which indicated how healthy we were, what our national productive temperature was in 1940. And in that best year we had eight and one half million people unemployed. In 1943 we were producing almost one and one half times the gross product we did in 1940 and had no unemployment. Not only did we absorb those formerly unemployed, but old folks, women, and kids were pulled out of the rocking chairs, kitchens, and schools to pitch in. And, on top of that, millions of men were taken out of jobs to use up and destroy much of the gross national product that the others were building up.

That's a partial picture of yesterday and today. Just a glimpse at tomorrow should make you come back for a closer examination of the past. If, after the war, we do no better than we did in our *best* peacetime year, the more conservative estimates insist that between ten and fifteen million Americans will be without jobs. That's what will happen if we go back to the production level of 1940—a year already touched by war.

There seems to be a general assumption that this best of our pre-Pearl Harbor years will automatically be peanuts compared to what's coming. The only way to find out if anybody's being kidded is a good look at the machine that makes jobs.

That's only the first step in finding out whether we'll have jobs for everybody. Actually there are two steps, each of them very important.

Step One: We've got to understand the raw material out of which jobs are made—our economy, its principles of motion (toward depression or prosperity), and what the war has done to it.

Step Two: There are a lot of contradictory forces and pressures working on this raw material, pushing and pulling in opposite directions. We have to examine the forces and trends that are moving toward the creation of jobs. Those forces and trends are our assets. We've also got to add up the pressures that are working against the creation of jobs, that are blocking full employment. All the wheels in our economic machine will not be turning in the same direction. So we'll have to add and subtract, find out if we're left with a plus or a minus. Which has greater weight—the pressures for or against jobs?

Working out the arithmetic of employment, the balance sheet of our future, is left for the next chapter. Our immediate problem is to get a glimpse at the answers involved in Step One.

The high tide of business activity, employment, and income— a situation called prosperity—is fed by two springs. One is consumption. It consists of all the goods and services that you, the consumer—and the government—purchase in the course of the year. Consumption also includes those goods and services bought by manufacturers, traders, and farmers to replace that part of their productive capacity which has been used up in the course of the year; the accountant gives it the impressive name, capital replacement.

The other source of business activity goes under the very undescriptive name "net capital formation." (The economist's description is not infrequently reminiscent of the doctor's insistence on writing prescriptions in Latin.) But don't shy away because of its name. It hides a significant clue to the mystery of prosperity. The hieroglyph "net capital formation" measures the amount of money that is plowed back into our economy to expand productive capacity and ultimately make more goods and services for you, the consumer. Net capital formation consists of the additions made by business, agriculture, and government in the form of factories, machinery, equipment, new construction, roads, and public works.

Our annual consumption and net capital formation, added together, make up the total of our "gross national expenditures." Academic? Maybe it's technical. But it's important. Examine it more closely and you'll find out how nicely the pieces will join— if our hands don't tremble in putting them together. There's a balance between what we normally do with our national dollar, received as income, and the level of activity we achieve. Where we put the bet determines the size of the winnings.

At any given level of activity our economy creates dollar income. What happens with that dollar income then determines whether our level of activity will remain unchanged, expand, or decline. The bulk of our national dollar is spent, almost as soon as received, on the things we consume. A small portion of it is saved. But here we reach the crucial fork in the road. In one direction lies prosperity, in the other depression.

If the savings are transformed into a demand for additional production, the immediate effect would be to create a total demand sufficient to absorb the same volume of goods and services that have created the income in the first place. But don't stop there. Investments in productive capacity also make possible a larger output than was turned out in the preceding period. If and when this greater volume is created, we have an expanded national income and a higher level of economic activity. Keep it up and you'll be getting more money than before; you'll be able to buy and consume more goods than before. You can also save more. But to continue the upswing, total expenditures must balance total production; and therefore whatever you save must go into added capital formation.

Your savings are part of the fuel that fires the furnace. Whoever uses your savings to expand productive capacity is the stoker. The heat in the furnace is jobs.

You consume the bulk of your income dollar. But what are you doing with the rest? *How* you save it is important. The wad in your mattress doesn't go to work. It's coal lying some distance from the furnace, out of reach of the fireman. It isn't heat; it might just as well be dirty black rock.

Idle money employs no one and produces nothing. Worse than that—it even destroys jobs. The market is looking in vain for your hidden dollar. The job which your dollar could support disappears.

It may be your job or somebody else's job. But it's your job anyway, because your employment depends on somebody else's having a job and the income to buy the things you turn out.

The economic Archimedes who discovered these facts might well have jumped from his bathtub shouting, "Eureka!" He had discovered that a nation, to keep itself prosperous, must constantly forge ahead. It's all in the way you use your dollar and in the way business investors use theirs.

That principle operates in wartime too. An enormous amount of money is saved. A good part of it goes to the government in the form of taxes; another substantial slice is invested in bonds and other investment outlets; most of the remainder goes into bank deposits. And through the government the receipts are then converted into goods and services of all kinds.

When the war is over a hundred billion or more of bank deposits, bonds, mustering-out pay, and mattress money will swell the nation's pocketbook. The problem is to find out whether the money from that pocketbook will trickle or spout.

During the war, production gained unprecedented momentum because the government injected billions of dollars into the economy without giving a hang as to the profitability of the investment. Other considerations replaced the question, "Will it pay?" Berlin and Tokyo at any price! Government agencies replaced individuals as decision-makers. The process was wasteful, cumbersome, bedeviled by all kinds of internal strife between different groups still operating as individuals. But the issues were novel: "Can we get enough of what we need to win this war? How soon? What do we need in order to get it?" It took two years of painful fumbling, costly mistakes, and much confusion, all of it well greased with income and investment, before the problems of producing for war were solved. And then a profusion of war goods flowed from the highest level of production in the nation's history, the highest level of capital formation, the highest level of employment.

National decision replaced the vagaries of the market and the gamble on the size of the pot. A directed flow of dollars moved the sights up and up and the range of the gun further and further.

After the war, though, the decisions to expand or not to expand will be made initially by a fairly small group of people whose lead will be followed by a much larger group of less powerful investors. The future of America's production will be determined then in large measure by a small group of men.

The decision as to what shall be done with savings money rests with individuals, even when they're individuals acting for corporations. You will make investments according to your judgment of their profitability. "Will it pay? How much? And when?" If the prospect isn't alluring, investments in added capacity won't take place, and if they don't take place—no jobs. And remember that they must take place at a constantly increasing rate since we have a growing population to employ. Just holding on at any old level won't do. The nation's economic future is a pole-vault contest. Every established record must be broken, and broken again and again.

But remember our Archimedes' discovery. Prosperity and high employment mean that the up and up must not end with Armistice. Jobs mean continuously raised sights, require that investments function with an ever-new ardor. From that investment will have to come an impatient and billowing production. And you'll have to buy the output. Then you'll have jobs; all of you.

Here's what it takes to bring full employment to America after the war. Make it, and you'll not only have jobs but you'll be rolling in your standard of living. Clean out your attic, move out the furniture, add a wing to your garage, stretch your basement, and hire yourself a piece of storage space. And get a good night's sleep before. To have full employment in 1946:

You must eat almost twice as much food as you did in 1940.

Smoke a third cigarette for every two you used to.

Take 27 per cent more drugstore potions to get over the effects.

Clean everything you have three times as often.

Take an additional bath every five days.

Read 16 per cent more newspapers, magazines, and books.

Write twice as many letters.

Heat and light your house twice as well as you do now.

Use 30 per cent more gasoline.

Buy another suit or dress for every one you used to buy.

Repair your car twice as often or just double the fog lights.

Really, you should wear three shoes.

For every two shirts, handkerchiefs, and ties you bought before, buy three.

You'll have to order three pieces of furniture for every two pieces you bought in 1940; almost double your floor covering; buy a radio, piano, phonograph, and organ twice as often as you did; break your dishes one third more often than you did, and learn to play another musical instrument.

Get a new watch and clock every two years instead of three.

Double your purchases of luggage.

And buy a new car twice as often as you did.

Even death must become more extravagant. In place of every two tombstones laid in 1940, you'll have to unveil three in 1946.

Go to the movies five times for every four you went before the war.

And to the doctor four times for every three.

Travel 150 miles for every 100 prewar miles.

Pay 30 per cent more rent or wear your house down that much faster.

There must be two and one half times more home building than there was in 1940 and an increase in all types of producers' goods two thirds larger than in that good year.

The government, on top of all this, must build 27 per cent more than it did in the year of Roosevelt's third election, and it must almost double its other peacetime services.

And even all of this is not the full list of the increases in our national expenditure that must take place, according to the Department of Commerce and the Committee for Economic Development, to absorb those Americans who are employable and seeking jobs in 1946. Of course, you will not have to budget your buying in accordance with a particular schedule like the one above. You may decide to take more of one item and less of another. But, all in all, you will have to buy more, eat more, use more—if you're serious about full employment. Consumption must go up if everybody's going to have a job . . . if *you* are going to have a job!

How close we will come to this mark will be the theme of the following pages. Success will hang on the results of America's industrial reconversion; the expenditure of its savings; its willingness, fear, or confidence; the weighing of all the vast quantitative changes wrought by war, and the making of timely adjustments; the staving off of inflation, the mitigation of eventual deflation, and the political maturity of the American people, their representatives, and the agencies of their government.

CHAPTER VII

Brother, Can You Spare a Job?

"HELP! Help Wanted."

As used by one desperate company in 1943, that sign told the story of the high level of employment to which the war lifted the United States. It also told your story. Tomorrow you'll be looking for that sign—and it won't be there.

It took more than eighty-five billions of government money annually and the switching of more than ten million men from jobs to uniforms to give us "full employment." Like an elevator that has a large part of its load removed and receives a terrific new shot of power at the same time. Of course it zooms.

We know that extra power under the employment elevator will begin to diminish as the war draws to an end—and will be almost completely shut off when the final victory is won. We know, too, that millions of men will be switching back from their uniforms to their jobs, making their weight felt on the elevator again. We know, inevitably, that the elevator will start coming down. The question is: How far down?

At war's production peak industry was running close to top capacity day and night, furnaces red-hot, never cooling. The grinding of wheels and stamping of machines pounding without a stop. We were producing at a rate of well over one hundred eighty billion dollars. About half of that was war production; about half was civilian production. All of it made jobs. The end of 1944 will begin to see the inevitable reduction in the quantity of war jobs. The year 1945 is likely to cancel out one third of the jobs that have been making munitions for the world's battlefields. The end of 1946 may leave the nation with less than 10 per cent of its peak production for war.

Here's a score card that shows you what that drop will do to your job, *unless* we get a substantial rise in civilian production to replace the wartime lifting power of our employment elevator.

People holding jobs, the war years	53,000,000
Returning job-seeking servicemen	8,000,000
	61,000,000
Retirement of emergency workers	· 4,000,000
Size of labor force available for civilian jobs at war's end	57,000,000
Number employed in 1940	46,000,000
Excess over 1940 at war's end	11,000,000

IF WE DO AS WELL AS 1940, 11,000,000 UNEMPLOYED . . .

Unfortunately, even that eleven-million figure doesn't tell the whole story. To turn out the goods we made in 1940 we'd need less hands than we used then. Technological improvements enable us to get more production with fewer workers. The Department of Commerce has estimated that between 1940 and 1946 we will have improved enough in efficiency to displace eight million workers. Figuring on this basis, it might be necessary to add additional millions to the eleven million which our score card shows, conceivably reaching a total of nineteen million men and women without jobs. That's the picture if we play the game at the 1940 level of "prosperity." It's the measure of the problem that confronts both the country and the individual.

The government's Bureau of Labor Statistics has made a state-by-state study of the employment in war industry which must come to an end. The result? A national total of more than six million demobilized industrial workers plus 8,500,000 demobilized servicemen. The Bureau itself hastens to add that this estimate of the magnitude of the coming re-employment problem "is, if anything, understated." In a defense center like Michigan, for example, the Bureau concludes that for every ten persons employed before the war there will be six persons looking for jobs. All in all, the Department of Labor statisticians fear that we will have twelve million unemployed on our hands within six months after the war. Government alone will release some two million persons from civil employment.

Private research organizations come to equally frightening, if not identical, conclusions. This is the way the conservative Brookings Institution sees it:

Twelve months after European armistice: 6,400,000 let out of war plants and the armed forces.

First six months after Pacific armistice: 6,900,000 additional.

Twelve months after Pacific armistice: 2,500,000 more.

Eighteen months after Pacific armistice: another 2,000,000.

In effect, says Brookings, 17,800,000 persons in the demobilization period will have to find new jobs, recover their old ones, or retire.

None of the agencies making such forecasts can tell you exactly where we will stand. There are psychological factors that will certainly operate, but their intensity cannot possibly be measured numerically. An important factor will be the avalanching of unemployment once it gets started. Every worker who loses a job is a threat to the job of another worker simply because a man laid off buys less and thus causes a drop in other economic activity.

The initial demobilization of workers would not be so serious if we had the capacity for reabsorbing them into new activity immediately. But even if new work is available, it takes time for the stream of job seekers to flow from one reservoir to another. The size and complicated character of a modern industrial economy itself puts a limit on the speed with which we can, blotter-like, soak up the jobless. The National Resources Planning Board, in trying to find out how long it would take to put our potential labor force at work *during wartime*, when it's easiest, concluded that "an average absorption of 2.5 to 3 million workers in the United States, and a maximum absorption of 4 millions in a peak year, is all that can be achieved." With millions in search of new jobs, the limits on our rate of re-employment will prove to be a tragic strait jacket.

Of course the hardest-hit areas will be those that boomed during the war. Over-all totals of unemployment become vivid only in terms of the individual communities that will suddenly become ghost towns. The Bureau of Labor Statistics has given an illustration of such a typical community. Into quiet Mayes County, Oklahoma, the war brought the Oklahoma Ordnance Works. Suddenly the farm population found itself living in an important manufacturing center. In 1940 there were only 101 manufacturing workers in the whole county; at its peak the Ordnance Works will have five thousand workers or more on the pay roll. When the war is over, the plant is certain to close down since it produces only smokeless powder. Between one and two thousand men are expected back in the community from the armed forces. Vague hopes stir the community; maybe the DuPont Company will convert the plant to plastics production. But, even so, the number of employees retained will be comparatively small.

What will be done with the excess men and their families, several thousand of whom moved into Mayes County only because of the plant? The state is not prosperous, and the community is even less so.

Some of the experts who have studied the postwar employment problem would argue that the estimate of eleven to nineteen million unemployed is too gloomy. They put a great deal of weight on two factors which might cut the number of those out looking for work. For one thing, they emphasize the reduction in the working force which will come with the voluntary withdrawal from the labor market of women, overage men, and students.

There's a large element of guess here, of course. But we start with the fact that by war's end four million additional women will have been employed in every conceivable phase of economic activity. They will have had a very pleasant taste of economic independence and large pay checks. There can be little doubt that many will hesitate to give them up voluntarily. The journey back to the old standard and old habits will never be completed.

On the other hand, the old folks and the children will retire in greater numbers. Suffering from job hunger cramps, America will write a Child Labor Amendment into the Constitution or enact legislation which the Supreme Court will uphold as constitutional.

It is entirely proper to emphasize the reduction in the number of job seekers which will follow the war, but it would be undue optimism to expect it to be much more than four million—the number used in the score-card calculation.

However, another method of cutting down on the number of job hunters is suggested as a possible way out. That is to cut the number of hours employees work, and use more workers, simply taking fewer hours from each. Certainly full peacetime employment at the wartime level of work and production—with regular shifts, swing shifts, graveyard shifts, and overtime—would prove to be an impossible chimera. Full employment at even forty hours a week will be tough to reach. Full employment at *thirty* hours a week would be another story. But America will not reach thirty hours a week without first having gone through another depression. There are too many basic difficulties in the way. In some industries even the thirty-hour week will still produce a quantity of goods not easily consumed by America.

Another difficulty involved in reducing hours is that it will mean cutting pay. Inherently, industry has no great passion for a long work week—and, obviously, neither has labor. But industry is hardly likely to favor a shorter work week at the pay of the former long one.

How well can we actually expect to do in minimizing the labor-supply problem through the technique of cutting hours? Here's one answer: The conservative, business-minded Department of Commerce concludes that with production as high as 1940, "even with an average work week five hours shorter than in 1940, there would be more unemployed at the full end of the war than the thirteen million in 1932."

If neither the voluntary retirements from the labor market nor the reduction of hours will make any substantial difference, then we are left with the original estimate of eleven to nineteen million unemployed at the end of the war *unless* . . . Unless we beat our 1940 level of production and boost it fifty per cent to make jobs for all the fifty-seven million people who will want them. Can we reach that level? Since we've turned out as much as ninety billion dollars' worth of civilian goods a year during the war, we'd have to add another forty-five to fifty billion dollars to civilian production as war contracts are canceled. And that's at prewar values. "We can do it!" say many industry spokesmen.

Their prophecy of boom is based primarily on the assumption that the American people have saved an enormous amount of money during the war, which they will be ready, willing, and able to spend for all the things they couldn't get during the war. This anticipated buying spree should, it is argued, prime the pump and get the wheels of our peacetime economy going again fast.

There are many reasons why the rush into the market may not materialize, why the wheels may not start turning as fast as some expect. There are hurdles of many different kinds, and all of them stand between you and your future security. If our economy stumbles over only a few of them, jobs will fall by the wayside—growing ranks of unemployed will line both sides of the road and, by their very presence, make it even more difficult to get over the obstacles still to be met.

The first hurdle looms as soon as Washington starts the reconversion race with the peremptory: "Your war contract is hereby canceled." Here are some of the complications which cancellation brings. First there is the basic difficulty of the enormous number of contracts and companies that have to be unwound. More than 100,000 contracts made directly with the government will press for final settlement between 1944 and 1947, and no one can even estimate how many times that number of subcontracts will be involved in the negotiations. It totals almost one hundred billion dollars' worth of special and intricate problems.

The critical point here is the time it will take to untie the knots. Our experience at the end of World War I doesn't give us much reason for optimism. There were only some 32,000 contracts, involving a mere five billion dollars' worth of uncompleted work, to be settled at that time. Two and one half years after Armistice less than 50 per cent of the contractors had received payment. A few contracts were still being fought over in the courts when World War II was already on us.

119754

A company executive who doesn't know how his war contract will be settled, how much money he will receive, what he's to do with half-finished articles, is hardly in the best position to take decisive steps toward the kind of civilian production which would result in maximum employment. Literally tens of thousands of sub-contractors will run into special problems here, because they have no direct contact with the government, and may have to wait until after the prime contractor achieves a settlement.

But don't overrate the employment difficulties that will be caused by this financial problem. Among the small fry it is inevitable that uncertainty about the payments on war-contract claims will result in hesitation about making new commitments and beginning the expenditures necessary for peacetime production. Some few will be completely paralyzed by the red tape or cash poverty. But there will be efforts on the part of the government to work out a settlement procedure that will minimize uncertainty, and fortunately most of big business, which is responsible for big employment, will not be upset by these financial troubles. Their war profits, even after excess profits taxes and renegotiation, will leave enough money in their corporate tills to pay the cost of quick reconversion.

Even before contract settlement is completed we will face another obstacle on the road to jobs for all. Plants all over the country will have to slow down or close down while they're changing over their machinery and equipment from the manufacture of their wartime products to their peacetime products.

DETROIT'S WORKERS:
War's End Will Mean the Overnight Firing Of 600,000 of Them

This headline in the *Wall Street Journal* of January 10, 1944, exaggerates the speed with which the problem will develop but accurately identifies the size of the problem. How soon will there be jobs for those 600,000 men and women in Detroit's factories again?

Few businessmen really know how long their physical change-over will take. It's not that they lazily refuse to plan ahead. It's simply that in the nature of the case many companies can't tell what machinery and materials will be available. Even a simple problem like floor space won't have simple answers, with government property littering the plants and storage space jammed with army and navy goods. But time is of the essence—precious time in which idleness and joblessness start. Time in which "the overnight firing of 600,000" Detroit workers spreads uneasiness across the country, sets people to wondering about the security of *their* jobs, sparks uncertainty into fear.

If the danger of the gap which must inevitably follow physical reconversion is so clearly recognized, why isn't something being done about it? It's when you probe the answer to that question that you begin to get a real sense of just how complicated, intertwined, and involved are the problems we face in trying to achieve full employment. For instance, one solution would seem to be to allow companies that anticipate lengthy reconversion shutdowns to start their peacetime programs early, at least where the materials they need are plentiful. But early in 1944 Donald Nelson, head of the War Production Board, said: "We would rather be two months late in reconversion than five minutes late in military production."

Other difficulties of reconversion are as various as the types of industrial mobilization required by the war. Consider, for instance, the war plants that were built for the sole purpose of making explosives and other purely military material. The engineering involved in converting these plants to some kind of peacetime production will not be justified with the presence of other plants already available to do that work. What happens to the people who worked in these plants during the war? More red ink!

Consider those mass-production industries which were converted to make a war article substantially different from their peacetime product. Or those basic industries, such as steel, aluminum, shipbuilding, chemicals, aviation, machine tools, which have expanded so hugely that serious question will arise as to what can be done with their output.

For many other industries the war has meant not greatly increased capacity, but full use, for the first time, of existing capacity. Shoe production, for example, became a war industry simply on the basis of changes in color, shape, and size of the products. Strictly speaking, industries like these don't present a reconversion problem in terms of physical change-over. About three out of every ten of the companies in war production will be in the position of the electric-clock factories that switched to timing units for bombs and will be able to get back to electric clocks without any great loss of time or money.

So far as that is true, it represents a reservoir of continuing jobs. However, at the same time that we pass this hurdle of physical change-over, we are confronted with a series of special obstacles that will make the going tough for particular segments of America's business—each one spelling its threat of unemployment. Here is an example of one of the most important. The proportion of workers in jobs producing metal, metal products, machinery, and transportation equipment is three times as great as the peacetime ratio. Nothing's the matter with the products except that you can't eat them, they don't wear out easily, and you don't want to be exploding them all the time. The peacetime reduction of the output of these industries will involve a terrific job of moving people around, and in the shuffle a good number of jobs will be lost.

And there are special problems of half-war-half-peace production. These will be hit hard, particularly such industries as automobiles, where contract cancellation will come gradually. The shift won't be from all trucks to no trucks, all tanks to no tanks. Plants will be left with some war orders to fill. This will mean a partial reconversion of many an assembly line, a race in two directions at the same time—with resulting confusions and dislocations in the final reconversion job.

These are some of the hurdles on the production side of the road. Distribution, too, has suffered severe dislocation and will undergo many reconversion pains. Paul Hoffman, of the Committee for Economic Development, says physical reconversion will be a difficult assignment, "but the tougher aspect of the task ahead is that of rebuilding and revitalizing our selling organizations." It will be no pushover to rearrange the molecules in the structure of enterprise so that we have the right working sequence again. What you have scattered to a thousand breezes can't be brought back on the wings of a single wind. More time lost! But again, fortunately for employment prospects, many of the giant companies have kept their networks of dealers.

Some industries are in for a good break on the hazards of both the physical difficulty of reconversion and the uncertainty of the market. The textile industry is one. It knows, for example, that it will have as added customers approximately eight million men returning from the wars. The clothes these men once wore will have been thrown away or eaten up by the moths, made into suits by their wives, or hung up in the closet for figures they will no longer fit.

Textile mills will continue to produce textiles. Some industries have enough peacetime orders on their books to keep operating at full capacity for years. The wartime famine in nylons, for example, will keep the hosiery machines humming for a long time to come.

Great stress has been placed on the new employment opportunities that our agricultural potentials will provide. In this case, however, some important reservations must be made. Although our farmers will find good foreign markets open to them in the period immediately following the European armistice, it is foolish to expect that there will be a great tide of men and women flowing back to the farms from the city. "How can you keep them down on the farm—after they've seen Paree?" Certainly Europe will consider us the granary—for a while. But one crop period may be all that Europe will ask for, over and above her usual prewar imports. By the time Tojo gives up, most of the "replenishment feeding" on the other side of the Atlantic will be over.

Government plans for the care of our demobilized veterans speak of settling a good number of them on the land. Department of Interior chief Harold L. Ickes promises that he can locate 165,000 men and their families on farms where they would become self-sustaining. In turn, they should generate the employment of others, because they will be purchasing farm implements, autos, clothing, etc. "We are charting a new frontier," he says.

Every little bit helps, but before we take the bite let's be sure we can swallow it. Will the heavy demand for agricultural products continue after the war, so that the crops these men wrest from the soil can be sold? The demand for food is sure to fall when the soldier becomes a civilian eater and the civilian diverts part of his shrinking income choosing among a larger variety of available goods.

And we don't dare to forget that agricultural techniques have improved, so that fewer farm hands can turn out bigger crops. Some observers in the United States believe that at least a million fewer farm workers will be needed after the war than in 1939.

The one certain characteristic of the early months after the war will be uncertainty—a multitude of uncertainties. The basic fact will be that Uncle Sam will no longer be the single or the main customer, the customer with the unlimited credit and the inexhaustible pad of order blanks. All the uncertainties of the ordinary peacetime market will reappear in magnified form.

In wartime the nation had definite goals—100,000 planes, a bridge of ships, an arsenal of democracy. With one monopolistic buyer in the market, the nation had its market defined for it, its production marked out and directed. If an automobile company refused to get busy on airplanes, a limitation order could simply prohibit the plants from turning out cars. There was no alternative but war production. The power of government won't be there to drive business back to peace, but there will be an automatic spur—the acute business realization that to the first in line will go the first markets, the first impression on the civilian consumer, the first profits, the best guarantees of competitive permanence.

So great will be the rush to get started on the problems of reconversion that the government will have to play the traffic cop. Just as war priorities channelized war output, so too will reconversion priorities channelize peacetime production. A business got a higher rating in war if it could demonstrate its ability to serve the best interests of war production; it will get the higher ratings in reconversion if it demonstrates its ability to give maximum employment.

That, at any rate, will be the plan on paper; but reconversion priorities will run even less smoothly than their war counterpart. Even if "priorities in reverse" do get materials to job-giving companies, there is the danger that bottlenecks will appear in the form of unbalanced reconversion. In many a plant everything will be ready to go—everything except one small part without which all else adds up to exactly nothing marketable. "For want of a nail, a kingdom was lost."

All sorts of other difficulties barge in with "priorities in reverse." One question alone will send government officials to their beds with headaches: What are you going to do with new producers? The easiest reply is to say that you will give priorities only to the firms that have been handling that type of production before the war. Yet a newcomer may be able to make more jobs. A Henry Kaiser may decide to go into auto manufacture. To give materials to the newcomer will inevitably penalize those whom the country still keeps on war production. To refuse to give him materials is to stifle competition and quick peacetime jobs for the sake of rewarding those continuing in military production.

The over-all attempt will be to direct materials first to those who can make the most jobs quickly—old firms favored, other things being equal. Taxation will be a good deal more effective as a method of speeding job-producing activity and slowing down less productive business operations. There will be tax premiums for those companies that "git thar fustest with the mostest" jobs.

Tax 90 per cent of an itching dollar and its owner is less likely to scramble for more. Tax a substantial percentage of corporate profits and the corporation will play the game for safety, security, and permanence—not risk, profits, or expansion. But if the government take is only 10 per cent, you know how business will break its neck for more.

If any businessmen are losing sleep about this hazard of reconversion, they are misreading the future. In this respect peace will be along business lines. Taxes will be made almost to order for what the specialist calls "risk capital." In a hurry to make the business environment after the war as pleasant and encouraging as possible, Congress is even apt to jump the gun and make the last phases of the war itself as comfortable as possible too.

Still, uncertainty will prevail. Businessmen are not likely to feel confident about undertaking large-scale activity when so many of the questions presented by reconversion are unanswered. These uncertainties after the war will emphasize a curious and prevailing characteristic of American business. Many people in America assume that because private industry has been able to produce an enormous volume of goods in wartime it will continue to do so in peacetime. Yet, oddly enough, in the period following the war most business organizations are likely to plan for too low rather than too high a level of production. Despite the lesson of business capacity and industrial output provided by the war, the effects of the long prewar depression will not have been fully shaken off. America will return to the usual concepts of "normal" business, again underestimating her own capacity both to produce and consume.

The fact is that peace does not have the "no-expense-spared" incentive of war. Costs become the basic argument in peacetime decisions. In war, money's no object; in peace, money's the only object. It must be. Decisions will be made by private business without the bottomless resources of a Federal Treasury at its disposal.

Within this framework America has not yet learned how to provide security for herself without paying the penalty of contraction by individuals and businesses which are concerned with their own safety. Risk, enterprise, competition, profit, and courage are the potential assets from which expansion and jobs will be made. They are the dynamics determining how much and how fast the wheels move as the gear of the economy is thrown from war to peace.

If the "wait and see" of reconversion takes hold, then back the nation marches to a restricted economy—and large-scale unemployment.

There is a very real possibility that business will take this fork in the road because of the greatest uncertainty of all, the market—how much you, the public, are going to buy and what you're going to buy. Every businessman would give his eyeteeth to know how you'll behave if he offers you goods. Will you step up dollar in hand or shy away like a skittish mare?

Of course you'll be able to afford to buy. In one form or another —cash, bank accounts, war bonds—you're going to have between seventy-five and one hundred billion dollars. But one trouble is that you won't part with your money except for value received—the best and newest value.

True, you left a lot of things unbought, but you really weren't too puzzled about what to do for goods during the war. The record is clear on that. There was more, not less, civilian purchasing during the war than before the war.

Of course there'll be a lot of catching-up buying. But you'll be watching war factories closing down, and when termination hits your plant you'll say, "Guess I better wait about buying that washing machine until I'm sure I'll have a new job and will be able to keep up the payments. The missus can wait." Even if you're still sitting at your lathe, you'll be slow about spending. "Can't tell what's going to happen now. The boys will be getting back from the war, and the boss is supposed to rehire them. Will he keep me on?"

There is genuine danger in this potential hurdle—a general deflationary psychology sweeping the consumers of the nation after the war.

Even assuming that the savings are liquid right from the start and begin to flow into the streams of trade, there is still the question of whether they will begin to turn the mill wheel of employment at once. If the manufacturer of a specific product can't be sure that you'll come knocking at *his* door, don't expect him to start full-speed production.

Nor can we overlook the fact that a lot of the purchasing power can be expended without making any new jobs. If it goes to buy government surpluses accumulated during the war, then it won't prime new manufacturing pumps. As noted in an earlier chapter, the government will make every effort to dispose of its surplus goods in a way that will cause the least possible dislocation in the country's markets. There is one possibility, however, that may change this policy and bring government-owned surplus goods flooding into competition with privately distributed merchandise. The possibility is the much-talked-about and much-feared specter of inflation.

The average citizen is able to recognize inflation by the fact that prices are going up. It can be a gradual process, a trickling off of extra pennies when he buys, or it can become a runaway process, every day more pennies, and then nickels and quarters, until the dollar is just a shadow of its old self. To the naïve, the explanation is simple—profiteers; to the knowing, it's the result of a complicated set of relations.

Inflation is due to the sudden upsetting of the balance between supply and demand. If there's more money around than goods, our economy tries to adjust itself by creating a new balance. By a rise in prices, some of the demand is reduced and eliminated altogether. It isn't true, as most publicists have been implying, that nobody wants inflation. It's like the old proposition about everybody being against sin. The fact is that both sin and inflation can be a helluva lot of fun while they're going on.

Inflation is a disease of the price system—and price is the focal center of the whole economic system. The prices that prevail on the day you go out to look for a peacetime job—and the trend of prices upward or downward at the time—may decide whether you are hired or not.

All of the conditions of the war make for inflationary pressure. But the existence of war also makes anti-inflationary action possible. With war's end we are likely to have inflation-brewing conditions at just the time when the loudest demands are for the release of government controls. With patriotic fervor cooling, there will be less willingness to accept the discipline of an anti-inflationary program.

What are the chances for inflation? Jobwise the question has enormous consequences. Inflation following the war would mean an automatic high level of business activity. If prices are rising, then more people are lured into production and you get a greater volume of goods. Deflation following the war would bring joblessness as a certainty. If prices are falling, production will be slower, since the high-cost producer won't be able to stay on and the normal producer delays, fearing he will get less for his finished goods than his cost. As usual, the dilemma has two horns. After the first intoxication, inflation would bring economic disaster to millions and the threat of chaos to the nation. Deflation threatens a contraction so acute that the paralysis we know as depression takes over. Which will we have?

At the end of 1943 the Office of War Information, in warning against the dangers of wartime inflation, drew up a rough inflationary balance sheet, listing the factors for and against. To figure out where we'll stand after the shooting is over we ought to see how each of them will shape up at war's end. Here they are:

FACTORS FAVORING INFLATION

1. High income payments to individuals.
2. The excess of income over consumer goods and services available.
3. Corporate profits (after taxes).
4. The government's war expenditures.
5. The amount of war-bond redemptions.
6. Money in circulation.
7. Money in checking accounts.

FACTORS AGAINST INFLATION

1. Personal taxes—federal, state, and local.
2. War-bond sales (excluding those to commercial banks).
3. Savings deposits.
4. Life-insurance premiums.

We already know what many of these items will look like after the war. High income payments are certain to drop with wholesale contract terminations and decreased working hours. Even if hourly wage rates after the war remain unchanged, Professor Sumner Slichter, at Harvard, tells us pay rolls will shrink by more than twenty billion dollars. With men laid off in the retooling period, the cut in the nation's pay envelopes will be even greater. In short, the strength will go out of one of the most direct of all the pressures toward inflation.

The disparity between income and available goods will be narrowed down from two directions: first, because income will decline, and, second, because there will be some substantial increase in the volume of goods, no matter how slow the progress of reconversion.

Corporate profits, the least important of the inflation factors, will start downward when termination comes and the production motor idles through the reconversion.

The biggest factor in OWI's inflation budget is the expenditure of billions by the government on war purchases. With the end of the war against Germany there will be an almost immediate slash, which will be reflected in the weakening of other inflation forces. Money in circulation and in checking accounts, much of which flowed out of the government's expenditures, will begin to diminish.

As for the anti-inflationary forces: Personal taxes will be reduced somewhat, but not to the extent that individual self-interest might hope. War-bond sales will not altogether pass out of the picture even after the Japs have been disposed of. Undoubtedly there will be a new bond drive around a slogan of demobilization like, "Bring Him Home with the Victory Loan," comparable to the final bond campaign in 1919.

But the big question remains: What will happen to the savings that could smash the inflation dam even if all other pressure were neutralized? If every dollar bill were rushed out of the mattress and the bank, if every war-bond holder were to disregard the loss involved and dash up to the Treasury's door with a demand for immediate redemption, we would certainly be sunk in the flood. But it won't happen here!

The United States will not suffer a serious postwar inflation because all the factors described in the first part of this chapter—slowness of reconversion, unemployment, both business and public uncertainty—will work against the "dis-savings" that economists fear so much. We won't have inflation because everything that will happen to you will compel you to hold on to your money rather than spend it. Here is a preview of the kind of *"deflationary"* developments that will occur.

First of all, there will be termination unemployment.

Secondly, there's the absolute certainty that take-home pay will fall. You'll hold on to your savings much tighter when your weekly pay envelope is thinner—and thinner it will be, because of the reduction in hours and overtime.

Third, you're going to wait for prices to come down. Wartime conditions forced prices up, you'll be saying to yourself, and you've waited so long, you can wait a little longer.

Fourth, you'll be waiting for the new products that you read about and haven't seen in the shopwindows. Why rush out and get a radio when that swell FM-television-standard-short-wave combination described in Chapter XII may be just a few months away?

Fifth, and most important, there's the basic fact of what the war economy *didn't* do to you. It didn't tighten your belt too uncomfortably, and there will be no real pressure for you to slip the strap out of the buckle immediately. You haven't been starved enough so that you'll want to rush out madly and buy. If you had been going without shoes, in patched-up pants, in a cotton overcoat—as our allies have been doing—then certainly you'd let loose in the greatest buying spree of your life. But no matter how long the war lasts, you won't be brought to desperation. Furthermore, however insufficient our future production, you will go into the stores and shops certain that you will be able to get all you need for your body's comfort, even if you can't get all you want for your heart's desire.

No, we will not be exclaiming after the war, "Good grief, how the money rolls out!" People will *not* be letting go. Instead of a flight from the dollar, we will have a desperate clinging to the dollar—until employment begins to pick up again and job tenure begins to look more real.

That doesn't mean we won't have some kind of buying splurge. Too much of our thinking is artificially narrowed down to two alternatives: boom or depression. We will have a third alternative in the early postwar years, and it will be this alternative that will shape your living at that time. Here are some of the things you can expect—consistent, inconsistent, reasonable, contradictory:

There will be a replenishment boom, but it will be spotty. Don't expect an over-all boom, with every type of activity plunging ahead.

The buying will be just as irregular as the resumption of activity itself. In fact, the demand for some types of goods will be so great it won't be met fully.

There will be a special scramble for certain kinds of consumer goods—furniture and household equipment, for instance. This is probably one field of human wants where there'll be no inclination to "wait and see." In the case of other goods, the manufacturers will be looking for you.

A lot of brow-knitting will be done by manufacturers, before the last shot is fired, to anticipate just what goods will experience the replenishment boom. The Department of Commerce, the United States Chamber of Commerce, trade associations, have already begun to make surveys with interesting, if not conclusive, results. They have learned that there will be a deficiency of almost four million washing machines, about five million refrigerators, three million vacuum cleaners. Tables have been worked out for everything from bedsprings to radios. Polls have been taken to find out what people *think* they will be buying after the war. For example, 3,675,000 families have their eyes vaguely fixed on new automobiles; 1,540,000 families on new homes.

That might sound like the makings of a giant boom, but the important thing is not what people think they are going to do but what they actually *will* do. And that may turn out to be quite different from the optimistic estimates.

It all adds up to a basic pattern: For about two years after the end of the war in Europe, America will experience a combination of boom in some fields and depression in others while you are catching up on your needs. With each month after European war has ended, the number of the unemployed will grow—a number fed by the demobilization of a sizable portion of the military and the contraction of as much as half of the giant called war production. With each month more and more of the reconverted industry will move in to take its share of both the employment and the dollar market. But the sponge won't quite be able to sop up the water leaking in.

In many ways the years after the war will constitute one of the strangest periods through which America has ever passed. Boom and depression at the same time. High national production—compared with 1940—and growing unemployment at the same time. Expanding civilian enterprise but mounting joblessness. Profits and bankruptcies both increasing. Prices starting high and dropping reluctantly while savings remain substantially frozen.

Had America not gone through the great depression of the thirties, the prediction might be otherwise. The next few years would probably be years of great inflation, high production, and speculation, almost full employment. But the naïveté is gone. We'll all "wait and see"—remembering unemployment as a burned child fears the flame.

If the pace of reconversion is slow, the tempo of policy-making will be even slower. This is the crucial fact. A two-year gap between the existence of a national difficulty and the taking of steps to cure or relieve it is not unusual. But the price will be mounting joblessness and shrinking confidence.

Policy will be the crying need. But how many of the following issues will have been decided before they grow critical?

Who will be canceled out of war production first and how?

Will the United States continue any munitions manufacture or stop abruptly as soon as the immediate needs are filled?

Which peacetime industries will get the first available material?

What's to be done with the war goods lying all over the plants?

What's the government going to do with its fifty billions' worth of goods?

What will be done with the vast government-owned plant?

Will price ceilings be changed to permit more profitable peacetime sales?

How long will rationing continue and on which products?

Will private money or government loans refinance peacetime business?

How deep will be Uncle Sam's participation in world rehabilitation?

How soon will demobilized men start re-entering civilian life—and which men first?

What will the tax setup be during reconversion?

Will monopolies be prosecuted or will the government permit the continuance of industry combination for reconversion?

How much government spending will be done and for what types of activities?

What will America's policy be on tariffs, payment for Lend-Lease, international exchange and monetary stabilization, export of vital materials, import of strategic materials, international cartels?

Will the payments to discharged workers be increased beyond the present unemployment-insurance provisions?

At what level of unemployment will the government step in to make jobs and in what ways?

The speediest reconversion of America to a production level that will yield the highest volume of employment is impossible without policy on each of these questions—and dozens more. Every question unanswered will take its toll. America will be confronted with these problems at the very time when circumstances will exaggerate our normal reluctance to act. The year 1944 is a presidential election year—and the questions of reconversion can't be solved on the political stump. The greater the political heat generated by these issues, the longer will action be postponed, the more remote will be the possibility of intelligent solution.

America will have started its reconversion with the threat of unemployment over its head. The end of the war with Germany will make that threat a reality. The end of the war with Japan will see that reality reach acute dimensions.

Despite a mounting supply of available workers and growing unemployment as the curtain goes up on 1945, manufacturers will seek to hold or set their prices at high wartime levels. The producers of raw materials will try to keep their prices up. Labor unions will seek to hold their wartime wages up. The new group of the unemployed will try to keep their chins up.

At first the dislocation will come with startling suddenness. The immediate shock will be that of remigration—the shifting of workers from War Plant A to Peace Plant B. That dislocation is unavoidable.

The hardest reality to take in the period between the two victories will be the shortage of manpower in the midst of growing demobilization and unemployment. This paradox will develop from two factors: Unemployment will be local and so will manpower shortage, and the localities will be many miles apart. Again the early experience of the war will be duplicated. Well after Pearl Harbor, with growing manpower shortage limiting many war operations, some American localities were still designated as "labor-surplus areas." Labor is human—it isn't so fluid or transportable as oil pumped through a pipeline.

The greatest heartbreak in the tragedy of unemployment, uprooted families, depressed communities, discontent, and rising friction, will come from the realization that some communities will not be able to get work going because others have idle men on the streets. An airplane plant closed in California is no answer—at least no immediate answer—to an idle refrigerator plant in Indiana that needs men to get started. Curiously, too, society's solicitude for the dispossessed will serve to keep some of them dispossessed a little longer. Relief and unemployment insurance laws in the various states are so framed that workers must show a considerable period of residence before they can qualify. Before they hit the road they will naturally want gold-backed promises of employment in the new community.

Men—just men—may be available in considerable numbers; but specific kinds of skilled men may still be tied up in continuing war production which will go on long after reconversion has started. A lack of five patternmakers may keep five hundred other workers idle.

In many of these projections into the future the probabilities are inescapable, the timing of them subject to doubt. There are those who expect depression but insist it will be preceded by intense inflationary spending which will create jobs. It is more likely that the replenishment spending will not cancel out the deflationary forces or bridge the difficulties of reconversion. Such is the probable course of events:

Assuming the end of the war in Europe by late 1944 and in Asia by mid-1946, the following seems likely: At the close of 1944 several million of the formerly employed will already be listed as employment liabilities. Decisive legislative action and government policy for 1945 seem improbable. The desire to run away, to escape, to let go, the growing distaste for bureaucracy and bureaucratic action, the split between the executive and legislative branches of government, growing pressure by blocs and a greater tendency to yield to it—all will add up to delay, confusion, and little more than isolated, inadequate action. The inevitable crisis will begin to threaten when the last months of 1945 find the ranks of the unemployed multiplied to perhaps ten million.

If, under this timetable, the winter of 1946 will be a period of stress, it will also be a period of crystallizing aggressive action.

Government, business, labor, and agriculture will be shaken by the crisis into "doing something about it."

Reconversion will already have passed through some of its most painful phases. The new products will have begun to emerge; new construction will have started to spread noticeably instead of inching across the land. The benefits of our technological advances acquired in the laboratory of war will become visible. After many promises to keep hands off, to give private enterprise free rein, government will begin again to pump money into the stream. The end of 1946 will find the hopes of America beginning to rise.

In these critical years America will have faced one of the most dangerous social and political storms of its history. In the process jobs will have become an increasing demand, echoed and re-echoed with new urgency.

The long march toward the goal of stability, security, and a sustained level of employment will have begun by the end of 1946. It may take the rest of your life.

After the crisis the economy will still rest on the base of private enterprise but it will have accepted government as an ally in producing employment. America will have changed some of its basic concepts in its struggle with the problem that dogged every step of our prewar years and that hung like a grim shadow over the land even with the first rays of peace.

III

The Future of America's Classes

CHAPTER VIII

Rugged Collectivists

"OKAY, so he stole the horse. We won't let him do it again."

But there's only one horse. He didn't give it back and you're not going to make him. There, in a nutshell, is the future of big business. In a vastly oversimplified form it tells the story of what happened to the American economic structure during the war and gives the pattern for the years ahead. But, like all oversimplifications, it's unfair. The horse wasn't stolen; we gave it. As a matter of fact, only its own decision prevented big business from becoming bigger than it is. The government offered to let business build and own the billions in new plants. Big business passed on that round; it may raise the next time.

Once again we turn to the two keys which open the door on the future. To know what business will be like tomorrow, you must know what it looks like today. And to project that picture, you must follow the conflict between our idealized attitudes and our daily practice—the gulf between our assertions that little business is the backbone of industry and the actions we take which stifle its growth.

It is of the utmost significance that the most articulate voice for the free, independent American way is itself undergoing concentration. The vehicles of opinion in America—whose untrammeled expression has traditionally been considered a basic safeguard of democracy—are rapidly being gathered in fewer and fewer hands. Town after town that had three newspapers now has only one. In more than one hundred cities the owner of the only newspaper owns the only broadcasting station. Of some eight hundred and

fifty radio stations in the country, more than three hundred are
under the wing of a newspaper; and the purchase of broadcasting
facilities by papers and magazines is continuing. Add the fact that
the four major networks get almost 75 per cent of their income
from forty advertisers.

The characteristic American attitude may be all for small business, but the publishers of the country's small papers—the home-
spun country weeklies which might be expected to voice that attitude—have frankly declared their admiration for the big fellows.
The American Press, a magazine for home-town newspapers, sur-
veyed opinion in forty-eight states. In its issue of January 1944 it
reported this consensus of more than five hundred country publishers:

THIRTY-SEVEN REASONS WHY COUNTRY PUBLISHERS LIKE "BIG BUSINESS"

1. It is the greatest factor in making this nation the best and most powerful on earth.
2. Hitler would be "World Fuehrer" if it wasn't for industry's amazing job.
3. The people in this country do not want a labor-dominated government.
4. The products of large industries have won the people's highest esteem.
5. Big business knows what to do in emergencies and has the capital to keep men on pay rolls when things are bad.
6. It is much better to have big business than big government.
7. The capitalistic system is much better than modified socialism.
8. Big business knows it must be worthy of confidence or it will lose its leadership.
9. Businesses get big because of fair dealing, honest products, and a long-view perspective of public demands.
10. Big business makes good business for little business.
11. If it weren't for big business there wouldn't be any America.
12. It will be American capital and big business—not academic theorists—who will bring America back to peacetime living.
13. If it wasn't for big business Mr. Roosevelt would take us over.
14. Big business is necessary for the success of newspapers.
15. Big business is the backbone of small business.
16. Big business keeps prices down where its products can be enjoyed by more people.

17. Big business is fairer than labor or any other single group.
18. Big business has saved this country.
19. Big business is simply an aggregation of the capital of numerous and widely scattered stockholders.
20. Big business cannot be held down without holding down small business.
21. The basis of democracy is to protect the right of small business to become big business.
22. We can't condemn an organization because it surrounds itself with the facilities to build better mousetraps.
23. A government which opposes big business is heading toward a communistic state.
24. Big industries have brought us most all of the modern conveniences we have today.
25. Competition is the life of trade.
26. Only big firms can afford the research needed to give us better and cheaper products.
27. Good pay by big business gives our middle class a high standard of living.
28. We are fighting this war to save free enterprise—which means big business.
29. We must get back to the day when a poor man with initiative will have the hope and chance of becoming an outstanding leader.
30. We owe big business a debt of gratitude for the luxuries and necessities we all enjoy.
31. It takes big business to make the wheels move.
32. It was ambition that made these organizations so powerful.
33. As big business prospers, so prospers the nation.
34. If we have to be exploited by any group, we prefer big business—they do it with more finesse.
35. Big business is as much a part of American life as hot dogs and Coca-Cola.
36. Take away big business and what is there for the little fellow to strive for?
37. Our country has developed through the capitalistic system of business.

Today big business is rapidly growing while small business just about manages to hold its own. This was the net result of war, and it was inevitable. America could afford to waste billions. The nation could even afford to sacrifice thousands of small enterprises. Only time, with lives in the balance, was precious, and time was the trump card in the hand of big business. Because munitions were needed quickly and because it could deliver, big business got the lion's share of war contracts. Under Secretary of War Robert P. Patterson told the story when he said, "Orders had to be placed with companies best equipped to handle them with speed. . . . We had to take industrial America as we found it."

Businesses operating with less than $100,000 capital might have delivered. They *might* have. But big business could and did.

Attempts were made by the government to cut small business in on war production. But, as Vice President Wallace said, "The Smaller War Plants Corporation came into the picture two years too late." That it came into the picture at all is a tribute to American sentiment. It was ineffective. Argue with General Blitz. He will still insist that he'd rather deal with one giant corporation and place an order for ten thousand planes than fuss around with a thousand smaller plants handling the bits and pieces from which the planes are made. It was no accident that before the reconversion period the chairmanship of the Smaller War Plants Corporation proved to be a one-way road to oblivion.

But don't get the idea that small business passed out of the picture. A glance will convince you it isn't so. As of July 1943, the total physical output of small plants was still at about the 1940 level. Small business survived—but its character changed. It made the bits and pieces, but only as one of the thousands of work horses for a General Motors with whom Uncle Sam did business directly.

At war's end this reality will be the base from which the business community starts to operate. It will shape public policy and determine the relative position of all the classes in America. By looking backward we pick up this crucial fact from which we can move forward. The nation may pretend that it doesn't exist. Indeed, with each wartime increase in the power and influence of large enterprise, prettier bouquets were thrown in the direction of the little man. With each restraint imposed on competition, a more effusive paragraph was written to extol the competitive way.

From one of America's important industrial organizations, the New England Council, come the words of its president, pungently describing the conflict between reality and what we think about it: "The great inconsistencies between what is being said about free enterprise and what is being done by owners of the capital that is essential to free enterprise. . . . Everywhere we encounter a reluctance to take risks. Everywhere we find a strong belief in private ownership, and everywhere we see a scarcity of persons willing to become owners when risk is apparent. The demand for security is not confined to the disinherited."

The implications in this statement are significant, for they indicate a distinction between a free-enterprise system and a private-enterprise system. Free enterprise is competitive; private enterprise merely means privately owned business which may or may not exist in a competitive atmosphere. Free enterprise is inconsistent with restrictive agreements, combinations, monopolies. It calls for a market in which the more efficient producers and sellers are free to set their individual production schedules and their prices. Every small business has at least a chance to grow, limited only by the managerial ability and resources of its owner. But if small business can't get bank loans just because it's small, if companies won't sell to small business, then we may be talking about private but not free enterprise. If a businessman isn't free to move into any line of activity he chooses, his freedom of enterprise is obviously limited. And if the life or death of his business is controlled by the power, policies, or whims of another company—his freedom at the very least is dubious.

Don't confuse capitalism or the private-ownership-profit system with free enterprise. Capitalism has a long-term future in America. There will be a greater amount of privately owned industry in America than ever before, but it may be controlled by fewer persons. A greater volume of business, yes; but not necessarily more competition.

Free enterprise and unrestricted competition began to retreat a long time ago. Even before World War I it had all but disappeared in some of the heavy industries and in most of mining. The decline of competitive enterprise has been most marked in all forms of industrial production. Concentration has occurred in agriculture, in the service trades, and in retail distribution, but not in comparison to the absorption of industrial activity by large enterprise. During the twenties and thirties free enterprise began to lose its grip on the manufacture of much of the goods you buy.

But it took the war to make a really striking change. In just two years, 1942 and 1943, the share of big business in the nation's total output grew faster than it did in the preceding twenty years. "By 1943, with the compressing force of war still gaining momentum, the hundred largest firms were already controlling about seven eighths of the nation's war output, with approximately four fifths of all prime war contracts in their hands."

That small group farmed out the nation's work to subcontractors who, in turn, passed on slices to sub-subcontractors. The pattern of American business was being redesigned. The thousands of independent little pieces that used to constitute American industry were linked together by the forge of war into an integrated chain, anchored to the prime contracts held by the giant companies. The small firms that remained in business—and most did—made more profits than they had in a long time. But they were operating as satellites. Initiative, direction, and planning stemmed from the big contractors. The ruggedness of the American businessman may not have diminished; his antipathy to external control has not diminished; but the former individualist was rapidly becoming part of new gigantic industrial collectives.

It was more than the concentration of contracts that shaped this pattern and strengthened the role of larger enterprise. Many other compulsives of war led to the one result. Suspension of anti-trust suits for the duration, for example, was only a logical admission that it isn't smart to distract the big fellow whose products you need for your salvation. The control of the distribution of materials through prime contractors, to take another illustration, was determined by the need for controlling the use of scarce supplies and getting them quickly where they were most needed.

Since Pearl Harbor large business establishments have been urged, and at times have been compelled, to merge their individuality for the common good. They were instructed to exchange facilities, pool their patents, share their know-how, join their former competitors in dividing functions rather than completing whole units on their own. Industry-wide teams emerged, frequently even interindustry teams. Much of American enterprise was reorganized toward one goal—maximum output for the single customer, the Federal Government. Industrial relationships were reorganized in order to produce the most rational combinations of productive facilities. National planning, national blueprints, national production schedules guided the machinery of America. They worked best where the industrial units were large and few and closely knit.

If this is free enterprise, Karl Marx should do a handspring while Adam Smith eats his hat.

The wartime organization of our industries into a single team or a number of teams was nothing new—in theory. Back in World War I, Bernard Baruch's War Industries Board prepared elaborate plans along the same lines, but the war ended while they were still on paper. In World War II they became economic reality. Because the plan was not put into effect in 1918, no real problem arose in 1919 and the years following. When World War II ends, the plan will have been a reality for at least four years, and America will have been permanently changed.

When Simeon the Stylite left his pillar after thirty years he could no longer walk. The same atrophy will prevent our economic mechanism from resuming its wonted ways and exercising its old flexibility.

It will happen despite all our intentions for tomorrow. The nation is as near-unanimous about those intentions as it can ever be. Not a single influential voice has been raised against a return to free enterprise. On the contrary, the demand is for an expansion of competitive activity. The will is there, genuine and sincere. But can we expect the development of an economic climate favorable to the growth of the kind of competition that existed yesterday?

The reality will be spun from a number of threads. For one, small business has not passed from the scene. Some 150,000 medium-sized and small manufacturing plants are in operation in 1944 as compared with 170,000 before Pearl Harbor. Small business, as a recognizable entity, will survive the war. But the opportunities of growth from small to large business will be still fewer than they were yesterday.

Ability to secure new earnings is the basic test of such growth, for the street adage, "Money makes money," contains a good deal of economic truth. The trend in the distribution of earnings is therefore our clearest indication of what's ahead.

Progressively throughout the last fifteen years, and more dramatically during the war, big business's share of the national dollar has been increasing. Its total of profits after taxes shows proportionately steady increases over those of smaller business, and the same is true in the matter of reserves. The relative position of big business grows stronger. There is enough information already at hand to demonstrate that its financial position, an essential prerequisite for profitable operations, will be extremely good, particularly in the first two years after war's end.

Then why the beating of the breast on the part of many large companies that taxes and renegotiation were preventing them from setting up sufficient reserves? The outcry is understandable enough. The war contractor is obviously better off the more money he can get; and the faster he can get it, the smaller the amount he is compelled to turn back when his contract is renegotiated. He can hardly be blamed for not wearing his dressiest clothes when he comes to plead for financial mercy.

Actually, however, in retrospect it will be seen that Uncle Sam has not been too parsimonious. The policy committee of one of the most acutely observant brokerage firms in the country summed up the situation quite frankly in a bulletin to its clients:

So far as the financial aspects of transition are concerned, there are many buffers in being or in the making. In spite of dissatisfaction in many quarters with the size and nature of taxation and with the terms and manners of renegotiating contracts, the fact remains that corporations as a group are making good earnings even after high taxes and are building stronger balance sheets. The liquidity of the reserves and current position in many cases depends on the government's policies and practices regarding contract settlements at the end of the war. To date these practices appear to be on the generous side.

From the narrow perspective of a single war year, opportunities for war profits may look mighty slim; 95 per cent of the profits attributable to wartime prosperity are now taxed away. And then the armed services insist on renegotiating contracts and recouping "excessive" profits. But with volume mountain-high, as compared with prewar output, the amount of profit retained in proportion to working capital is a nest egg of nice dimensions. And don't forget to count the 10-per-cent postwar refund on excess profits taxes paid during each of the years since 1941. If the war comes to a close at the end of 1945, corporations will be getting the refund on taxes paid through five years. Big business is hardly slated to go over the hill to the poorhouse when peace comes.

A further advantage for big business in the tax law is the "carryback" provision on corporate income taxes, aimed at minimizing reconversion difficulties.

Unfortunately there is no simple, brief explanation of the way these provisions operate, as many businessmen have learned to their discomfort. Their essential nature can best be illustrated by taking United States Steel as an example. Suppose the company just breaks even on operations in 1944. Normally, it would then have a deficit of twenty-five million dollars, representing the obligations on its preferred stock. Under the carry-back provision, however, it would receive a tax rebate of $49,600,000 on its 1942 tax payments. And the net result would be that the preferred stockholders get their dividend. There would even be enough left over to pay the common shareholders $2.80 per share. Converting a twenty-five-million-dollar deficit into a twenty-five-million-dollar net profit available for dividends isn't bad business nor will it hurt stock-market quotations any.

These refunds and credits were not intended to help just big business. Small business is not excluded. But the very size of big-business operations magnifies the benefits it will receive, as contrasted with those the little firms will get. The multiplication of income and profits enjoyed by big business will multiply the reimbursements when the tax collector begins to shell out.

Peace will not bring financial worries to the big organizations which have accumulated a tidy refund for the rainy day of reconversion. The larger firms, which have never had difficulty in getting money from the private-capital market, may not even have to look to that source for operating cash. But, as we've already seen, small business may hit its head against a financial wall and be compelled to turn to government for financial assistance.

Small business will really need the hay, and private channels will not provide very much of it. As *Fortune* magazine has frankly noted, "Big business, even when it is not self-financed, usually has special pipe lines to the money markets; and Wall Street, for a variety of reasons, has shown little interest in finding or placing high-risk capital. . . . It will be difficult," concludes *Fortune*, "for the would-be entrepreneur in a new or small business who has long been faced with special disadvantages, chiefly financial." All of which means that, as usual, the squeeze will be on small business. The only difference is that this time the smaller man starts a little closer to the position behind the eight ball.

Accidents of government policy will also help larger enterprise. As we have seen in an earlier chapter, the government will want to unload the plants it built during the war. Government officials will talk about making the facilities available to small business. And they won't be kidding.

But ask Bill Jones, who has that hatbox factory around the corner, if he'd like to expand and buy an airplane company. An attractive buy, with very exciting possibilities. He'll certainly be very interested. Instead of one hundred people on his pay roll—four thousand. Instead of twenty thousand square feet of space—whole city blocks to run around in. Instead of an annual income of $100,000—why, millions. Sure, if only he could pay for it and get it running; if only he knew what to make with it and whom to sell to; if only he didn't have his hands full with his own little business in the first place.

Small businesses buying big businesses? The odds are all against it, even with the government doing the selling and lending the cash. Of course the government's plant-disposal policy will aim to stimulate competition where none existed before. But the competition so stimulated will be between industrial giants—between a Reynolds Metal and an Alcoa, for example. Most of the facilities are in fields where medium-sized or small enterprise just hasn't a chance of getting a foothold, except in those few cases where it's feasible for the government to break the plants down into bits small business can digest. During the transition period and after, the dynamics of business life will call for quick and decisive action. Economically and financially, big business will be better able to do both: decide and act.

That doesn't mean little business will be left entirely out in the cold. There will be some opportunities in the form of government merchandise, machinery, and tools. Plenty of good buys that can lengthen the life of individual businesses as well as increase their profits will come into the market. Small business engaged in distribution may not only prosper but may enjoy an expanding future. Though the department stores and mail-order giants won't grow smaller or the chain stores disintegrate, small retail distribution will not be supplanted by big business. It's here that the government surpluses of goods will have their most marked business effect. Bargain counters, displaying what were originally government wares, will draw crowds, and many an easy dollar will be made by the small distributor.

But the small manufacturer will suffer his heartaches. To some who were fortunately placed in relation to war production—the small-town machine shop, the whistle-stop maker of bits and pieces —the war brought unexpected growth. But it will be dissipated even before the clouds of dust and smoke lift from the battlefields. The more enterprising saw possibilities of emerging from the war as near-big businesses. Resourceful and ingenious, they got the government to finance new plants or extensions to old plants and new equipment. With an eye to the future, they plowed back all the profits from their war contracts into the business, hopeful that they would be able to own a big business, free and clear, when it was all over.

Renegotiation of contracts by the armed services has dashed their hopes. Repayment of excessive profits made on war work is required—and the starting point for calculating fair earnings is the initial investment made by the firm. A striking illustration is the case of Jack and Heintz, Inc., which got going on an investment of $100,000. By the end of 1942 the government had invested more than $3,000,000 in plant and equipment and had advanced more than $11,000,000 in cash payments against contracts to provide working capital. On the original $100,000 the company earned more than $8,000,000. "Much too much," said the government renegotiators; "you'll have to hand back seven million."

The company's plea is that without the money it won't be in a position to reconvert to large-scale peacetime activities after the war. Its fight against renegotiation, which will be a long one, will strike a responsive chord in the hearts of businessmen similarly situated, but its plight will not engage the active sympathy of potential competitors. The *Journal of Commerce* comments editorially:

Jack and Heintz has done a fine production job in turning out aircraft starters, for which the company and its employees should receive full recognition. But whether concerns newly established during the war period, mainly with government funds, should be provided with sufficient earnings after renegotiation to finance their entry into civilian industry on a large scale is a separate question. Were such a policy adopted, the government would in effect be providing the capital for a number of new concerns to compete after the war with established businesses operating solely or chiefly with their own capital.

Situations of this kind will present one of the paradoxes of the future. Congress, like the public, will not be able to shake off its affection for small business. Middle-class aspirations in America, strengthened by the war, will demand a real measure of assistance. But small manufacture can be helped only by preferential legislation; only if the government steps in to equalize the chances can the varying types of enterprise play an even game of cards. Yet, for reasons to be examined in the next chapter, it is the small- and medium-sized businesses themselves who will be among the first to resist such efforts in their behalf.

An interesting illustration of this paradoxical situation is the opposition of the United States Chamber of Commerce to federal aid in favor of one class of enterprise. The Chamber, as distinguished from the National Association of Manufacturers, relies on the support of a vast number of small American businesses. Yet a report prepared for its Committee on Economic Policy throws its weight against various kinds of small-business relief which have been proposed to Congress. Comparable to the assistance given agriculture, one proposal would establish expert consultant services for firms that can't afford their own. Business research would be subsidized through state universities and special federal credit made available to the little businessman to whom Wall Street has consistently turned a deaf ear. The Chamber, declaring that several of the measures had merit, added that "the aid should not be restricted to business of any given size." But there will be no avoiding the fact that if the odds are made even for all participants, the chap with the biggest bank roll will continue to get the gravy.

In the basic contest between the big and the little the hands of government will be stayed by the most important pressure we shall know in the years ahead—unemployment. Big business makes big units of employment. For the sake of jobs government will grant many concessions, no matter how hostile it may be to big business. Such concessions will involve not only a substantial cut in the tax burden, but permission to continue some wartime agreements between firms in the same industry, government subsidies in the form of price inducements on government-owned facilities, the careful disposal of government-owned supplies in foreign countries, and controlled, gradual disposal in the domestic market. True, some of these measures will be favored by smaller enterprise, but the consequences will benefit most those in the upper bracket of business. If only because big business is the key to big employment, the average American will applaud such policy. And big business will continue to grow.

That continued expansion will not be due to the "greed of rapacious business." The truth is that the decisions will be made not by individuals—inside or outside the companies themselves—but by the compelling force of an economy already resting on the foundation of big business. The economic atmosphere, too, will help decide the outcome. Given an extended period of prosperity, there will be room for small business; prolonged depression will find small business unable, as usual, to cope with the pressure.

Newcomers who decide to enter business for themselves may find it possible to get a start, and in the same fields that were open before Pearl Harbor. But, once in the field, they'll find the going much tougher. For one thing, the gap between big and small will be far greater. Among the large companies which have grown bigger, competition will have been reduced, while among the small it will have become keener.

Many little enterprises that survive the impact of our war economy will have done so at the price of their independence. Like suckerfish clinging to a shark, they have been able to get along because they attached themselves to the big firms and served as subcontractors. Finding sustenance on their own would be extremely difficult; motion and direction of their own not easily restored.

The most formidable difficulty for many of the smaller businesses will be the loss of contact with the civilian market which wartime operations entailed. The distributor is an indispensable link between production and the ultimate consumer. Without him the flow of goods is either retarded or completely blocked. During the war big manufacturing companies will have continued to engage in effective marketing and advertising, even where they have nothing to sell. Most of them will have succeeded in keeping their distributive channels pretty much intact. This will be true of automobile companies, manufacturers of radios, refrigerators, phonographs, washing machines, farm equipment, and other durable consumers' goods which depend on a well-organized network of dealers.

The International Harvester Company, for example, estimates that it will have 95 per cent of its marketing machinery functioning at the end of the war. The Packard Motor Car Company still has more than 90 per cent of its dealers in business. Fewer than 15 per cent of the tire dealers have gone out of business since Pearl Harbor. Why should they? The large tire manufacturers have supplied them with everything but tires. The Firestone Tire and Rubber Company fed its distributive network with three thousand different items from a catalog that covers sixty-eight pages—books, paints, wallpaper, garden tools, clothes, etc. Big business will weather the storm. The wave that engulfs smaller enterprise may be little more than a trickle across the ankle of a corporate giant.

Fortunately there is hope for some small business in that the large war contractors will still need subcontractors after the war. But they won't need so many. Some large establishments will choose among the best of their present subcontractors, letting the others go. To those retained, tempting offers will be made. Acceptance will mean a chance to stay in business; profits, though no more than a fair return on investment, will be secure. Only independence, the opportunity to expand production and profits, will be hurt. It will be a bold entrepreneur who decides to face the risks of independent action in the market. Either way, little business will make a sacrifice.

Even when the urgency of government regulation is unquestioned it is, at best, tolerated. The heavy hand of government grows more uncomfortable with time. In the first years of reconstruction the nation will feel "tired" of government regulations. It will refuse to accept the need for regulation once the occasion which gave it birth has passed. Much of the government control is plainly labeled "war." It will be rejected once peace provides the rationalization. The discontent with government interference will carry over to other forms of regulation which preceded the war. Administration and enforcement, however necessary, will be much less vigorous in the first period after the war than they were before Pearl Harbor.

But eventually the cumulative impact of economic problems and the developing crisis will release a new wave of controls. Disappointment over big business's failure to decentralize will stir some antagonisms. Disappointment over the failure to achieve high employment by a government hands-off policy will arouse other irritations. The deeper the crisis, the greater will be the focus—unwilling, to be sure—on Washington. The hands-off period is likely to be short-lived.

Attempts will almost certainly be made by the government to restore the competitive market. The dwindling of government control will bring into bolder outline the economic power of big business. When government exercised primary power, big business could sit in the shadows unnoticed.

In a belated effort to create the competitive environment that everyone wanted and assumed would automatically come, vigorous enforcement of the existing anti-trust laws will be undertaken. It will be the path of least resistance. For a while we will believe that the anti-trust laws can restore free enterprise and unrestricted competition in the market.

Yet, in the light of past experience, it is impossible to escape the conclusion that the results will be negligible. Anti-trust laws have never successfully restrained bigness. In fact, as well as in law, *big* business is not necessarily a "monopoly." Consequently, an attempt to completely overhaul the anti-trust laws can be expected ultimately. Disappointment after disappointment in attempting to halt the industrial mammoths will finally be expressed in new statutes that will specifically label the following business practices as evidence of illegal action: identical bids, uniform price increases, higher domestic than export prices.

As now interpreted, the anti-trust laws require proof of the actual existence of an agreement to restrain trade. Price similarities are not sufficient by themselves to support a case. Before the Department of Justice can demonstrate that they are illegal it must prove that they flow from an agreement, written or oral. In most cases that proof is unobtainable—simply because no formal agreement is entered into. An agreement is hardly necessary when the parties have no desire to engage in price competition.

If the campaign against big business becomes intense enough, every kind of corporate merger will come under close federal scrutiny, perhaps through a new federal agency determining whether the union of two firms is in the public interest and permissible.

As the years pass and the small become no bigger and the big no smaller, the movement for a federal incorporation law will gain headway. Such proposals have been brought before Congress previously. In the mid-thirties Senators Borah and O'Mahoney pressed for their adoption without success, primarily because of the prevalent fear of further concentrating power in the Federal Government. In addition, state governments had a direct economic interest in the issue since corporate fees have been a sizable source of revenue. More important, though, in dooming the legislation, was the fact that two generations had passed since the country became very excited about big business.

But resistance of this kind will grow weaker as the big corporations grow stronger. Treating the entire continent as their market and reaching into the distant corners of the globe, the big companies will be clearly beyond the reach of the separate states. The antipathy to strong federal government will give way under the hammer blows of the years after the war. And once more all eyes will be turned toward Mecca-on-the-Potomac and federal power will be invoked.

A federal incorporation law, if it comes, will be much less flexible than the present requirements of the states. For example, charters will not be granted permitting a corporation to engage in any activity it chooses to enter. Nor will it be permitted to acquire property, to merge and consolidate purely at the discretion of its directors or the will of its stockholders. Instead the federal charter would probably define in specific terms the exact sphere in which a company could do business. Most important, the law would have teeth that are likely to compel adherence: violation would mean the end of the privilege to do business. The only catch is that the teeth themselves may be so sharp and the company so big that the government would hesitate to use them lest it commit economic suicide.

More immediate than any basic change in corporate structure will be certain compulsory changes in corporate practice. Refinement of existing patent laws can be expected in the not-too-distant future, even in a period of retreat from regulation. The war will have brought to light the extent to which processing of vital raw materials and the manufacture of finished goods has been restrained through domestic and international patent control.

The war has ripped the veil from patent mysteries in many an industry and spread the secret "know-how" of many a technical process. In 1941 the Temporary National Economic Committee recommended the recording of all sales, licenses, and assignments of patents. It urged that safeguards be established to prevent their restricted or monopolized use. One proposal that has been offered is to make patents available to anyone who is willing to pay appropriate royalties. The patent will be in the spotlight for some time to come.

The war will also have sharpened America's concern with the cartel, a type of industrial structure that was almost unknown to the average American before the war. Once again it was war that lifted the curtain, revealing this time certain close and intricate relationships involving some American companies. Similar associations of companies, for the purpose of limiting production, fixing prices, or distributing markets, have long been an accepted international institution. In no country other than the United States has their operation been viewed with alarm. Here alone has the anti-monopoly tradition brought about articulate reaction.

But that doesn't mean that the cartel will be rigidly barred from our shores. At home the technique has already been used as a partial answer to economic problems in some industries and in certain conditions. Even before the war the precedent was already prepared in the Bituminous Coal Act of 1935. All the bituminous coal companies were given the right to fix uniform prices and selling policies subject to approval by a government agency. During the war co-operative division of markets was introduced in many industries in accordance with plans for maximum war production. If acute depression brings plummeting prices and cutthroat competition, like that which almost wrecked the bituminous coal industry and brought wages down close to starvation levels, some of the principles of the old NRA are in for dusting off. NRA was the antithesis of free, unrestricted enterprise. Such cartelization, permitted within limited areas and under government supervision, will again be a strong probability in America.

Many an eloquent speech will be delivered against the international cartel, but there is little likelihood of strong governmental action. In the past, American companies were allowed to join world-wide combinations. Before Pearl Harbor, American companies were linked to forty-five international bodies. After the war such ties will be subjected to greater control. Not only will the firms be required to register with the Federal Trade Commission, but it is almost certain that all cartel agreements that bind American companies will be subject to the scrutiny of government. For a time America will argue that international cartels are immoral and undesirable. As usual, America will mean it. But the rest of the world will not feel that way. Cartels will continue to be an instrument in international trade and power. Uncle Sam won't pick up his marbles and go home when faced with a game as critical as this, nor will he want to.

It is much more likely that America will decide to participate more aggressively in the game. It may yet emerge as a master of the cartel, using it for international power. A marked shift toward an American imperialism would be characterized by intensified business participation in such international relationships—under government sponsorship, supervision, and inspiration. Side by side with these evidences of economic internationalism will be found a recurrence of tariff isolationism.

But the most direct influence on all private enterprise will be the government's attitude toward the business tills. Senator George says that postwar America lies within the four walls of our tax laws. The senator will be forgiven the exaggeration, for at worst it is only a magnification of a major truth. Taxation will determine the course of American business more significantly than any other governmental action. Taxes can make or break private property. More subtly than any other instrument, the tax laws can alter the distribution of American wealth, the relative power of the economic classes, the respective weights of big and little business.

Once again the gulf between problem and solution will be great. The escape from reality in taxation already began to take hold during the war.

The unavoidable reality is a national debt of about three hundred billions. When the full expenses of war have been paid and demobilization completed, that figure may even be exceeded. The future basic budget of government will be at least three times higher than it was in the most expensive peacetime year. Just paying interest on the debt will take more than the whole cost of government in the depression year of 1934. Figuring at the optimistic interest rate of 2 per cent, six billions a year must come out of the Treasury just to carry the three hundred-billion load, without reducing it. Add to that a minimum of seven billion dollars a year—and perhaps double that amount—to maintain the military machine after the war. Wendell Willkie estimates that other government expenditures are not likely to be less than seven billion dollars, under the best of circumstances. Right there you're looking at a rock-bottom budget of twenty billion dollars a year. And that's only federal expenditure; you'll be paying another ten billions to the states and cities of America. Any attempt to pay off a portion of the national debt goes on top of that. Any further pump priming or depression-filling activity pushes the tabulator hard for another fistful of billions a year. In short, the nation faces a gigantic government cost for years.

These are the realities. Few economists believe them to be oppressive realities, but they may become oppressive if we refuse to face up to them. An unwillingness to tax hard during a period of prosperous activity and the impossibility of taxing hard during a period of depressed activity can be dangerous, although the debt itself is not risky unless the national income falls drastically.

An attempt will be made to balance the budget—a budget not much under twenty-five billion dollars a year. With individual taxes high and corporate taxes reasonably light, an annual national income or level of production measured at one hundred and fifty billions or better can carry that load. The most conservative economists now believe that a country's internal debt is bearable if it doesn't exceed twice the amount of the country's national income. They also say that a country's total tax burden should not exceed 30 per cent of its national income. With a national income of one hundred and fifty billions or better, assuming no continued inflation in prices, the budget can be balanced, the interest on the debt paid, and high levels of production and employment can be maintained.

On the other hand, national income which falls below that level means that employment and production are dropping. Then tax rates must be made lighter to encourage business. Not only would it be impossible to balance the budget by taxation in such periods of deflation, but an effort would have to be made again to fill the gap in employment by increased government expenditure. That means new debt, knocking the budget completely out of joint.

The problem of government debt is therefore in almost every respect a secondary one. Production and employment are primary. In a period of unemployment every national problem will be multiplied, every danger to the political and economic structure aggravated. Solve the problem of employment and the other sores of our political and economic structure will heal quickly.

One of the certainties of the first years after war is that the taxes on business organizations will be much lighter than they were during the war. The excess-profits tax is doomed; it may not even survive the final stages of war itself. The coming job fear assures that every employment-giving instrument will be viewed with awe and treated with a long-forgotten respect. Opinion will be united on that. Some will argue that the best employment stimulant will be to eliminate taxes on corporate income altogether, except for levies on that portion frozen in unreasonable accumulations and not plowed back into business or distributed to stockholders. In this approach to taxation, similar to the old undistributed-profits tax, the corporation's treasury is considered a conduit through which money flows. It is only when the money comes to rest that the tax is to be applied. Once the corporate income ceases to work constructively and fails to stimulate employment, taxation would begin to exact a penalty.

As far as personal taxes are concerned, everybody is agreed that taxes on individuals will remain high during the years after war. It is unlikely that they will come down substantially throughout the next generation. National borrowing, already overworked by the burdens of war, will be due for a good long rest. Traditionally, America has always opposed "perpetual" debt. For a good while we can expect considerable clamor for a balanced budget, for paying the current costs of government out of taxation, and, if possible, for paying off a little piece of the debt each year. The noise will die down when the size of the national debt fades from public consciousness.

Taxation will be one of the most active battlegrounds of the future. Business has been accustomed to think of it merely as a device for paying the costs of government; business will get to know it as a device for economic planning. It may not be so used, but it will exert its influence, at least, as a potential weapon. In a period requiring intense business activity, resumption and expansion of activity, the tax system could be used to stimulate productivity through a reduction of rates on business, coupled with production incentives. Once the wheels are turning under their own momentum and the danger is boom rather than depression, a higher tax structure could counteract the inflationary tendency by resting more heavily on business.

This approach has a long way to go before it can come into operation. A perfectly synchronized system of future taxation would need an almost acrobatic agility. As the industrial and monetary scene changes, fair turns to foul and foul no less abruptly to fair. Legislative delays make such taxation far from "scientific" and keep it from functioning automatically in response to economic developments. The mechanics of taxation are such as to deprive it of the chameleon versatility needed for quick adjustment to shifting business purpose. It takes considerable time, for instance, to gear administrative machinery to a tax on undistributed corporate profits or on idle bank deposits in order to keep money moving. The lag between the needs of the hour and the effective date of a tax law can conceivably result in just the wrong action at the worst possible time.

Besides, in democratic countries political expediency has always played a greater part in tax legislation than the combined wisdom of fiscal and economic experts. This will continue to be true where federal taxes are concerned and certainly where states and municipalities are concerned. Where pressure is free to operate most directly, you can forget economic justification altogether. Consequently, any radical overhauling of the federal and state taxing systems or combination of both is chimerical in the period ahead.

These defects are not inherent in taxation but in our methods. They are inherent in what we'll probably do with our tax laws. Any attempt to bend the present system to new functions will arouse irritation and lead to dubious results, except in one important respect. Growing emphasis will be placed on the use of incentives to stimulate production. No longer will the tax law's sole concern be the raising of money. The incentive principle has already sunk deep roots into the nation's tax structure. During the defense period and in war, taxation was used to encourage plant expansion through the privilege of writing off the cost of war facilities over five years instead of over a longer period. Even before the war many states provided that the employer's social-security tax rise or fall with his failure or success in diminishing labor turnover. For a brief period of time the federal corporate tax was framed to stimulate the distribution of earnings. In the future the motivating force of incentive taxation will be employment, investment, expansion.

Proposals like C. W. Hazelett's tax on idle money will rally impressive conservative support. Literature like that of Arthur Dahlberg, urging taxation of bank deposits, will not be filed quite so quickly in the congressional wastebasket.

The urgent need for swift reconversion and maximum employment will win recognition for tax-free reserves, reconversion credits, and accelerated depreciation. Certain taxes that are burdensome to the corporation and not too productive in revenue will be abandoned—notably the capital-stock tax and its corollary, the declared-value excess-profits tax. To stimulate increased sales and consumption a good number of the federal excise taxes will be lowered or removed. Liquor and tobacco will still carry their burden of taxes. So will gasoline and a few other articles of that kind.

In a subtle way a number of these peacetime changes in the tax law will serve to multiply the advantage of the larger corporation. With individual taxes high, with gift and estate taxes made stiffer, corporations will have every incentive to plow back their earnings into expansion and new production. Big business will have enormous funds with which to diversify output, expand markets, conduct aggressive campaigns against the smaller competitors.

Eric Johnston, president of the United States Chamber of Commerce and the acknowledged spokesman of progressive business, said, "There is a people's capitalism. I come from it. I want to see it survive for every poor girl and boy in America after me. And not only survive but triumph. Only America, I think, can light the world toward an ultimate capitalism of everybody."

Capitalism—on the march again. It will continue to supply the dynamic energy that will run at least this most important of the world's productive machines. It will continue to turn out goods with an abundant profusion. The future of capitalism in America is undisputed. So, too, are the cycles of capitalistic development—its successions of boom and bust. So, too, the growing crystallization of classes and expanding barriers between them, for which no effective antidote has yet been found.

In the years after the war, capitalism and government will face in the most acute form the questions that have troubled both most painfully during the last generation. How to make jobs for the largest number and protect freedom of enterprise at the same time. How to provide security and enlarge the liberties of most at the same time. How to win safety without contracting. How to stabilize and grow. How to keep the big from growing bigger and the small from becoming smaller.

CHAPTER IX

They Make America

THE ECONOMIC PROPHETS have doomed the middle class. If they are right, America is doomed. The nation's future is the future of those groups who are the numerical majority in America, those groups who think and act for America. It is the future of the aspirations and identifications that have shaped the American culture, that have dominated its political life, have determined its origin, course, and direction.

The phrase "middle class" has come to be epithet and encomium as well as description. When it is used descriptively it is least effective. How else could that be when the term can refer accurately only to a state of mind and not to a definite economic status? The aspiration that millions of you hold in common is the basic characteristic that joins you. In almost every other way you differ. In almost every other respect there is no middle class at all. There are a number of middle classes which have little except their dreams in common. Yet you have little hesitation in insisting that you *are* "middle class." The vigor of your assertion and the enormous number who agree on that identification will not only help to determine your future but the future of your country.

By your own identification the middle class includes the $20-a-week clerk, the small factory owner who squeezes out his $10,000 a year, the $12,000-a-year branch manager in a General Motors office, the $70-a-week union linotype operator. Throw in the rural minister struggling along on $2,000, the successful urban lawyer whose yearly income rarely falls below $25,000, the 120-acre farmer whose income is what the wind and the rain, the market and the government permit. And the crackerjack, one-call salesman who makes and spends $50,000 with equal aplomb.

The sociology textbooks, of course, raise more rigid tests. Some say that if you are judging by income, the middle class must include those between $1,200 and $10,000. Some others say that you can label as middle class those dissimilar people whose incomes provide not only the necessities of life but a surplus that is saved. A small bank account, perhaps a few shares of stock, some war bonds, a few souvenir theater programs, a new roof on the barn, a new shelf of books in the minister's rectory—these are the trappings of middle-class status.

But no matter what the standard, the result is a motley amalgam of shopkeepers, small merchants, struggling manufacturers, the vast number of people in the service businesses, a large part of the farming population, supervisory employees, technicians, government workers, professionals, and even a fair slice of labor.

A good number of these you can easily recognize; they are part of the old traditional American middle class—the tradesmen, the professionals, the landowners—who first shaped the American dream. But there are newcomers—the corporate-employed technicians, the white-collar workers, the government employees, the higher-skilled craft workers sometimes called the "aristocracy of labor"—who constitute the new middle class.

Since most of you, standing on so many different economic and cultural levels, huddle under the same middle-class mantle, the weakening of any one sizable section of the group will be important to you. It will be critical for America. The future definitely does not belong to the independent proprietor with his own means of production. To the extent that you have identified yourself with him, you've climbed on a band wagon headed downhill. To the extent that all or most of you identify yourselves with his aspirations—instead of those which flow more realistically from your own economic and social position—America is threatened by dangers that might not otherwise confront her.

Groups are always passing out of the economy in the course of its unavoidable evolution. The invention of the automobile dispossessed many a carriage and bicycle maker who didn't or couldn't make the shift. The growth of the railroad displaced the thousands associated with the stagecoach. The mechanical cotton picker may yet doom hundreds of thousands whose roots are in the cotton fields.

The fate of none of these unfortunate groups implied a major threat to the entire country. There was no national self-identification with any of them. New groups and interests took their places and the balance was not upset. "The King is dead! Long live the King!" has enabled the evolutionary process to continue without critical battles at each of the crossroads of change.

But where the middle class as an entity is involved, that won't be true. Traditional middle-class aspirations have become a part of the American tradition itself, and they have been strengthened emotionally by the pressure of World War II. If the future is one in which the growth of large enterprise snuffs out smaller independent business, the American way of life itself will be the victim and you will cry out with its pain.

Your imprecations will be loud and deeply felt despite the fact that you yourself may work for big business, prefer to shop in the largest department store, deposit your money in the largest banking chain, or buy an automobile made by the largest Detroit company.

Your daily bread is probably baked in the ovens of a plant that turns out millions of loaves. You eat it because you hear it advertised over a big radio network. The food you eat is mass-produced in good part by one of a few mammoth companies. And you buy your favorite brands not only because you like them but because an advertising budget in the millions has brought the tempting pleasures to your attention. You've linked your hopes with those of the small independent enterprise, but you won't fill your tank with Murphy's High Test Gasoline when the familiar sign of Esso or Tydol or Gulf may be a mile further down the road.

There are many good reasons why you feel for little business and deal with big business. The basic reality of your life is the domination of the large corporation. What you buy from it gives you much satisfaction and little reason to complain. On the other hand, your self-association with the independent flows with equal logic from your traditions, your background, your desire for democracy itself. A country with many thousands of small businesses, completely competitive enterprise, individual unrelated units, is closer to economic democracy than a country governed by an exclusive industrial caste made up of a handful of big companies. If the big should take over, the fear is that you will have lost an essential phase of the democratic heritage. The understandable effort is to recapture it, to resist the change rather than to recognize the new conditions and shape them to the old desires. The small business structure that was America and the economic freedom it represented can both be lost in the frustration resulting from your inability to turn the economic and technological clock back. The future of the middle class depends on the outcome of the contest between the desire to hold on to the old and the willingness to effect an adaptation to and of the new.

Those who have predicted the doom of the middle class have been certain that all of you will cling unavailingly to the old as it passes from the scene. Were it not for this conflict, there would be no need for a separate discussion in this book of the future of the middle classes. Since *they* are America, all else within these covers is actually the future of the middle class. The only questions here are the validity of the bleak prophecy, a more accurate knowledge of just who is doomed, who will join them in their losing fight, why it will occur, what the consequences will be for the future of America.

Senator Walter F. George, chairman of the Senate Finance Committee, has insisted that any further increase in personal taxation will wipe out the middle classes. As long ago as 1887 the end was being predicted by W. G. Sumner:

It is the tendency of all social burdens to crush out the middle class, and to force the organization into a society of only two classes, one at each social extreme. . . . It is the tendency of all the hardships of life to destroy the middle class. . . . The rich man . . . can endure the shocks of material calamity and misfortune with less distress the richer he is. A bad season may throw a small farmer into debt from which he can never recover. It may not do more to a large farmer than lessen one year's income. A few years of hard times may drive into bankruptcy a great number of men of small capital, while a man of large capital may tide over the distress and put himself in a position to make great gains when prosperity comes again.

The bell tolls and the prophecies multiply. On the eve of the war Hilaire Belloc warned, "A process is now continuous all over Europe. The middle class is dying and with it our civilization is dying too. For the middle class made, and, until yesterday, still sustained, our culture. . . ."

Perhaps the most extreme—and most erroneous—prophecy of all was the one made by Karl Marx: "The lower strata of the middle class—the small tradespeople, shopkeepers, and retired merchants generally, the handicraftsmen and peasants—all these sink gradually into the proletariat . . . all these fight against the bourgeoisie to save from extinction their existence as fractions of the middle class." The irony of this Marxist error is that, far from disappearing or merging with the proletariat, the middle-class ranks have actually been swelled by the ascent of a substantial portion of the class below them. This enlarged group not only fails to fight for its existence in terms of self-interest, but has been the most vigorous force for the preservation of the industrial capitalism which Marx visualized as its own bitter enemy.

Only one important group consistently refuses to share the gloom about the middle classes—the middle classes themselves. Even before war brought prosperity a representative group of the population, when asked, "Do you think that the years ahead hold for you, personally, a good chance of advancement or the probability of any improvement over your present position?" voted its confidence in tomorrow. Only a third of the over-all group saw dead end ahead —and this degree of pessimism came from the aged and the poor.

"Do you believe that the great age of economic opportunity and expansion in the United States is over?" was another of the questions asked. Only 13 per cent thought so. Fifteen per cent didn't know, and 72 per cent thought that "American industry can create expansion and opportunity in the future." Even two thirds of the unemployed agreed.

The chances are that they're nearer the truth than the prophets of doom, though history will demonstrate that both have justification. For one of the middle classes the future ahead is a struggle against oblivion.

Hardest hit in the middle classes will be the small property owner engaged in production. His future will be but a shadow of the impressive past. The oft-praised sturdy character of the old property-owning middle class equipped its members to beat a path to economic success, but the evolution of the economic mechanism which once allowed success has made it harder and harder, with the passing decades, for any large number to reach the highest levels.

As mercantilism developed into capitalism, and later individual enterprise became the giant corporation, the chances upward diminished. The standard of living for the entire group was increasing at the same time. But the relative distances between the top and the middle were widening. Increasing luxury obscured the fact that the control of the instruments of production, the control of property itself, was passing into fewer hands. The concentrated control of owners of corporate property will not necessarily affect the standard of living of the average American. But the freezing of property and ownership by giant enterprise will inevitably cancel out the basic aspiration of the old middle class—the desire for ownership, the social position it gives, and a chance to move to the top. What was once a status becomes only an objective. A myth of direction is invoked: what was once fact becomes purely belief that middle-class status is a steppingstone up. But for the greater portion of the proprietor middle class it is merely a way station on the road down.

In the preceding chapter we have seen the dramatic extent to which control over American industry has been concentrated in fewer and bigger hands. The assembly line has, for all practical purposes, barred an expanding future for small independent manufacture. In the automobile industry, where 75 per cent of the entire output in 1930 was already in the hands of two companies, Ford and General Motors, the fact is perfectly clear. But even where the assembly line and technology have not revolutionized the industry, that trend has been almost as marked. The sales of Swift and Armour, among the meat processors, make the output of the smaller firms microscopic.

It is only in retail distribution that the gates have not been slamming shut. Over the years the chain store has been inching in, but it has been an inch-by-inch encroachment. The independent retailer who survived the war years was in many instances helped by the war. His compliance with the rationing and price-control regulations was frequently a good deal less punctilious than that of the chain and large department store. The pressure of the OPA was less direct on him than the pressure of his customers. Many customers who formerly passed him by returned. True, an estimated 20 per cent of the group failed to survive. But the balance did, and they enter the peace alive and kicking, some of them more so than ever.

Access to opportunity was the essence of a frontier society where the basic problem was to discover and exploit a pioneer nation's resources. As long as the frontiers remained, the middle-class dream of crossing the barrier and ascending into the capitalist level appeared realizable. But with the passing of the frontier, the progress of technology, the depletion of natural resources, the rationalization of industry, the organization of distribution and mercantile establishments on a grander scale, the dream of independent enterprise begins to grow dimmer.

The diminishing number of property owners is only a small part of tomorrow's problem. It's the extent to which everybody *wants* to be a property owner that makes the fact significant. Don't underestimate the every-man-an-owner psychology. This amalgamating aspiration that combines the diverse group, from typist to tycoon, is the consistent thread which has run through the history of the middle class in America. It is, as a matter of fact, the consistent thread of America itself. Whatever happens to the middle class will affect not only those distinctly in the middle by property or position, but millions of Babbitts without a swivel chair to squat in.

Here is an illustration taken from the lowest end of the economic ladder. In the black agricultural days of 1936 unionization had taken hold for the first time among the sharecroppers. Under a leaking roof in Muskogee, Oklahoma, where the most prominent and most noisy decorations were pans scattered across the floor to catch the rain, the agricultural dispossessed of seven states, white,

Negro, Mexican, and Indian, representing 35,000 sharecroppers, came together. In a meeting characterized as few are by unanimity of both opinion and privation, only one conflict occurred: Who is to be eligible for union membership? The Executive Board unanimously recommended that eligibility be limited to those who are tenants working the land of others. But the landless sharecroppers and farm tenants insisted that the constitution explicitly provide that even land*owners* who work the soil be permitted to join. *For secretly each sharecropper saw himself as the ultimate owner of forty acres and a mule.*

But even the absence of property, or, more seriously, the absence of any real hope of attaining it, as in the case of the sharecropper, has never weakened the middle-class focus on ownership. The "American dream" persisted, though for each member of the middle class who reached the top rung through ownership a dozen were driven lower in middle-class rank or into the working class. Jerome Davis has presented a parable which pointedly describes the anomaly. In a lake there were thousands of minnows and several large pike. The pike constantly devoured the smaller fish. The minnows finally formed a committee to plead their case before the pike. After deliberation the chairman of the pike reported: "We have decided that from now on one minnow in every thousand will be allowed to become a pike." The minnows went away happy.

The war has, of course, affected the separate middle classes differently. The smaller producer has been pinched by the successive restraints of price control, priorities, rationing, credit restrictions, transportation limitations, standardization of production. Others of the middle classes, however, will have come through without damage. Those whose future is by no means as dreary are the new middle classes, the groups whose roots are not in enterprise, or at least not in the ownership of their own businesses. Those on the government pay roll are one illustration. Aside from loans by government and its agencies, the people of the United States depended on government for more than 18 per cent of their entire national income in 1940. Another 3 per cent and public service would, in that peacetime year, have been the largest industry in America, just nosing out all of manufacture.

The position of the technician, the foreman, the engineer, the craftsman, and the host of other administrative and supervisory employees will also have been made more secure and even more promising. In common with everyone else in the community, the white-collar worker had a job—usually a better one than he had before. But the office workers, the government employees, and the fixed-income recipients, who don't identify themselves with labor, have suffered one wartime effect peculiar to unorganized workers. Their wages will by no means have kept pace with the rising cost of living. The proportion of the national income dollar that went to them will have diminished at the very moment that their position became more entrenched and the need for their abilities increased. It is estimated that as many as fifteen million heads of American families received little or no increase in their weekly pay envelopes during the war period. Louis Stark, labor editor of the New York *Times*, who studied the effect of wage stabilization on the unorganized groups, estimated that "while wages of industrial workers increased about 37 per cent from 1939 to 1943, salaries of teachers increased less than 8 per cent. This figure is used in the light of the fact that 66,000 teachers received less than $600 a year."

The significance for the future is plain. Both the unorganized salaried workers and the fixed-income groups in the community will start their postwar living on a weaker economic base. Their savings will be proportionately smaller, if at all existent; their margin for protection against disaster, weak; but their role and place is secure in the industrial community, secure except against the hazards of nationwide depression.

Despite the security of its position, however, this new middle class, because of its identification with the old middle class, shares the fears of the latter though frequently with less intensity. Even though the major threat comes from the class above, the middle class has traditionally looked with hostility at the class below. One clue to this anomaly lies in the middle class's fear of losing caste and the ever-present hope that it will rise into the controlling economic class itself someday.

Another clue is found in the fact that the nature of its undertakings exposes it to much closer contact with the pressures of the working class than with those of the capitalist group. Jealously guarding his small margin of profit, the middle-class producer generally fears trade-unions with an intensity born of desperation, for when a union strikes against him the very existence of his business may well be threatened. Furthermore, the small size of his enterprise makes him an easier object of attack by unions. Again, the middle-class distributor finds himself in daily conflict with lower-class consumers, whose sole aim is to reduce his prices and cut down his profit. The pressures directed against him by the big producers do not reach him with the same immediacy or intimacy.

Actually the great difficulty of the middle class arises from the fact that it does not strive to strike a balance in its relations with the class below and the class above. At certain points the interests of the middle class will conflict with those of the working class; at certain points they will conflict with those of the upper class. But having identified itself, as a result of its aspirations, with the top group, it will not be so free to fight the aggressions from that direction.

This inability to strike a balance will sharpen the schizophrenic conflict between middle-class ambition and the realities of its economic position, a conflict already revealed in its past. The Populist tradition, which epitomized the most vigorous middle-class action, produced its anti-trust laws, its Federal Trade Commission, its Robinson-Patman Act, and the fair-trade laws. But, like whispers against the wind, these failed to stem the inevitable agglomeration of small property into big property and the evolution of laissez faire into monopoly. The laws were the expression of political attitude; their uneven enforcement the expression of the conflicting economic ambitions.

This is no new discovery. It was best described by Peter Finley Dunne in one of his Mr. Dooley stories when he attributed to Teddy Roosevelt the following view: " 'Th' thrusts are heejous monsthers built up be th' intherprize iv th' men that have done so much to advance progress in our beloved country,' he says. 'On the wan hand, I wud stamp thim unher fut; on th' other, not so fast.' "

History has placed on Theodore Roosevelt the trust buster's

halo. But the truth is that his famous "big stick," his Anti-Trust Division, consisted of only five lawyers and four stenographers! None of the corporations under attack would have considered retaining for their defense a law firm so poorly staffed.

Robert H. Jackson, once head of the Anti-Trust Division, has appraised the validity of the middle-class attacks against monopoly:

> While the country has forbidden monopoly, it has also been subsidizing it. Monopoly has had tax advantages that have aided its rise. While the sale of a small business to another who wished to continue it as such would be subject to a capital gains tax, if it were absorbed by a big business the matter could be arranged in the form of a tax-free "reorganization." The tax-free reorganization privilege has been a powerful incentive for the concentration of business. The advantage in single transactions, at the cost of the Treasury, has often exceeded the whole annual appropriation for anti-trust enforcement. . . . Moreover, the privilege of paying dividend profits free of tax from one corporation to another operated as a subsidy for the holding companies, one of the most favored forms of creating and operating monopoly.

It is the self-identification with the upper class that makes it impossible for the middle class to defend itself against attack from above. At the same time it cannot find protection in any alliance with labor. Most white-collar workers share the employer's attitudes toward the unions. They have no greater income, no more security than the "worker," and are as dependent on their employers as any "worker" is; but their greater education, training, culture, social veneer, and closer prideful relationship to the work they do establish unquestionably their middle-class character. Peculiarly, within the ranks of industrial labor there is a craft-union aristocracy whose sense of vested interest is more firmly middle class than that of many persons traditionally regarded as such. Such unionists even consider themselves more "separate" from labor than do many people in management, and their unions are in great part an effort to preserve the barrier between themselves and the "workers."

But the new middle classes will not feel their resentments and fears of those below them as deeply as will the old. The frustration that besets the property owner will not be present. It is more difficult to dislike when you're moving up or holding your own than when you're sliding down. For many of the "new" middle classes, peace will offer the greatest prospect for economic advancement and political control they've ever had. They will enjoy the psychological lift of knowing that they are not declining in the community. Wage workers, salaried employees, and professionals jumped from six hundred thousand in 1870 to more than ten million before the war. From 4 per cent of the community they've become more than 20 per cent. For them the future is not a fight for group survival.

For America it means, though, that the future of the middle class is in large measure the future of a non-propertied class; more exactly, it's the future of a class that doesn't own its own means of livelihood. One hundred years ago sixteen out of every twenty people in America owned the means by which they made their living. Today seventeen out of twenty don't. A drastic change in the traditions of liberty and independence will result from this fact alone. America will be as much a middle-class nation as it ever was, but there's a basic adjustment ahead in middle-class aspirations and many conflicts before the adjustments are completed.

This new middle class has been growing much more rapidly than the number of industrial workers. The trend will continue, as Lewis Corey says, because they are the core "in collective, large-scale industry, and in the state, without whose functional services the economic system could not carry on because they now perform the tasks of industrial organization and direction that individual capitalist owners performed in the age of competitive, small-scale capitalism."

The future of the middle class will eventually involve an open struggle to achieve *place* in America—as the employed managers of big business. Tomorrow and the day after are made for the manager. The growth of large enterprise, the complexity of its operations, the trend toward specialization within the administrative activity of business, all emphasize the importance of the new industrial functionary. The stratification and "layering" of intricate modern industrial organisms make inevitable the growth of the specifically trained stewards of power, the new industrial bureaucrats. Here is tomorrow's aristocracy of the middle class.

As for the old middle class, it will be increasingly ground between capital and labor, its roots torn from its economic and philosophic soil. It will stand as the major problem of modern society. An instrument of democratic-capitalist revolution, father of the French and the American republics and the English industrial revolution, Europe's middle class has ironically paid the ugly fee of fascism as the price for its own frustration.

The substantial American middle class in agriculture is another participant in the gradual march away from property. The number of separate individual owners has been declining. The family farm has been declining.

Three notable trends have left a lasting imprint on the land. The marginal landowner is becoming the farm tenant. The smaller, less secure, independent farmer frequently becomes the farm contractor, selling his entire output to a specific food processor. The mechanization of agriculture has enlarged the farm and reduced the number of individual owners. With mechanization calling for ever larger capital outlays, this most important of the trends is unlikely to be reversed. The farm community will look to the nation for subsidies, price support, and similar guarantees against the competitive struggle.

The old middle class, the enterprisers, will find their democratic ideals tested by severe pressures. These are the three dynamic factors already in existence and destined to become more pronounced: the organized effort of those below to dominate the economic and political society; government action tending to destroy the effect of accumulation and acquisition; the forces which will close the escape upward.

The war has multiplied the effect of each enormously. The traditional middle-class group—those whose key incentives and inherited philosophies have centered around the concepts of "property," "economic freedom," "getting ahead," "laissez faire"—represents, from the social standpoint, the dynamite of tomorrow.

Tired and confused, the emotional uplift of war removed, these beleaguered middle-class entrepreneurs are the most susceptible to the infections of a postwar disillusionment. Every postwar call for new-style isolationism, every chauvinist appeal, will seek to enlist their loyalties. In every successful fascist revolution in Europe the basic appeal was directed to just such elements as these, bewildered, frustrated, and embittered. The fascist line dangled before the middle class is baited on two hooks, the first of which is protection against the pressure from below, and the other, the promise of a restoration to the old status of power and unlimited opportunity.

Of the major social entities in America, only one clearly sees its role, its direction and future—large enterprise. The little entrepreneur looks up while slipping down. The manager has not yet fully recognized his key role in "the managerial revolution." Unorganized labor is harried, incensed, and confused. It sees itself as part of America's middle class, wears few of the identifying garments, and resents the overtures from a group with which it prefers not to associate. Union labor worries, fears attack, and hopes for salvation.

CHAPTER X

Organized for Retreat

THEY APPROACH TOMORROW widely and actively disliked. They're not sure they like themselves or each other. A drubbing awaits them; internecine warfare will divide them; the economics of the hour will shake the ground from under them. Organized labor is on the threshold of an unwilling retreat. But it will emerge from that retreat undestroyed.

That organized labor will weather the storm created by the attitudes of the community is but another indication of the dichotomy between belief and reality. The survival of organized labor will be less a tribute to its own tenacity in the fight to come than it will be an evidence of how reality has its way with us despite our attitudes.

Modern labor organization is a by-product of the machine, stimulated by the business cycle, strengthened and made secure by the growth of larger enterprise and the impersonality of distant management. Since none of these will cease to be real, despite the fervent desire that they should, neither will the instrumentalities of labor.

After a turbulent century of violent conflict the unions have dug in. They will continue to be a recognizable landmark on the scene in which you spend the rest of your life. The certainty of their indefinite survival, though, skips a lot of territory. There will be marked changes. As the most important minority bloc in the community, they can't help but be affected by the ups and downs of public opinion, of production levels, of the fall of old products and the rise of new ones.

The influence of the labor unions in American life has been

growing. When fairly substantial sections of organized labor hitched their destiny to the New Deal wagon they got a long ride. The strength attained by labor and the growing cleavage between the labor organizations and the Roosevelt administration have suggested to some labor leaders that the ride with Roosevelt ought to be called to an end. They see in the labor movement the new political force that will come to dominate the economic and political life of the country. But they are taking their drinks too strong. But there is little likelihood of any such development in American life within the foreseeable future.

You may see it come to England during your lifetime. There the war has pushed labor leaders into positions of high government importance. The British unions have consolidated far beyond any position achieved by American labor, and the war has given them added social, psychological, and political stature. In England, according to Ernest Bevin, Minister of Labor in Winston Churchill's cabinet, the war must be followed by "economic reconstruction of the old foundations of society . . . The task of rebuilding the world has to be done by the working class." Language such as that used by Bevin is taken seriously in England.

There are many reasons why American labor won't move in the British direction, or at least not for a long time. The most important is the long history of class consciousness in England; in the United States it has hardly put in an appearance. Both the youth of the American republic and the stronger economic position of the republic have delayed the stratification of classes. It has been possible for a Rockefeller to start out on a shoestring and wind up with a fortune. That crossing of class boundaries has frequently been achieved in the United States. American workers believe in the same philosophy as their compatriots in the middle class: "I am here today, but tomorrow—who knows?" Even in the Garment Workers Union, one of the oldest of the organized trades, almost every member looked forward to the day when he'd become, as the expression goes in the industry, "a cockroach capitalist." The phrase, incidentally, was no aspersion on the class to which the worker aspires. It was a description of the size he hoped initially to attain.

Challenging frontiers have inspired the upward aspirations of the American worker. Now the geographic frontiers are closed. Only new economic frontiers—the development of new industries under conditions that favor the appearance and growth of newcomers— can maintain a free flow from class to class. We have seen, in looking at the future of enterprise, that the new industries will appear, but it is also inescapable that the entry of newcomers will be more and more limited. The aspirations will not disappear as quickly as the economic ceilings grow fixed. It takes a long time for history to seep into the consciousness even of those who live through it.

America after the war will emerge with some increase in class consciousness. There will be a growing cohesiveness within groups and widening gaps between them. But even the average labor-union member will not read "dead end" on the signpost of the future. The buffeting the unions will receive, however, will begin to affect him. Unemployment will emphasize the diminishing hope.

Labor will meet the peace with a deceptive show of strength. On Armistice Day the labor unions will be able to show a membership of twelve million on their books. To begin with, that figure includes men in the armed forces who will never return to their old jobs or their old unions.

A good number of members are in the unions only because closed-shop and maintenance-of-membership clauses imposed by the War Labor Board have compelled their membership. As war-expanded industries begin to contract, union members will be squeezed out of jobs and will drop out of their labor organization. As a general rule, union membership rises in periods of prosperity and contracts in periods of depression.

The unions that have gone through the wartime inflation of membership will be most likely to experience a sudden membership deflation. Relatively, the CIO is likely to suffer a sharper drop than the AFL. In fact, AFL leaders have been staving off the demands from some sections of their organizations for unity with the CIO until after the war because they look forward to the weaker bargaining position of the CIO when the storm blows up. Dan Tobin, leader of the AFL's powerful Teamsters Union, says: "We do know this: that all organizations of labor will lose substantially in membership when the war ends. . . . It is safe to say that the membership of organized labor will go back one third shortly after the ending of this war. . . . Many of the CIO unions are war organizations. Certainly there will not be 40,000 employees in the Boeing Airplane manufacturing plant."

The bulk of CIO's strength lies in the war industries such as auto and aircraft (with more than a million members), steel, shipbuilding, rubber, chemicals, and so on. Union war babies will suffer a high rate of infant mortality.

While most of the loss in membership experienced by both AFL and CIO will be due to unemployment, other factors will make the drop steeper. The war will have shaken up the composition of union membership. The migration of workers from peace- to wartime industry will have caused confusion in union books. Unionists lost to their organizations as a result of this migration and as a result of the draft may never reappear on the original rolls. Some old union men will come back from the war with a resentment against their old unions—a resentment similar to that of the other servicemen.

The severest shake-up, though, will come from the dilution of labor that has taken place. Because less skilled workers had to be used to overcome the manpower shortage, industry found it necessary to subdivide skilled activities into simple, separate operations. The vast changes in technology have caused some skills to disappear completely, others to lose their importance. The chief economist of the AFL says, for example: "In one lens-grinding operation I was analyzing the other day that has long been maintained as a single operation, the skills have been broken down into nineteen separate jobs. Nineteen separate workers can now be trained in a short period of time to perform those individual operations, but they have not the slightest idea about the related operations in this line."

Out of such change will flow jurisdictional disputes which will weaken the organizations involved. From this, too, will stem the defection of skilled workers who no longer have a place in the economy as craftsmen following an established trade. In this one case the AFL will be harder hit by a wartime impact than the CIO.

The AFL relies more completely on the organization of skilled crafts; it will feel more keenly the trend away from the slowly acquired skills.

The other repercussions of war, however, will hit harder at CIO because its membership is new, less attached to union ways, and less likely to cling to membership out of habit or inertia.

The unions are far from unaware of what's ahead. Some will make desperate efforts to meet the crisis and hold their membership with every variety of attractive bait. Unemployment-insurance funds have already been established by some union organizations to supplement state payments. Accident and health insurance, toward which contributions have been made over a considerable period of time, will be pushed in order to convince members that they ought to remain in the organization to protect their "investment." Here again AFL unions are likely to prove stronger because they have had a longer time in which to build up such resources.

Of advantage to the AFL, too, will be the fact that their members have already gone through periods of stress. They've learned in advance to protect themselves against coming threat. Not so with the CIO. All factions among the leadership of the United Automobile Workers, the biggest union in America, combined to urge their 1943 convention to approve special assessments, ranging from two to six dollars a member, to enable the union to build up a fund of five millions as a cushion against postwar knocks. The pleas were forceful, the future pictured as frightful indeed, the effort a failure. The UAW, with a membership of more than one million, will start the retreat with a treasury of less than one dollar per member. The AFL Teamsters Union, on the other hand, with less than half of the UAW's numbers, is so strong financially that it was able to make eight million dollars available for bond purchases and other war purposes.

The drive to hold on will be vigorous. It is always present. Sanitariums, educational programs, patriotic drives, cultural activities, political outlets, servicemen's dances, cocktail parties, marches on Congress, and even the Broadway presentation of all-union musical comedies are the sandbags heaped on the riverbanks to stem tomorrow's flood of difficulties.

All in all, the picture is one of weakness—greater weakness in the CIO than in the AFL.

Retreat for the labor organizations will not, however, mean retreat on some of the planks which carried them to their present strength in America. For example, no matter how weak union organization becomes, collective bargaining will remain a legal requirement. Changes will be made in the National Labor Relations Act, but the fundamental compulsions will continue. The war has strengthened them. There are more collective-bargaining agreements in the United States today than ever before. Some industries which had been partially successful in their fight against unionization before the war will emerge almost 100 per cent organized.

The contest will not be over the principles of collective bargaining as such. It will be over the practical issue of whether there is a sufficient number of union members to require the bargaining of the employer. The weakening of unionization will create situations where management will not be obliged by law to bargain with the union. For one thing, a surplus labor market will enable employers to find an abundance of non-union labor.

A period of difficult labor relations is ahead—a period of keen management-labor conflict. When unions are strongest, strikes are less frequent. Their very strength makes it unnecessary for them to strike. The most highly organized industries show a record of few strikes. The wartime strike experience may seem to contradict this, but a new factor was involved: in most instances the strikes were like those of the United Mine Workers—against the government, not the employer. The fight was against wage control, not a struggle for bargaining power.

One of the principles established by the Wagner Act will have an important bearing for tomorrow. While the law requires that employers negotiate with the representatives of their employees, there is no compulsion to agree. After the war employers will continue to negotiate, but agreements will be fewer and the strikes that occur when there is failure to agree will be more numerous. It will not be just the weakening position of labor that will stimulate management resistance. Employers will have increased difficulty in meeting the demands of their employees.

The first occasion for large-scale strikes will come when reconversion gets going. The period will be marked by sharp grievances. Workers will have to be shifted to new types of jobs; employees who were upgraded because of the drafting of other men from the plant or by reason of the intense labor shortage will have to be moved to less important work; veterans will begin to replace employees hired during the war; men will be taken from one type of machine and put to work on another. Even under ordinary circumstances such changes would foster discontent. But with insecurity growing, the atmosphere will be surcharged with the quick resentments of deepening fear.

All these difficulties will be heightened by the fact that some employers will consider the occasion made to order for an attack on union organization. A surplus in the labor market always finds unions at a disadvantage. In a period of layoffs it is comparatively easy for an employer to dismiss union members along with those who are no longer necessary for his production, despite the provisions against discriminatory discharge in the Wagner Act. It will be harder for labor to enforce those provisions.

It would be remarkable if many employers did not continue to use a labor source that has been enlarged by the war—a source not too affectionately regarded by the unions. The women who have been brought out of their homes into industrial activity will not all retire. The war has demonstrated that in many cases they are as well equipped as men to carry on the functions they have been performing. Female employment may prove to be the most important battering-ram that industry will use in the siege of union organization. Pay scales for women are ordinarily lower than men's; and the war will not have permanently equalized the pay, despite the permission granted by the War Labor Board. The new feminine employees have not proved as susceptible to the blandishments of unionization. Since they challenge the vested interests of the male unionists, they are not likely to be welcome. Even during the war the unions were reluctant to permit women to come into the plants. With the war over, unions will be way ahead of management in the drive to chase the women home.

Some of the weaknesses of organized labor after the war will be due to an attitude that will characterize the entire community—a sense of guilt originating in the war itself. Compared to those who served directly, who risked the complete sacrifice, no discomfort can seem adequate. The Timken Roller Bearing Company knew this when it ran its full-page ad carrying the following caption: "THEY OFFER THEIR ALL! CAN WE OFFER TOO MUCH? The Timken Roller Bearing Company proposes seniority rights to every employee for double the time spent in military service." Who can object? There can be no protest, as the company says, "from those of us whose sacrifices by comparison have been negligible or non-existent—to this humane and reasonable treatment of our returning heroes." But the result of multiplied seniority for servicemen will be the laying off of men who have been with the company all along. The resentment, the widening cleavage between the serviceman returning to his job and the civilian losing his job because of reduced seniority will hardly be minimized even if a sense of guilt prevents protest.

The widespread application of the Timken technique would create a serious problem in labor relations, particularly where union contracts defined seniority rights. A deeper alienation between ex-servicemen and unionists is inevitable. The Achilles' heel will trouble labor.

The inevitability of labor retreat does not mean that the demands of labor will be modified by its knowledge of the difficulties it faces. On the contrary. Labor organization is a business. In bad times holding your customers is more important than ever. Unions suffer from the same dread of bankruptcy as private enterprise. It takes a lot of money to run a major labor union, and the only important source of revenue is the dues paid by members.

In Europe union members have acquired the habit of hanging on during fair or foul weather. Foreign labor organization has offered the economic advantages and the cultural and political attributes which keep the union member even in periods when there is no monetary advantage in belonging and paying dues. That kind of loyalty is characteristic of growing class stratification. Union membership gives status, and for this you pay dues willingly.

But in America this European attitude has never taken root. If the union can't produce, no sense paying dues.

Unable, for reasons beyond their control, to deliver the goods, unions will try to compensate by promising more—in the form of bigger demands. The most immediate question will be that of wages, threatened by the dislocations of reconversion. Labor will strike out for a speedy lifting of the wage-stabilization regulations. The War Labor Board hasn't exactly had smooth going during wartime. Its final days, until the threat of inflation is over, will be rough indeed. Wage stabilization will go by the board when pay rolls begin to plummet and jobs disappear. Unions, with redoubled ferocity, will attempt to hold something approximating the wartime levels. The struggle against a drop will be a bitter one. As the hours of work diminish, both AFL and CIO leaders will concentrate their energies on raising the hourly rate of pay so that the weekly take-home total bears some resemblance to what it was during the war. Adjustment to a lower standard of earning will not come without resistance from labor.

That labor's wage demands will be rejected by industry is equally assured. With profits falling, production going into a slump, and markets uncertain, industry will not yield. In the economic environment of the first transition years there is no possibility that the unions will meet with more than slight success. The retreat will be on—though neither willing nor strategic.

In the reconversion period the unions will fight for dismissal pay or for some sort of holiday pay to bridge the time it takes to retool. Pressure will be brought to bear on industry, and, failing that, the heat will be applied to government; but no expansion of government spending is likely. Here and there employers with sufficient reserves will work out some arrangements, but by and large the attitude will be, "Look to your unemployment insurance." Benefits, however, will not be increased in time to meet the first wave of reconversion joblessness. All in all, the unions will do poorly on the money questions.

Major conflicts will surround the issue of union security. Union recognition on terms that favor permanence is more important to the average union than working conditions. In the course of union negotiations many an employer has been startled to find, when the compromising stage was reached, that the unions will sooner recede on an economic demand than on an organizational demand like the closed shop or the checkoff. From the organization's point of view the first job is to get the foot in the door; then plant it firmly; finally bring out the sample case. If the union gains a foothold, it can win back in the future the gains it has temporarily surrendered. On an even more pragmatic level, the union officials and organizers have personal considerations that may supersede the monetary interests of the members they represent. A union without contracts is a store with merchandise on consignment and no business. Union recognition secured from an employer will keep the customers waiting on line and will bring others. It's capital from which a more permanent vested interest can be built.

Among the industrialized countries, only in the United States has the closed shop been a basic concern. In Great Britain, where the Trades Union Congress is a powerful and completely accepted organization, the shipping industry is the only major one in which the closed-shop contract exists. A government report on industrial relations in Sweden notes: "The closed shop is not a significant issue in Sweden, because of the very large proportion of workers who are union members and because the employer no longer tries to break down union organization, preferring to deal with the workers through strong trade-unions."

The zeal with which American labor has fought for union-security agreements has been in direct proportion to its own feeling of insecurity in the American scene. Surrounded by union men on every hand, a non-union worker is fairly certain to be pressured into joining. The situation is typified by an exchange that took place between Sidney Hillman and a member of the Judiciary Committee of Congress early in 1941. One of the committeemen asked, "Now, my understanding of an open shop is a place where union and non-union men work together. Is that true?"

"Oh no, Congressman," Hillman answered, "they just work in the same place. They don't work together."

For a number of years American unions will continue to fight for the closed shop. In fact, the economic atmosphere and the sting of retreat will make the fight more bitter. But with the eventual resurgence of union organization and the ultimate unification of the major labor organizations in the United States, the experience of European labor organizations will be repeated here and the closed shop will cease to be an issue between management and labor.

No instrument gives the labor leader more complete domination over his union membership than his control over the individual's job under a closed-shop provision. Its ultimate elimination will make labor leaders more responsive to both the needs and the will of their own members.

A new demand that will be made by unions after the war—and it will cause many a strike in the years to come—will be the guaranteed annual wage. For years negotiators have thrown it across the table at management in the process of contract bargaining. When Father Coughlin was organizing "Social Justice" cells in a number of the larger unions, he plugged for a guaranteed annual wage in his radio broadcasts.

In the past there has been very little genuine insistence on this point. Only one union has been pressing consistently for an annual guarantee—the United Mine Workers, who for two decades have sought a yearly minimum of two hundred days of work. In 1942 Philip Murray's own United Steel Workers of America joined the fray. More recently, the Brotherhood of Electrical Workers (AFL) let it be known that it would be willing to reduce its hourly rates of pay in exchange for a guarantee of some 290 days of work a year for its journeymen.

It is in the seasonal industries that the issue will be especially prominent. In one of the two major seasonal industries, automobiles, the union argued for a consistent flow of work throughout the year as a method of securing a regular annual income. Leaders of the United Automobile Workers propose that the humps in the purchase of automobiles be leveled out through the device of reducing car prices in off seasons.

The war will have resulted in a temporary guarantee of uniform employment throughout the year in industries such as coal, but with war's end will go the steady job. In most instances the guaranteed annual wage will not be possible until seasonal industry is in a position both to plan its yearly output and to even out the irregularities in production. Industry will have to be certain of a continuous market throughout the year. That will certainly not come in the period of reconversion. It will be difficult even when America stabilizes for the long pull ahead. That difficulty will not be the measure of the interest and demand. Elmer Roper, for example, reports that "three times as many workmen believe that guaranteed wages are 'important' as those who believe that a voice for labor in management is 'important.' " Nevertheless, the demand for labor participation in management will be heard increasingly, although at the time labor is in the most unfavorable position to make its voice heard. The demand for participation in management will not diminish with union strength. The traditional position of the unions is that they "have no desire to control industry." The statement is made with equal fervor by the president of the AFL and the president of the CIO, and it comes out of labor's traditional policy, set by Samuel Gompers. Labor organization in America started out by saying that management is industry's job, doing a fair day's work at a fair day's pay is labor's job. That philosophy has been and will be repeated like a litany by labor leaders—revealing again the conflict between what we believe and what we do.

The whole history of union organization has been a gradual encroachment on functions which were formerly the sole and exclusive jurisdiction of management. From the original campaign for a ten-hour day to the most recent drive by the International Ladies Garment Workers Union to make the dress industry in New York more efficient, labor has moved in on management prerogatives. The ILGWU's "There can be no security in an insecure industry" is a forerunner of similar attitudes that will guide unions in many American industries.

The evolutionary process of union interest will run something like this: First, there will be the contest to be recognized. Then the contest for exclusive recognition. Simultaneously with these the demand for higher wages, fewer hours, better working conditions. Finally, the demand for guaranteed wage security. In a risk-enterprise structure which is not susceptible to ironclad pledges the unions will find themselves seeking to regulate the economic and managerial processes of industry itself.

In the New York dress industry the situation was made most graphic when the union came forward with a proposed contract clause reading: "Should the employer fail to maintain and operate his shop in an efficient manner as herein defined, the workers shall be entitled to be compensated for any loss of earnings resulting from the employer's failure to comply." The New York *Times* commented: "Neither consumer nor employer can have any real quarrel with a union statesmanlike plan to raise its members' incomes by increasing their productivity."

Not many employers will quarrel with the unions' successful effort to improve worker efficiency; few, though, will accept the unions' efforts to improve the employer's. It's one thing to have a "suggestion box" in which workers may drop their ideas; it's quite another to have a formalized labor-management committee. A long step, however, was taken when, despite resistance, such joint committees were formed in some four thousand war plants throughout the country under the sponsorship of the War Production Board. Many of these wartime labor-management groups will pass out of existence with the end of the war which introduced them. But the "muscling in" on what formerly was management territory will not.

The very crisis which will confront America's industrial structure will provide the atmosphere in which labor will insist on offering its solutions through such a mechanism as the labor-management committee. And management resistance will, except in the rarer instances, be a good deal less polite than was the case during labor shortages.

The public generally will be unfriendly to organized labor. A whole series of irritations which have been accumulating in prewar years and which in some cases have been heightened by the war will erupt. One of the most disturbing will be the returning jurisdictional dispute.

Inter-union warfare existed long before the conflict between the AFL and the CIO. Many a cattle-rustling AFL craft union sought the herds competitively corralled by another. Industrial unionism, the principle on which the CIO functions, does eliminate contests between crafts. But inter-industry rivalries take their place. Among the most savage internal contests within the CIO, for example, was the fight for jurisdiction between Harry Bridges' longshoremen and Sam Wolchok's warehousemen. The big battle, however, will begin when the war is over—when union membership begins to decline and the AFL and CIO are no longer bound by their no-strike pledge.

The war itself will have jumbled union jurisdictions. For example, transformation of civilian industry to war production meant a shift in the type of products turned out by many factories. A former manufacturer of silk dresses found himself making parachutes; another firm that turned out rubber aprons in peacetime may also have converted to the same activity. During the war the unions tacitly agreed that whatever organization was on the scene was to remain there. But when reconversion comes those manufacturers will not necessarily return to their former peacetime products, and the unions will want to hold on regardless of the nature of the subsequent manufacture.

In the case of new products the situation will be even more confused. Who gets jurisdiction of the cameramen who run the iconoscopes in the television studios—the movie operators' union or the radio technicians' union? Who wins jurisdiction over the manufacture of television sets? The AFL carpenters already have an eye on the manufacture of television sets, but the electrical workers will insist that television is an electrical contraption, not a piece of furniture. The difficulty is that industries have no clear-cut boundaries, as Joel Seidman pointed out in his study of union functions. "The men's clothing industry merges into women's clothing; women's clothing borders on both textiles and rubber; rubber runs into automobiles, and automobiles into steel, electrical equipment, and other industries."

Sometimes you don't know who's who. One of the most peculiar jurisdictional disputes arose between Dubinsky's ladies' garment workers and Hillman's men's clothing workers involving the manufacture of bathrobes. The sex of a bathrobe is determined by whether the pocket is on the left or the right. Frequently the same manufacturer turns out both in the same shop.

It took almost a year to solve this mystery of the patch pocket. It will probably take a good many years before labor settles down on the basis of a knowledge of who's got jurisdiction where. Meanwhile public resentments will mount.

The internal policies of unions will also be responsible for considerable public opposition. The high initiation fees which attracted attention during the war grated on the public.

Fortunately for the unions, the public will be less concerned later on, because there is little likelihood of a decrease in initiation fees—except for servicemen. The high initiation fee is frequently used deliberately for the purpose of discouraging an influx of workers into an industry where employment is tight. The postwar job hunger will reawaken the desire to keep the fraternity small—and to keep the jobs among friends.

But public opinion will watch democracy within the unions. High initiation fees are obviously a limitation on democratic participation, particularly where the unions, under the Wagner Act, have gained legal authority to bargain collectively. The closed shop is another limitation, so far as it vests power over the individual in the hands of the union officials. Individual members who come into disfavor with the leadership or who function as a dissenting faction can be subjected to severe discipline by direct deprivation of their livelihood.

Nor will union membership be made available to groups which have been traditionally excluded. During the war a small stream of Negroes has been grudgingly permitted entrance in limited instances where the doors had previously been closed. Even that trickle will dry up with the job competition of tomorrow. It is improbable that the internal structure of labor unions will be made more democratic, considering the economic stresses which will follow the war. In most unions the election system provides at least a method of controlling the policies of union officers. Enlarged democracy in these cases depends on wide participation by the members themselves. In the small number of cases, where the election machinery is either rusty or, for practical purposes, fake, there is no short-term likelihood of any thorough house cleaning.

The same will be true of the attempt to reverse the policies of those unions which have learned that restriction of production brings immediate monetary dividends. Thurman Arnold's efforts to break up labor abuses of this kind by applying the anti-trust laws to the unions have not been successful, nor will they be without additional legislation. Public hostility will mount high, especially when union restrictive practices begin to interfere with new products.

Where maintenance of high prices is the only possibility of retaining the wartime wage levels, labor will join with industry to enforce inflexible prices.

One factor blocking legislation will be the fact that business is a party to the conspiracy in many of the cases. It will be difficult to attack labor without at the same time bringing up corporate restraints of trade. But that subject is not going to be long avoided. When it comes up, labor will take a greater beating in the legislature while business will get it in the courts under existing anti-trust laws. But until the attack starts the specific restrictive practices will have an important effect on living and employment. For example, the inhibitions aimed to prevent the use of cheaper material, improved equipment, or more efficient methods are among the most important barriers to the growth of prefabricated housing, as described in the next chapter.

When jobs are again at a premium, unions will strengthen their rules to compel the hiring of useless, unnecessary labor. Featherbedding, the making of otherwise dispensable jobs, will increase. The restraints designed to enforce systems of graft and extortion will, in the rarer instances where they exist, break out in stronger form because of the retreat from law, the disorder, cynicism, and escape of after-war morality and practice.

Labor's resistance to the elimination of practices which had their birth in the economics of the time will be fiercer when economic pressure becomes burdensome. With economic advantage at stake, labor will be no more temperate than business pressed to the wall. Even when the heat was hardly on, George Q. Lynch, president of the Pattern Makers League—a strategic union, though its membership is comparatively small—condemned Thurman Arnold's proposals for legislation in these words: "Mr. Arnold can only be recommending the creation of new definitions of crime so that Mr. Arnold may more successfully prosecute and enforce his ideas of proper conduct toward the state. That is the general idea involved in 'totalitarianism.' It has created the Gestapo and the concentration camp. In Germany Mr. Arnold is called Mr. Himmler."

Labor's contact with government, though, will not be solely as victim. If it doesn't like those whom it characterizes as Himmlers, it is inevitable that it will try to put in office men who are more friendly to its objectives. Labor in America has never been without political interest, though it has generally followed the dictum, "Reward your friends and punish your enemies." Remaining independent of either political party, it has played both for value received.

Labor's alliance with the Roosevelt administration was a profound break with this tradition. Here and there individual labor leaders continued their preference for other political figures. Some, like John L. Lewis, developed a profound dislike for the New Deal, but they weren't typical. When the temper and orientation of the administration began to change with war, labor's hurt was that of a rejected mistress. Before war's end labor will find itself once again attempting to simulate an independent role, jockeying for bipartisan friendship and support.

The formation of a labor party is extremely unlikely. There are major immediate reasons that will compel labor to pass up this moment in history to organize a parallel to the British Labor party. First of all, labor unions will be too busy trying to hold their present members. Besides, sharply drawn issues between candidates will do much to prevent the organization of a third party. Labor will be discouraged by the legal bars to placing a new party on the ballot in many states and the difficulty of pushing it with any degree of success.

Another obstacle—about which union leaders prefer not to talk— is that they can't deliver the labor vote even in local contests. The influence of the union on the political opinions of its members is weak and won't become stronger for some time. Furthermore, labor's sincere and articulate advocacy of the free-enterprise system is a bar to the creation of its own political machine. A labor party with no substantial deviation in economic principles would be an anomaly not destined for any striking success.

Add to these difficulties the feud between the AFL and CIO, a division in labor which will weaken both its representation and its strength in politics. That doesn't mean labor won't go in for politics, but its participation will have few of the political and economic earmarks of a real labor movement. In local communities, where labor organizes politically, it will parallel the local machines from which American political development has traditionally sprung. And just as frequently, in both tactics and organization, it will have many of the "boss" characteristics of these machines.

In such political maneuverings the Communists on the American scene will be active. More and more they will try to set themselves up on approximately the same basis as Tammany Hall and with little deviation in method. Even while professing not to be a political party but only a "political association," they will attempt to become a power-wielding machine. They have announced their conversion to the traditional American two-party system—a delicate way of saying that they intend to bore from within both parties. It was not coincidental that while fighting for control of the American Labor party in New York State the Communists sought to prevent the organization of such parties in other states.

Don't interpret this as labor movement; it is labor politics. It will be significant because of the resulting confusion. For years it has been the purpose of the American wing of the Communist party to get control of the unions in order to enlist support for Soviet foreign policy. Captured units can be used as fronts to simulate liberal American opinion in the tortuous shifts of the party line. These efforts will not be less pronounced as a result of the dissolution of the Third International. The Communist-controlled labor unions will more and more strive for the function performed by district leaders' headquarters in the local political machine.

This confusion of union and party will ultimately raise new problems for labor. The courts will be called upon to decide whether a Communist-dominated union is entitled to the protection of the National Labor Relations Act in view of the commingling of political and economic functions. An employer who is prevented from opposing such Communist unions is in effect deprived of his right to resist a political party with which he disagrees.

The war will have helped the Communists to gain more influence in labor's ranks. Russian heroism and success will be a valuable commodity on which the Communists will be able to trade for some time to come. But if Soviet foreign policy should deviate from our own, the Communists will again be isolated. Even without that development the Communists will have a long row to hoe before they can achieve more than local domination in labor circles. Most union leaders fear the Communist drive for power in their organizations and see in it a threat to their own positions. Their ineffectiveness in meeting the wave of unemployment and wage cuts ahead will make them more vulnerable to Communist attack, but they are sufficiently well entrenched to survive nevertheless. However, this internal fracas will also serve to block immediate action for a labor party.

The political ambitions of labor as a whole will be put off until the public antipathy to union organization has worn away. Meanwhile retrenchment will be the business in hand, and it will continue until the major contest between labor and industry over recognition has been relegated to a place in history, until the stratification of classes in America has become more marked and depression has weakened the individualistic American aspirations. On every step of the road ahead labor will quarrel with the community and bicker within its own ranks.

For the nation the most significant feature of labor's immediate future is not so much what labor will accomplish but rather what will be done in American life because of its presence. The depth of public hostility and the degree of labor ineptness will determine how extreme the community's protective action will be and how useful a whipping-boy labor will prove to be. An ineffective minority may determine the conduct of a majority by throwing it into a rage. This negative result will be an even more certain consequence of Communist activity. A fire in the theater may do less damage than the panic it causes.

Of all the groups in the entire nation the only economic class that emerges with a substantially accurate appraisal of its place, the only one which will seem to know where it is going, will be big business. Small enterprise thinks it does and will be disappointed. The middle class knows where it wants to go but will only multiply its already existing frustrations. Labor isn't sure where it's heading, except that the road directly ahead is retreat. It will be right.

IV

Your Life Tomorrow

CHAPTER XI

Six Million Bathtubs

"WE CAN'T GO BACK TO 1929 because those days weren't good enough. Even in 1929 there were six million American homes without bathtubs," said a former president of the National Association of Manufacturers, Walter Fuller.

You can't go back to six million bathless homes, says Mr. Fuller. But we're likely to. That doesn't mean there's no future for housing in America. But for most of the people now living in homes without bathtubs the future, at least for some time, will bear a striking resemblance to the past.

The homes of the American people will be one of the most dynamic centers of interest, planning, and action for at least the next generation. We know the houses of tomorrow will carry the imprint of today's technological advances. We know, too, that housing activity holds what may be the greatest promise of mass industrial activity and employment *some time* during the coming generation. We know that both actual need and pent-up demand for better living quarters will provide the base for possible action. But we also know that housing has failed to keep pace with the engineering and manufacturing techniques that could catapult this industry forward. And we know that it will take at least a decade for the traditional pattern of the industry to change. Until then folks in middle-class quarters may move into better middle-class homes, while those directly below them may move up into the places thus emptied. Although the wealthy may not become any wealthier, their homes won't show it. For the very rich and the very poor, woe. The opulent will find their big estates a pain in the assessment. The poor will live on in their present estate; the walls will just become a little older.

The opening pages of this book emphasized the importance of the two keys to the future. The first one says, "Look to the past and present." The second tells you to look for a gap between attitude and action. In no other area of the future are these keys more important than in determining the physical environment of the rest of your life. There are few people or groups who want the present city and rural slums. Yet the slums are likely to be with us for many a postwar year.

The backyard outhouse with a half-moon cut in the door may seem picturesque to the traveler passing by, but it's not so "quaint" to those who have no other bathroom facilities. As a matter of fact, when Mr. Fuller emphasized the six million missing bathtubs he was talking only about city families. Right up to the beginning of the war the over-all figures—for farm and city—showed that more than *sixteen million* of America's thirty-seven million dwelling units had no private bathtub or shower.

It may sound fantastic, but these are the official census figures for 1940, published in 1942, telling us that just about one out of every two dwelling units in the country still uses the bucket on the kitchen floor for the Saturday-night bath!

By conservative housing standards, cold statistics indicate that more than thirteen million families have been living in substandard dwellings. The inventory is eloquent. Here, for instance, are the farm homes of America, as of 1940. Here are the families who live on the land, 93 per cent of them with an annual prewar income of less than $2,500. Here is rural America:

Five out of six families had no running water.

One out of ten had no indoor toilet or privy at all.

Nine out of ten had no private bath or shower.

Nine out of ten had no central heating system.

Three out of five had no refrigeration of any kind.

Seven out of ten were without telephones.

Two out of five owned no radio.

Seven out of ten had no electric lighting equipment.

And here is urban America:

Just about one out of every three city families in homes, apartments, or tenements that could stand some major overhauling or some basic plumbing.

More than ten million city families living in substandard slum dwellings—too many jammed into too small an area, lack of recreation space for children, dark, vermin-infested rooms.

Forty-two per cent of all city tenement houses with no central heating—and even in 1943 many buildings in which only one toilet and one cold-water faucet served as many as a dozen families.

Twenty-five per cent of city dwellings with no private bath.

More than one million with no gas or electricity.

Almost two and one half million with no refrigerators of any kind.

Two million people are living in New York City in 1944 in "old-law" tenements that were officially condemned in 1885 as "foul, unsanitary, and unfit to live in." That was the official description of the Tenement Housing Committee in its investigations sixty years ago.

Lest anyone think that these New York slums are exceptional and not characteristic of the rest of the country, here are a few other examples chosen at random. In Hartford, Connecticut—before that city's war boom made things worse—one out of every four people lived in a slum area.

Or cross the country to Butte, Montana, where more than one quarter of the residential buildings were "not fit to live in or needed major repairs," according to official surveys.

Or out to San Francisco, where that city's Housing Authority declared in 1942 that one out of every five homes was substandard.

Or down to Dixie, where the situation in Louisville, Kentucky, is all too typical, with "96 per cent of the families living in substandard homes," according to the Municipal Housing Commission in that city.

There's one thing about the housing surveys that are always going on. They discover amazing facts, which somehow or other manage to reach or interest remarkably few people. Like the survey of a typical New England town. Anyone driving through this town would certainly remark on the beauty of its homes, but the study showed that eight out of ten of the admired houses were in bad condition.

Bad is a relative word, of course. What's your measuring rod? Living in the Ukraine? Housing in Syria? The average home in France? The thatched misery of Puerto Rico? Those who insist that America's standard of living is high can make a convincing case. So can those who point to its low standard.

Aside from "good" or "bad," the facts speak for themselves. For example, between 1930 and 1940 only 2,734,000 new dwelling units were built for 4,503,000 new American families. On top of that the war-imposed restrictions on construction hiked the housing deficit another half million units a year. The Commerce Department estimates a total demand at the end of the war for between four and four and one half million new dwelling units. This shortage, together with a large percentage of worn-out and substandard homes in every section of the country, is both the base of the future and its challenge.

The problem breaks into two pieces: apartments for city dwellers, and homes to wipe out the rural slums. The nub of the question in both cases is whether decent housing on a large scale can be provided at a cost which can be met by families in the lower-income groups. In terms of city apartments this question is not likely to receive either an early or an effective answer.

The dream pictures of handsome buildings with wide windows, spacious playgrounds, helicopter landing spaces on the roof, parking facilities for your car in the basement, large modern apartments at low rental are going to remain a dream. Actually, even those families who can afford to pay middle-class rentals will be unable to find accommodations much different from what they had before the war. To be sure, the construction industry estimates that the early postwar years will bring a building boom to the tune of some fifteen billion dollars annually. Maybe it will come, but many observers, including experts of the FHA and the National Committee on Housing, characterize the boom estimates as "pious hopes and wishful thinking."

There are several reasons why the boom may not materialize.

It won't be anybody's "fault." Prices of construction materials and labor costs will be up. The uncertain economic atmosphere of the early postwar years is likely to make apartment-house construction a risky proposition. Private capital isn't likely to flow into this field until we either return to prewar costs or succeed in stabilizing the wartime inflated price level. You may have forgotten, but builders and investors remember vividly and painfully the speculative housing boom that took place in most American cities after the last war. The buildings started to go up like mushrooms, but many a builder and investor was wiped out when the depression hit in 1929. Once burned, twice shy. . . . The construction that does take place after the war will put up high-rental buildings because the investor will have to cover his risk with a larger profit margin. Come peace, rents will be no smaller, though the apartments will.

Still there's no real problem for families in the middle-income group. They will continue to find comfortable, if not "super," apartments. The lack will be in low-rental city quarters for low-income families. There is no indication that the building boom predicted by groups in the housing industry would do very much in this direction even if it did materialize.

Realistically, there is not much more chance for any substantial amount of low-rental city building after the war than there was before. The same problems will be with us. Whether slum clearance is undertaken as a public-housing project or as privately financed low-rental building, there are several high hurdles to get over before blighted city areas can be rebuilt. First, getting land at a sufficiently low cost. Second, providing utilities at low cost— streets, sewers, water supply, service lines, schools, park areas, etc. Above all, the persistent housing bugaboo: high cost of materials and labor. With the best intentions in the world, a building project may, in the end, find itself *compelled* to charge higher rentals than the families for which it was designed can afford to pay.

Realistically, how are these drawbacks likely to be overcome? Or, in other words, how much low-rental city housing is likely to be available in the first years after the war? If you're figuring this up in the margin, you'd better put down something close to a zero for low-cost projects built by the traditional building industry. If there were money in it, they'd have done it before. There'll be even less money in that type of construction after the war, because the returns are low.

But that doesn't mean there will be no private building for low-income families. You'll undoubtedly see a sprinkling of developments like the Metropolitan Life Insurance Company's mammoth "Parkchester" in New York, which offers modern apartments at moderate rentals for families of lower-middle-class income. Two gold stars go to Metropolitan Life, one for providing badly needed low-cost accommodations and the other for finding an investment outlet for the funds of insurance and similar companies. But there are flies in this ointment too. For instance, a second Metropolitan project for New York City ran into strong opposition and legislative difficulties because, among other things, it would have included public schools which children living outside "the walled city" could not attend. This spotlighted the problem of race discrimination involved in the project. Similar difficulties may beset and delay other such developments. More important, though, is the fact that the "Parkchesters"—necessary as they may be for low-income middle-class families—are still no answer for the slum dwellers.

No one has yet found an adequate answer to the resistance of real-estate interests to slum clearance. It's not that those interests object primarily to the slums being torn down. For some, of course, slum ownership pays out handsomely. But why does most of the real-estate fraternity object? It's what will rise in the slum's place that they're afraid of. Housing developments for the underprivileged, whether constructed under government or private auspices, tend automatically to weaken real-estate values and to undermine established rental rates—or at least that's the fear. A newly constructed housing project that provides adequate modern apartments at thirty dollars a month is hardly calculated to protect the sixty-dollar rental of a not much better apartment near by.

So much the worse if the government does it, but it isn't pleasant to have your economic throat cut by private enterprise either. Henry Kaiser had better not have his back turned when he enters the construction and real-estate arena to produce low-cost houses by the carload.

Well, if the large private projects will little more than tickle the problem, if private building won't whittle down the size of the difficulty, if resistance to slum clearance exists and has an economic explanation, what's going to change the picture?

There is some hope that wartime developments in building techniques and in the use of new materials may help hurdle some of these obstacles, the obstacles that are labeled "cost." And there will be some state and city slum-clearance work. New York State, for example, has authorized one hundred and thirty-five million dollars to be used in New York City alone, and an additional fifty million dollars for other cities. New York City itself is planning a number of public-housing projects. Three of these will accommodate over sixteen thousand families. But, projected against the admitted need in New York City, merely a fraction of the "deficit" will be wiped out. And New York's plans are lavish compared with those of other cities.

What then? Well, the federal government will take up where it left off when war altered the construction programs. But all these will add up to better living quarters for only about 10 per cent of slum-living families. We'll still have 90 per cent of them with us. They are the ones whose walls will grow just a little bit older.

In general, the outlook for people who live in America's cities is not bright. Here and there a slum will be cleared; here and there new buildings will rise—but these will be conspicuous by their rarity. In this disproportion will lie the challenge of America's housing opportunity, which, so far as present signs indicate, is not being and will not be accepted in any real measure.

But all of America doesn't live in city apartments. What are the postwar housing prospects for the millions of American families who live in rural or suburban homes, or who want to move out of apartments into their own homes?

There'll be a demand for no less than three million new one-family homes alone, according to a Commerce Department estimate. And the big need in the case of these rural or suburban houses has been for those that can be sold for about three thousand prewar dollars.

But if you're in one of the millions of American families now projecting plans for such a home, prepare to bump into several hard facts. Assuming no inflation at all—assuming that your dollar will buy what it did just before the war—land would cost you about $600 and materials about $2,400. Then you would have to add another $1,500 for labor and another $500 for the contractor's profit. Total cost—$5,000.

Can that $5,000 be cut to $3,000? Certain other things will have to happen first. In part, building costs have been high because a house is a "custom-built" affair. You pay a premium for it just as you would for a specially built limousine. Equally important is the fact that the construction industry is prepared to keep the cost of individual houses high, rather than seek expanded profits by larger volume. The unions in the field, the suppliers, and the contractors are almost equally responsible for limited production on the one hand and the higher-than-necessary prices on the other. In most sections even the smallest modern houses must rent at more than twenty-five dollars a month to yield a profit. And in those sections of the country where some fairly modern houses rent for less, as in the South, the wages of most of the workers are also proportionately less.

An important element of cost has always been the interest paid on borrowed capital. Since interest rates will fall even lower than they did in the past decade, it is possible to have some lower rent without government subsidies.

The war has brought no answer to the basic problem of high cost. If anything, it has made some of the difficulties more acute. Every sign points to the fact that labor and material expenses in the first postwar years, though declining, will be higher than before the war. And the more inflation, the more the prospects of cheaper housing will evaporate.

If there were no elements in the picture other than these, if there were no basic changes awaiting the dawn of the years to come, this chapter would end on the next page. There wouldn't be much to tell.

But there *are* other elements. And their strength and probability are such that before the rest of your life is through housing in America may be sharply shaken up. These are the fuses attached to tomorrow's bombshell. They may get wet, they may not go off, they may sputter, or they may be a long time burning. But they're lit already.

If any one element of national activity is selected for depression-licking purposes by industry and government, there is little doubt now that it will be housing. This is merely another way of saying that the nation's housing deficiencies and opportunities are so great that little controversy exists about the need for action. The argument starts when the specific kind of action is suggested. But in any concerted drive to make jobs and stimulate prosperity, whether government-inspired, industry-operated, or publicly financed, housing will be picked to head the parade.

The building and construction industry, as now constituted, is doomed. Only the date of its execution remains to be determined. That both the practice and composition of the building industry, almost from top to bottom, are outdated is no longer questioned seriously. But that it will be quickly overhauled is by no means certain. It will not change of its own accord.

However—and this is in many respects the most hopeful harbinger of change—new and vigorous industrial and financial forces are ready to enter the housing field and bang things up a bit. When Lockheed Aircraft purchased a mammoth finance company dedicated to consumer financing of its housing activities after the war, the present real-estate and building corporations probably shuddered. An even brisker breeze chills the stagnant air when Henry Kaiser announces, "Housing after the war—that's me."

One of the most stimulating outgrowths of the war will be the large quantity of capital and industrial facilities in the hands of a group of new-style empire builders. Their wealth, energy, and equipment spell trouble for a number of sectors of established enterprise. But the new energetic tycoons are not the only ones who hold out this promise. Given even modestly favorable conditions, there will be an important overflow of capital and equipment into new competitive fields in the years following the war. In business circles this movement is called diversification of activity. Less obscurely, it really means that when you think you're exploiting the maximum opportunities in your own field and still have money, machinery, and energy left over, why not move into the other guy's field as well? A rubber company goes into radio. The automobile industry annexes a piece of refrigeration and air conditioning; aircraft muscles in on farm equipment. Watch out, housing!

Perhaps the first fuse that will be detonated is one that has been with us for some time—prefabrication. Prefabrication, either of entire houses or of parts, says to the present housing industry, "You're to me what the bicycle was to Ford." It may just be bragging; so far the fuse has little more than fizzled.

More than ten years before the war, prefabricated houses were beginning to make their appearance on the American landscape. Many were still in the experimental stage. Many were expensive. But a new idea had taken root: the idea of applying the principles of mass production to housing—as they had been applied to automobiles some years earlier. Just as the first Model T that rolled off Henry Ford's assembly line ushered in a new era of low-cost automobiles, so it was hoped that the first houses coming out of the factories would be the forerunners of a great, new, low-cost housing industry. "A car in every garage" would become "A house on every lot."

The hopes died down almost as quickly as they had sprung up. One reason why so few prefabricated houses were built before the war was quickly apparent. People didn't want them. In the first place, the prefabricators had overlooked the fact that they could not *create* public taste but would have to follow it. The early prefabricated houses were spurned by the average American family as "egg crates." The architects might acclaim the design as "functional," "advanced," "forward-looking," or what have you. The people stayed away in millions. They wanted their Cape Cod cottages, their New England designs, and the other traditional styles they knew, trusted, and liked.

Closely linked to this is a difficulty that has troubled some of the normally constructed homes. Many banks and other lending institutions have been loath to lend money on any other than the orthodox styles in home designs. Even the government's Federal Housing Administration has not been without this prejudice. No, there's nothing sinister; the bankers have not ganged up on progress. They've just been worried about the resale value of these homes in the event of a default on the mortgage. If you've ever tried to resell a used Cord car you know what they mean.

Another reason prefabrication failed to take hold in the thirties was that it didn't quite come through on its promise to beat the price of homes constructed on the site. The factory might be able to cut costs by turning out hundreds of "prefabs" on the assembly line, but by the time a house was shipped to Jones's lot in Connecticut or California it cost him as much or more than a conventionally built house.

Still another impediment that operated to block prefabrication may continue to dog all attempts, prefabricated or otherwise, to sell the Smiths their own private home. The Smiths, at least until the war, had become more and more persuaded that they didn't want their own home. They'd rather the landlord took the headaches while they remained free to enjoy and move. However, there's little doubt that the element of cost entered somewhat into these calculations, and if prices come down this obstacle may disappear.

Obviously, also, prefabrication suffered from the fact that there wasn't much residential construction *of any kind* during the prewar decade. Not exactly the climate for novelty!

Nevertheless, several centers of intense prefabrication activity persisted; men and companies continued to experiment. By 1940 they were selling more and more of these houses—better built and better designed than the first attempts. Some companies were manufacturing and putting up as many as twelve houses a day by the time the war crossed America's shoreline.

The war gave factory-made houses the first real chance to prove their mettle. War plants were being expanded all over the country; new industrial centers were springing up. The shortage of housing for war workers threatened to disrupt the entire war-production program.

Prefabrication's years of bitter experience finally stood it in excellent stead. In those places where they were called upon to perform, the prefabricators frequently turned in an astounding job. Houses appeared on bare plots of land overnight, as if by the magic of an Aladdin's lamp. One morning, just an expanse of bare earth; by nightfall, a community of one hundred houses or more, completely finished, ready for living. Lines of trucks rumbling to the empty places with the "makin's"—and presto, floor down, walls up, roof on, and a "For Rent" shingle hanging outside the front door. Thousands of prefabricated houses have been built in home-hungry war-production centers. Technical experts of the Army and Navy who examined these prefabricated structures found some "pretty bad," but the vast majority were characterized as excellent.

It is another of the less lamentable aspects of the war that it furnished a tremendous laboratory for the study of assembly-line mass production of houses. In the words of a leading architect, "This knowledge will give us better-built and more quickly available houses in the postwar years."

The war has dispelled any doubt that we have the know-how, the ability, and the resources necessary to develop comfortable low-cost houses for the average American family. But, as has been the case so many times in our history, we must face the fact that there's many a slip between the possibility and the actuality. Whether *you* will be able to buy yourself a modern prefabricated house at a price you can afford to pay in 1944, '45, or '46 depends on the outcome of the "Battle of Housing," which will continue for a long time.

There are several forces which will operate to delay the widespread availability of factory-made houses. The strongest force is the opposition which has come from the construction industry and the building trades-unions in the United States. Their opposition is understandable enough.

The thorny fact here is that the millions of dollars' worth of machinery and capital equipment of the construction trade and the many highly skilled crafts involved cannot, for the most part, be switched over to the techniques of prefabrication. An irreducible minimum of machinery without function and men without jobs will be left over. As in every case of a far-reaching industrial change, some of these men and machines will be headed for the scrap heap if they cannot be adjusted to some other possible function in the economy.

But the tenacity of the opposition to prefabrication certain to flow from the industry and the unions may be met with equal vigor by the new industrial elements already mentioned who look to housing with mouths watering. Rival labor unions will join them, and the conflict will be sharp. Devastating strikes and severe industrial warfare will mark the advance of prefabrication. We had a foretaste in the fall of 1941, when the Currier Company submitted a bid for constructing three hundred defense houses in Michigan. Although the bid was lowest by 44 per cent, the Office of Production Management rejected it rather than risk the labor blowup that was threatened. Whether you can get the "house of your dreams" tomorrow will in part depend on whether labor puts *its* house in order.

Local and state building codes will be another hazard in the way of factory-made houses after the war. Building in almost every locality in the United States is wound up in tangles of red tape. In some instances the only reason for the code is to protect the status quo and the groups dependent on it. In all too many cases, according to leading architects, these codes are outmoded, if not indeed benighted. However, owing to their complicated nature and the mass of detail involved, they are hard to change.

After the war, prefabrication will undoubtedly be able to offer a well-made, comfortable home for less than the cost of a similar house built by traditional methods.

You won't be able to tell a "prefab" from a conventionally built house. Advertisements in magazines like the *Architectural Forum, Better Homes & Gardens,* etc., have been showing prefabricated houses designed to suit almost every personal whim. The phobia about "standardization" and "box houses" has been successfully dispelled by the prefabricators, although anyone who has ever seen the deadly array of city brownstones or small-town houses echoing each other row on row may wonder why the public should suddenly rise up in arms against factory-built homes.

Probably the strongest indication of an early availability of prefabricated houses is found in the definite sales plans which many companies have already set in motion. For instance, department stores will be widely used as a consumer outlet. One leading department store was ready in 1943 to help you select your house, choose your site, supervise construction, and take care of your financing problems—thus relieving you of most of the bother. You can even order your house complete with furniture, appliances, and furnishings.

Moving another step in the direction of reducing the cost of "prefabs," one company has arranged for the establishment of a central sales organization in each large community. In a single office in your city you will find an architect, a real-estate expert, a builder, financial and legal advisers, and even designers to help you with the landscaping and decorating problems. You sign one contract for the whole works—and then start getting ready to move, because your new home will be ready in a month or less. Under this scheme each community office will be drawing on one central company. That will offer you all the savings of large-scale operations, and at the same time will help you solve the particular building problems of your locality.

If you're one of the restless few, you will even be able to order a house that can be taken apart and moved, so that you can enjoy a change of scene. One manufacturer has developed a portable home, complete with kitchenette, bathroom, living room, and two bedrooms. He is now planning to offer this house for less than $2,000.

In general, however, you are likely to find that although factory-made houses will cost less than comparable dwellings built on the site, their prices will probably not be much lower in the first years after the war. Material costs will not drop suddenly. In short, the prefabricated house you might have bought in 1940 for $3,500 may cost $4,000. But in terms of comparative value it will still be a good buy, and will represent a definite advance toward better housing at lower cost. Builders are predicting that houses will roll off assembly lines at a cost of 10 to 30 per cent under similar ones built by traditional methods.

The savings result from a more efficient use of materials and the elimination of material loss. According to one builder, you won't have enough waste at the site of your prefabricated house to "start a fire in the furnace." Another saving results from the reduction in the number of pieces that go into a house. Before the war an ordinary four- or five-room frame house, for example, contained 30,000 to 40,000 separate pieces. The industry predicts that houses of the future will probably consist of less than half as many parts. Another large economy, of course, will come from reduced labor costs.

More basic is the fact that as long as unemployment and insecurity threaten to paralyze the consumer's pocketbook, prefabricated houses, like their more traditional forebears, will be "available" in the sense that they can be bought, but there will be no spectacular home-buying spree. Curiously, the outcome of the housing battle between the construction industry and the building trades on one side and the new, war-strengthened prefabrication industry on the other will itself greatly influence the economic condition of the nation. Will manufactured homes accomplish part of the job that mass production of automobiles did for the period following World War I?

The answer to that question will tell how many "prefabs" are built. It will decide how great a slice of the housing "problem" is solved by mass production. But if you have the money and are not reluctant to spend it, that contest will not prevent you from buying a prefabricated home within a year after the war. And 10 per cent of you new homeowners are likely to buy a "prefab" in the first five years following the war. In the opinion of some people in the industry that figure may jump as high as 50 per cent.

As a matter of fact, it may be easier to buy a factory-made house within the first year or two after the war than to *build* one. The limitation on materials and the lack of manpower brought wartime private construction to a virtual standstill. The war has almost completely squeezed the small or medium-sized conventional building contractor out of business, while it strengthened the prefabrication industry. It is possible that the prefabricators will therefore get the jump on the traditional builders when the housing market begins to open up.

No spectacular opposition to the prefabrication industry is anticipated from the large suppliers who used to serve the construction industry. Companies that sell lumber, building materials, glass, etc., will be just as happy to offer their products to a "house manufacturer" as to a "house contractor." In some cases they will be over-anxious for fear that the restless war manufacturer moving into prefabrication may decide to make his own materials unless he is supplied promptly, politely, and cheaply.

On all evidence, then, we reach the following conclusions: There will be a battle royal between the opposing housing interests. Old and new materials and techniques and separate sections of private enterprise will be fighting for survival. The struggle will continue for as much as a decade after the war. When it is over the present building and construction industry will *not* be altogether dead, but it will provide in housing what Cadillac and Lincoln provide in automobiles.

Some 1,540,000 American families have indicated their intention to build or buy a new home within six months after the war comes to an end. That's a man-sized housing boom—if it happens. But there are three conceivable deterrents that should be appraised: You may not have enough money; you may not be able to get financing terms that will allow you to go ahead; you may be afraid of the future and of the instability of your income.

As for the money, that's no real problem. The savings left in individual hands when the war is over will be sufficient to float a housing boom of huge dimensions. Bank accounts, untouched insurance, the staggering quantity of war bonds, and just cash in hand add up to an amount that disposes of the first possible deterrent to your housing plans.

Nor is financing apt to be a serious drawback. The most important single factor here will be the continued operation of the Federal Housing Administration. FHA's authority to insure additional loans was scheduled to expire July 1, 1944, but in October 1943 the power was extended by Congress in contemplation of your buying a home after the war.

FHA, which had insured more than five billion dollars' worth of loans by Pearl Harbor, will have available an estimated $500,000,-

ooo for use at the end of the war. The President has the power to triple this sum. Compared to the string of zeros at the end of war-appropriation figures this amount may seem small, but it will be sufficient to finance the construction of about 400,000 homes. Any further increase would require congressional action. But don't worry; if the money is used up, Congress *will* approve.

FHA financing will unquestionably be the best assurance against housing stagnation after the war, even if the economic atmosphere is gloomy. You can see that from the terms of the loans. Assuming that the home you plan will have an appraised value of between $1,111 and $6,000, you will be able to borrow 90 per cent of the money on an FHA loan. This means, of course, that you will have to pay only 10 per cent cash. The down payment is slightly higher, rising on a graduated scale, for the tonier, more expensive homes.

The top rate of interest on your FHA loan is set by law. In November 1943 the maximum was 5 per cent, but many mortgagees were paying only 4 per cent or even less. An FHA official has predicted that under the competitive conditions likely to prevail after the war the interest rate might even drop to 3 per cent.

Assuming that the rate is 4 per cent, and that you want to build a $5,000 house, you will pay $500 down and then a little more than $30 a month to take care of the interest charges and your payments on the principal, which would be completed by the end of twenty years. Of course there will be additional expenditures for taxes, water, etc. If you happen to own your own lot, it may be valuable enough to serve as the down payment.

The real threat to any large and sustained housing boom comes from the unsettled and fear-creating economic conditions which will begin to emerge after the defeat of Germany. Partially because of its cost, and even more because of its permanence, purchase of a home is not undertaken lightly. Any mass uncertainty as to the future of jobs will have a depressing effect on housing operations.

Economic conditions may then slip so low that there will be a resumption of federal pump priming, as in the last depression. This time low-cost housing for the lowest-income groups will play a major role in the governmental depression-fighting program. If this sequence of events occurs, we will find a curious result: the middle class will have deferred its purchase of homes as confidence declined and the poorer groups will have been equipped with homes first. Sooner or later, though, the middle class will start buying homes—and in considerable quantities. That will come when the upswing begins to thaw the mass of accumulated savings.

And when that happens you will be able to buy many of the promised improvements about which you've heard so much. They are of interest not only to the prospective homeowner but to the modern apartment dweller as well. Here is how the houses and apartments of tomorrow will be made. This is what those who can afford the living of tomorrow will enjoy.

Many of the tricks the war has taught us in the use of materials will be applied to your living space. As a result of new molding processes, made possible by electronic developments in high-frequency electrical heating, thick plastic sections and laminated structural members will be available to add to the strength, durability, insulation, and beauty of tomorrow's houses. Plastic pipe and tubing, used widely in wartime houses, will probably be called for by many blueprints to simplify plumbing problems at lower cost.

Long before the war, plastics were already in wide use as knobs, handles, shower heads, drains, hardware fittings, etc. After the war you will find plastics in every room, adding color and convenience at little expense. The use of glass in the house of tomorrow will not be limited to windows or glass-brick walls. The war has expanded our knowledge of glass enormously. Because we now know how to make glass resistant to high temperature and temperature changes and durable under all kinds of stresses and strains, you may even have glass plumbing, pipe fittings, and fixtures.

Also, the home is likely to be not only more cheery and stronger, but safer, as a result of developments in producing new types of fabrics and surface coverings that are water and fire resistant.

Other "modern improvements" include window screens that you will be able to roll up as you do your window shades. This would eliminate the need for storage space for screens and the bother of putting them on and taking them off with every change of season.

Your house will be kept cooler in the summer and warmer in the winter, at lower fuel costs, through the use of improved insulation techniques.

You may be able to rearrange the rooms of your home at will. "Long-span construction," as the engineers call it, makes it possible to carry all the weight on the outside walls, and inside walls need not be permanent. This is a direct result of the wartime use of resin-bonded plywood, laminated structural members, and light-weight metallic girders—a clear example of the way in which wartime developments in the use of materials can be directly applied to postwar homes. Your house may be a completely open structure which you arrange into rooms by the simple use of prefabricated partitions, curtains, and standardized closet units. Since these partitions and units will not have to bear the weight of the ceiling, they can be moved readily or taken down completely, to give you any interior design you want. This will offer a practical and easy way to meet changing family needs or the requirements of different owners.

Low-cost houses have already been built on this principle. They were going up at the rate of six a day as far back as September 1941, when six hundred units, costing $2,000 each, were built for the Glenn L. Martin workers at Middle River, Maryland.

Don't forget that the advances in materials and techniques will be applied to houses constructed in the traditional manner as well as to prefabricated units. We have learned a lot about heating, lighting, plumbing, etc., which can be used with either type of housing to give you greater comfort at lower cost.

Home safety will be a bigger consideration than ever before. Prewar methods of fireproofing were so expensive that it wasn't practical to apply them to houses costing less than $15,000. As a result, there hasn't been much fireproof construction, except in office buildings, large apartment structures, and hotels. New developments in fireproof construction give every promise of much wider use in smaller buildings. Architects and builders assure you that the fireproof home can be designed as attractively as the more conventional, non-fireproof houses. Fire-resistant chemicals will help make your floors, walls, buildings, and decorations incombustible without making them ugly. Incidentally, such fireproofing will also help discourage vermin.

The key to what's ahead in the direction of general home improvements is that the war has given impetus to an *engineering approach* to the problems of housing.

Compare the developments of the automobile over twenty years with the lack of change in, say, bathrooms. *Fortune* magazine has aptly pointed out that if the average bathroom had improved as much as the automobile, "the shower would automatically deliver water of the right temperature. The tap in the lavatory would open by knee or toe pressure against a convenient lever or pedal; hot water would run instantly; the towel rack would be formed of hot-water pipes to keep towels warm and dry. Electric heaters and sun lamps would be built into the walls or ceiling. The shower would be enclosed in transparent plastic and would not steam up the room. The floor would be warm enough to walk on barefoot. The bathtub would preheat itself automatically. The washbasin would be big enough to bathe the baby; like a kitchen sink, it would be flush with the counter containing drawers and storage space. Soap would never turn to jelly because built-in soap dishes would drain properly. Space in the medicine cabinet would be sufficient to store the medicine for an army. And the mirror could be pulled close to a man's face and would actually be equipped with enough light to shave with ease."

Setting the challenge, *Fortune* declares, "The mass-production technique that made the auto what it is today may make the bathroom what it should be tomorrow. Small bathrooms could be made in a few easy-to-assemble pieces, priced to undersell even the cheapest of home-installed jobs." It would be possible to buy a complete bathroom of advanced design for $700. It would be possible for a homeowner to provide extra bathrooms by buying smaller units at $150 or even $50.

The kitchen and everything that goes into it is likely to get a big dose of modernization. The average housewife spends about half her waking hours in the kitchen, cooking, serving, washing and drying dishes. Her kitchen might more appropriately be called her "living room." Keeping this in mind, many designers have been working on plans to make things easier for Mrs. America tomorrow.

Any woman who has strained her back—and perhaps ripped her nylons—bending down to the oven at the bottom of her stove will hail with joy the new designs that call for oven and broiler above the cooking ranges. Incidentally, that's where they were in the old days before stoves were "modernized." The idea of a vertical broiler which will cook your steak on both sides at the same time has passed the blueprint stage. One designer has planned a kitchen that has no stove at all. His thought is that you ought to be able to use your various pots and pans as individual stoves simply by plugging them into electric outlets.

Aside from the obvious improvements, such as better light, more kitchen windows, and larger, more convenient working surfaces, you will probably be able to get, in two to five years after the war, vastly improved mechanical dishwashing machines, sterilizers, and similar devices.

A leading designer has cast a critical eye on our prewar refrigerators and is especially annoyed by the fact that the bottle of milk you want is frequently hidden by several beer bottles (or vice versa), the jar of cheese by a dish of fruit, while to reach the bacon you have to empty a tray of a dozen assorted items. This designer has suggested a round refrigerator built on the principle of a Lazy Susan, so that you can easily reach inside for whatever you want. It has been proposed that refrigerators might be broken into separate units and placed around the kitchen in a series of separate drawers. Such improvements, however, will be a long time coming.

There are several encouraging indications that some major improvements will be on the market within a year or two after war's end. Before the war several companies were experimenting with prefabricated bathrooms and kitchens. In the October 1943 issue of the *Architectural Forum* page after page of advertisements was already offering both bathroom and kitchen units incorporating many of the most advanced ideas. There seems little doubt that these will be generally available after the war, although their cost may continue high for several years.

There is no doubt, either, that you will be able to get such new devices for comfortable living as the "Precipitron," which filters dust from the air electrically. This appliance has been developed far beyond the experimental stage. It costs from sixty cents to one dollar a month to operate, and, before the war, sold for $300. Westinghouse engineers say that both figures can be reduced substantially after the war. The "Precipitron" has been hailed as the mechanical housemaid for the home of tomorrow. No more dusting, because there need no longer be any dust in the air.

The advances made before the war in developing small air-conditioning systems for homes and even for city apartments will continue after the war. The industry feels it can bring the price down to a level where it will be attractive to people of medium-sized incomes.

You can also look forward to more quiet and better lighting. You will be able to soundproof your home or apartment scientifically, at a comparatively low cost, within a short time after peace comes. Similarly, advances made in fluorescent lighting will make it possible for you to get better illumination and cut your electric bill at the same time.

"Radiant heating systems," which make the temperature more comfortable without warming the air of the room, will also be available. Radiant heating is hailed as more healthful and more comfortable than traditional types of heating.

New types of glass for windowpanes will allow all the health-giving rays of the sun to penetrate. You will be able to take a sun bath and work up a nice coat of tan without ever stepping out of your house.

Obviously it will be easier to incorporate these comforts in the building of brand-new houses; but many of them, like the air-conditioning units and the "Precipitron," can be used to make your old dwelling more comfortable without requiring serious alterations.

It is easy to be overoptimistic about the large-scale availability of better-living devices soon after the war. Here again those who are sustained by the present will resist the future. But this battle in the market place will not be of sufficient vigor to hold up the materials, appliances, gadgets, and conveniences. They will be available at a price. By today's standards they are luxuries and will remain at luxury prices for some time to come. The widespread use of many of these developments in living, as with most things, will have to wait until prices come down.

All in all, the dream house is not around the corner. Like heaven, it will remain to tempt you for the rest of your life. But, unlike heaven, you'll be able to enjoy some samples in this world. The picture of housing as a whole is one of the few areas of tomorrow that offer clear ground for optimism. The postwar world *will* give more people a chance at better living. In physical developments, at least, we do move forward to greater comfort—some greater comfort for all the people. But the larger problem of "one third of a nation . . . ill housed" will be little nearer to a solution in the earlier years after war.

The "quickies" which government-financed building provided for wartime housing needs will do very little to fill the gully between a poor family's pocketbook and a decent house to live in. It is true that more than 700,000 units were built beginning with the summer of 1940, but more than two thirds of these were scheduled for the scrap heap even while they were being built—for two main reasons. In the first place, scarcity of materials made it impossible to build durable houses in many areas. In the second place, nobody wanted the receding tide of war production to leave a series of permanent ghost towns in its wake.

One example, typical of hundreds of similar cases, is Vanport City. The war boom made it the second largest community in Oregon. Before the Kaiser yards brought some forty thousand people to the area the city did not exist. The ten thousand federally built houses in this "temporary" city are slated to be torn down and trucked away for salvage when the war is over. To have built permanent homes would have been to gamble with the possibility of enormous waste if the Kaiser yards close or slow down when the pressure of war is lifted.

As a matter of fact, legislation already requires the dismantling of war houses within two years after the Armistice, unless there is a contrary order from the Federal Housing Administrator. Local conditions may keep some wartime houses on their foundations for years, but there is no doubt that new homes will have to be found for thousands of the families who took part in war-job migration from coast to coast and border to border.

The people have seen that the country was able to plan housing— even if "temporary"—to meet the special requirements of the shifting war-job population. Inevitably the question will arise, in the minds of those who must move, whether postwar developments of towns and cities should not also be planned. Their insistence will echo stridently in the political consequences of the peace.

In London, where the Luftwaffe's bombs leveled whole sections, planning commissions have been working on blueprints for a better city. Even with this rare opportunity, earned at a fearful price, it is unlikely that the London of 1947 which rises from the ruins will be as well designed as her architects could make it or as well blueprinted as her city planners would like. It is not sheer obstinacy or stupidity which will dissipate the dreams of a great new city with parks and open spaces and tree-lined streets laid out to take comfortable care of the rush of modern traffic. The trouble lies deeper; it is impossible to rebuild a city within a period of a few years. The growth invariably comes slowly. The men who are planning London's changes write:

One of the chief difficulties of every constructive scheme of boldness is that it shows a vision of the future assembled in a single report and group of maps. It appears as though the whole were to be carried out at once, with a corresponding shock to the uninformed who are led to imagine that it is much more ambitious than is really the case and very chimerical. Actually it is always intended that it shall be carried out in periods or stages. . . .

If the planners of the new London see so many difficulties ahead, it is hardly likely that our unbombed cities will take many drastic steps toward improvement. The efforts of the many community and local planning agencies in the United States will have very little visible effect, even as long as ten or twenty years from now. Not many of these agencies have any power to enforce their decisions; there are too many legal and financial problems involved, aside from the inertia which keeps us from moving forward unless and until we are faced with absolutely intolerable conditions. The sweeping changes will be largely in public activities: highways, speedways, parks, bridges, tunnels.

Lacking a national housing program of the kind which brought modern homes within the range of low-income groups in Europe, America will fight her housing question in the political grandstand, not in the arena of accomplishment. Individuals and families here and there will be able to take advantage of what the war has taught us about housing, but for the nation as a whole the prospects are little brighter in the early postwar years than they were before the war.

There is at least one rift in the cloud. Many an American city has been forced, under the pressure of a war-swollen population, to a new understanding of the larger needs in housing. That knowledge will come in very handy after the first major postwar depression. It will then be put to use. You can be sure that basic change will still occur in your lifetime.

Your home will be the center in which you enjoy a host of new mechanical achievements. To be sure, resistance and inertia will take their toll of time. But patience, science, and technology hold a stacked hand in your favor.

CHAPTER XII

To Your Enjoyment

Wood that won't burn, glass that won't break, window screens that contain no wire, and machine bearings that contain no metal are just a few of the things in the offing.

Better and yet cheaper homes, finer and less costly automobiles, radios, and refrigerators, more nourishing food, superior medicines—a greater abundance of almost everything that adds to the comfort and satisfaction of living —all of these will be awaiting the home-coming soldier when the war is won.

Spurred to extraordinary efforts by the extraordinary needs of the past two years, we have gone ahead thirty or fifty years as measured by the old rate of development in many fields.

LAMMOT DUPONT,
Chairman of the DuPont Company

Many manufacturers fear that the public has been oversold on the prospects of revolutionary changes in postwar life as a result of plastics, light metals, and other new or relatively new materials, and new designs which they might make possible.

An automobile manufacturer recently said: "The postwar car is bound to be the 1942 car. It can't be anything different." Similar statements have been made by refrigerator manufacturers and others. Time will be required to perfect new models. The men, machinery, and materials for experimentation, testing, and perfecting will not be available until after the war.

Peacetime Plans,
THE NATIONAL ASSOCIATION OF MANUFACTURERS

THEY OUGHT TO GET TOGETHER. The age of miracles will not be "awaiting the home-coming soldier." Capricious promises of a chromium world are feeding false hopes for tomorrow.

The bright new things will come—but it's a question of time. From a historical point of view the waiting period will be short indeed, but from the perspective of day-to-day living it will aggravate and disappoint you. Those who predict revolutionary changes in your daily life point to the technological advances made in the course of the war. True, they are realities; the war will have speeded up the processes that would otherwise have lumbered along in more leisurely laboratories. But there is a wide gap between knowledge and use. Otherwise a good number of the developments promised for tomorrow would have been available yesterday.

Under normal circumstances, even in the absence of war's dislocations, the forward march is hobbled. The economic interests of those who have pioneered an existing product are perhaps the greatest deterrent to the introduction of the new. The contest between prefabricated housing and the traditional building industry is a classic example. The opposition of labor unions to the "canned voice" of the sound film is another; Petrillo's contest with the recording machine still another. The inventor of the razor blade that wouldn't wear out discovered the power of established economic interest. So did you, or you would be shaving with it now. The chemical compounds that step up the driving power of gasoline, the cloth with durability far beyond your present clothing are all illustrations of the friction between the new and the old, between the general interest and self-interest.

The enemies of progress are not merely special groups, but all groups within the community. Some may have more to protect in a given case, but the past has given copious illustrations of the vigor with which both labor and capital will resist the march of the machine where present interest would be affected.

For years the patent system has been an object of scrutiny. The growing strength of larger enterprise and its emphasis on secure and stable markets have done very much to prevent an unrestricted contest between inventions, developments, products, and markets. And from this standpoint the war has strengthened the resistance, not minimized it.

Perhaps even more fundamental is the fact that patented processes themselves have changed in character. Once an invention was a rare combination of luck and genius; today it is more often the normal product of organized research. Ordinarily it is owned by the companies which paid the costs of scientific and technical study. Sharp competitive struggle is less frequently set off by innovations produced under this procedure. The rush of the individual inventor-entrepreneur is supplanted by the corporate anxiety not to disrupt the market.

But there will be countervailing forces. The mere fact that technological development has leaped forward and in five years has accomplished what might otherwise have taken a generation is a guarantee of some acceleration. In one way the vested interest has declined. Many machines have been worn out in the course of war production or rusted out in the course of disuse. That will eliminate one of the important reasons for delay—the investment in the old machine. The great variety of machine tools that will be available at bargain prices will be an added stimulant.

The exchange of patents and "know-how" demanded by war will have weakened the secrecy of what before was privately held information. Patents and processes owned by enemy nationals have been made available to American business by the Alien Property Custodian. Perhaps most profound of all among the guarantors of change is a psychological, rather than a physical, characteristic of tomorrow. The people have been sold on the impressive changes ahead. The market for prewar models may prove very disappointing in the face of a public demand for the widely advertised miracle products. Industry will be moved by its fear of the consumer, or, in other words, fear of what the competitor may offer. In normal peacetimes you have a pretty good idea of what your competitor is going to do next. But in the hectic struggle for markets during the reconversion to peace, suspicion and uncertainty will be the industrial bywords.

It has been said that every businessman has two postwar plans—to use plastics and to get into another business. It's an exaggeration, of course, but both are portents of more sensational technical progress than would ordinarily occur. The businessman's determination to continue using traditional materials is far weaker than

it has ever been. He's approaching the future with an open mi[
and is ready to experiment.

The decision to move into greener pastures will be particularly
important where the larger businesses are concerned. We've already
talked about diversification of industries—the tire manufacturer, for
example, moving into radio. If the airplane manufacturer starts
turning out farm equipment, you can bet your boots that his products will not be exactly like the equipment being turned out by the
veteran industry. When he moves in he will use one or both elbows
—lower prices and better goods.

The balance favors advance. It will be impossible to withhold developments more than temporarily. The change will not come so
soon as the ads have enthusiastically promised, but it's only a matter
of time.

The world of tomorrow will not arrive wrapped up in a neat package. It won't be here one year after the war, or two, or five, or even
ten. The first decade or two after the war will be a transition period,
merging our "old" technology and the new. The promised world
will be for your children and theirs. Probably not for you. But you
will certainly see its major outlines sometime before the rest of your
life is over.

The industrial revolution, of course, marked the great turning
point in the history of the modern world. It altered our social,
political, and economic environment so radically that one hundred
and fifty years later we still have not found solutions to the problems it brought. Today we stand on the brink of new change. Modern physics and chemistry are shifting the course of the industrial
revolution, promising in a generation a greater rise in the standard
of living than perhaps all the past one hundred and fifty years have
accomplished.

The coming era of light metals, plastics, expanded use of electronics and aviation may fashion a world which our parents would
have considered beyond the ken of even the most fantastic visionary.

Tomorrow's world began to take shape more than fifty years ago.
Almost every advance made today goes back to the revolution in
physics and mathematics. The current advertisements wave the
mystic word "electronics" before your eyes as if a new discovery

has been made. No, the war hasn't pried open a long-kept secret. It simply has made extraordinary use of already known principles. "Electronics" was already in your house with the radio; you saw it in operation every time the electric eye opened the door in a railroad station.

A revolution of long standing is for the first time being accurately identified. Some of the theories of that revolution are familiar, at least in name, to many people. Einstein, for instance, and his theory of relativity. And others less famous are equally important—such men as Planck, Heisenberg, Schroedinger, Riemann, Kantor, Lawrence, Neils Bohr, and Willard Gibbs.

These scientists threw a bombshell into classical physics. They blew it sky-high by proving that our basic concepts of matter, space, and time were inadequate and that the world needed new fundamental concepts if scientific and technological progress were to continue.

They opened the door to the microcosm—the world of the atom —and made available to chemists, biologists, physicists, and engineers a treasure-trove of new knowledge, which has already brought us great new industries and new products, new techniques, and the promise of more to come. The new scientific explanation of the nature of matter and the universe has fascinating philosophical implications, but it is in the field of industry that its effects are being felt more directly. In synthetic chemicals, for instance. In radio and television and radar. In the whole field of plastics. In artificial rubber, and silk. In new types of glass. The transmutation of metals is no longer an alchemist's dream but a daily routine in many a commercial laboratory.

Just as it took years to realize the potentialities of the machines introduced by the industrial revolution, so has there been a lag of some fifty years and more between the new scientific revolution and its fruits. Under the impetus of World War II, however, we are approaching the time when the full impact will be felt in our everyday lives.

What follows in this chapter is a picture of the world which will be built by the new physics, new mathematics, and new chemistry. Ultimately, there is no doubt, it will be as different from today's world as today's world is different from the eighteenth century. Some of the developments will come suddenly, dramatically; most will come gradually. The advent of new products, new industries, new materials, new techniques will bring staggering problems of economic readjustment, along with the hope of better living.

It will be our problem to learn how to enjoy the expanded life that technology will provide.

Probably the most apparent and most dynamic change will take place in the air. There's a special excitement in the announcement that you'll be able to fly from New York to London in about fifteen hours, or to Rio and Buenos Aires in only twenty-four hours. No capital of the world will be more than two or three days distant. With the new jet-propulsion plane, distance will shrink even more.

There's a deep stir of anticipation when we hear about the seadromes, which are planned as "artificial islands" dotting the ocean to make overseas flight safer and more comfortable. They will offer hotel accommodations, motion-picture theaters, swimming pools, tennis courts, and so forth, in addition to the necessary filling stations, repair facilities, weather bureaus. Planes will be able to carry more passengers in place of the tremendous gas load now required by transocean hops. By increasing the payload the cost of operation would be cut so that, as one expert wrote in 1942, "there is no valid reason why a two-cent-a-mile coach rate couldn't be set, making the one-way cost to England $70." Everything that's said is true. The only hitch is time. It is likely that a number of years will pass before the seadromes actually move from blueprint to the ocean and before rates are down as low as $70 for a transoceanic flight. But, with rates from New York to London already at $200, one certainty for the immediate future is that over-ocean air travel will become a matter of daily routine.

What will happen to the ship lines and the "floating palaces" like the *Queen Mary* and the *Normandie?* There will still be plenty of business for them. They offer comforts which are still impossible in planes—the leisure of a cruise for its own sake and the pleasures which require more room than you can get on a plane. As aircraft grow bigger, however, competition between plane and ship for overseas passenger traffic will undoubtedly develop.

There has been a common misconception that air freighters would deliver a deathblow to cargo ships as a means of moving international trade. In part these misconceptions have come from the dramatic stories of military cargo planes making eleventh-hour deliveries of much-needed munitions to isolated battle fronts when the slow speeds of cargo ships would have meant disaster. In part, too, the picture that has been painted of one huge "locomotive" plane towing a string of glider "freight cars" has also stimulated the public imagination to conclusions which the facts don't warrant.

The critical factor in all transport of cargo is the cost per ton-mile. Even in the case of the most advanced design on the air engineer's drawing board, planes could not, in any foreseeable future, compete successfully with cargo ships in terms of freight charges. Even if ocean-flying airplanes could get their costs down to the point where they could operate at from ten to fifteen cents per ton-mile, the ship carriers would still have an enormous cost advantage of as much as fifty or seventy-five to one. The plane's speed advantage of about six or ten to one will not, in the opinion of experts, be sufficient to offset the cost disadvantage.

The fundamental fact is that only commodities valued at $1,000 a ton or more are reasonable prospects for international air cargo. The general limitations on the types of freight which can profitably be flown overseas will, in the opinion of the Air Transport Association, limit imports and exports by commercial air freight to from 100,000 to 150,000 tons per year, a fraction of the United States total.

International air travel of any substantial scope would literally be impossible under a confusion of multiple regulations varying with each country. "The air has no boundary lines." In the conflict between this fact and the very real boundary lines which exist on the ground below, the early peace years will witness one of the most delicate problems of international peacetime relations.

How to handle the competitive interests of the various national airlines will be the subject of many an international conference. Before the war many foreign airlines received large subsidies from their governments. They, or their successors, will be back in the air: the Royal Dutch Airline, known more popularly as KLM;

Imperial Airways, now called "British Overseas Airways Corporation"; and Air France. Competing American airlines have sometimes been dissatisfied with United States policy in resolving opposing interests. There will be domestic fireworks on the question.

The international air problem is further complicated by the flying fields built by the United States and Great Britain on foreign territory for military purposes. Who is to own and control these bases when the war is over? Since these problems raise the question of sovereignty, their solution will not be simple and may be long delayed, with a consequent lag in the development of international flight.

It is dangerous to try to describe the plane of tomorrow. Revolutions in design come too quickly—witness the jet-propulsion plane, which has no propellers and can fly higher and faster than ordinary planes because it is less dependent on "biting the air." Rocket planes are an old dream—as old as the dream of flying to the moon—which may now be coming true. What man can say, in the face of today's discoveries, that tomorrow will not produce a plane as far in advance of today's jet-propulsion plane as that craft is from yesterday's traditional design? New speeds for passenger flight are now practical. Experts assure us that jet-propulsion planes will be flying the Atlantic in six hours. Breakfast in New York, dinner in London. Once such a schedule was limited to Superman, Flash Gordon, and Buck Rogers; tomorrow it may be your timetable. We thought we were doing pretty well when we reached the point where San Francisco was only an overnight trip from New York. Tomorrow's jet-propulsion plane may make it seem as slow as a covered-wagon trek.

There may be excitement in the anticipation of taking a picnic trip to London or Paris after the war, but for most of us the more immediate influence of aviation's future will undoubtedly be felt right here at home. When war came United States airlines had already established a tradition of safe and efficient service in almost every part of the country. In the ten years after 1929 the speed of our domestic planes soared from 110 to 180 miles an hour. The passenger fare of eight cents a mile in 1930 was cut to 4.9 cents. Only 58 per cent of the scheduled trips were completed in 1930; but in

1941, 91 per cent of the greatly increased number of scheduled trips came to a "happy landing." Only a very slight percentage of the uncompleted trips was due to accidents.

As for the plane itself, experts suggest that the first peacetime plane used by our domestic airlines will disregard all present types, and even skip over those already projected for future use, and start with a new ship called the "Lockheed Constellation." Most of the details remain under the lid of military secrecy. This much we do know: It can carry fifty-five to sixty passengers, fly as much as four miles above the earth at a cruising speed of three hundred miles an hour, so that it could make New York to Los Angeles in nine or ten hours, non-stop.

These are momentous prospects. The factors on the credit side of the ledger seem to give the impression that the airplane and the airplane industry have an unlimited future. Unfortunately there are a number of serious challenges which stand in the way of that possible future.

The automatic limitations on the volume of international air cargo have already been mentioned. There are also very real limitations on the amount of passenger traffic that may be expected in international flight. For instance, a total of 291,000 ship passengers traveled from Europe to the United States, with 276,000 going the other way, in the twelve and a half months ending June 30, 1938. Of these, 74,000 and 54,000, respectively, were first- and cabin-class travelers—people most likely to use transocean planes when they become available. Pure mathematics would indicate that all these passengers could easily be handled by only thirty-four planes of the Martin Mars type. But mathematics may be quite unrevealing. Past experience indicates that you can't compare changing forms of transportation. Because of the reduction in travel time, the busy executive who would like to spend a week end in England may for the first time take that trip. Tourists who can get away for only a two-week vacation, and others like them, will constitute a large contingent of the new air passengers. One leading aviation expert estimates that one million persons will cross the Atlantic by air in 1950, with more than a thousand large transports in operation.

There's a similar story for domestic flying. If every individual who traveled by rail during 1941—both in coaches and Pullmans— decided to fly after the war, less than sixteen hundred planes of the Commando type could do the job. Yet, by 1950, more than three thousand—and perhaps as many as five thousand—large-sized air transports will be required to handle the passenger load. Translating today's travel into an estimate of tomorrow's passengers is an unsatisfactory process. But the mathematics, though unsatisfactory, does indicate some limitations for the immediate future.

But they will not prove to be sufficient to delay the availability of plane travel to you. Yet they are important to the mammoth industry that first flourished in war and to the vast number of aviation employees who cannot be sustained according to even the most optimistic view of immediate aviation possibilities. But aside from the question of size, commercial air transport is one of the first deliveries the promissors of a bright tomorrow will make.

Not so with the private plane. There is no doubt that the public has been oversold on the extent to which the private plane will crowd the skyways after the war. It is worth noting that in the year before the war there were only 17,351 private planes in the country. Many companies were operating successfully in this field —Piper, Taylor, Luscombe, Cessna, and others—and they had more orders than they could take care of. They had made such progress that it is now predicted that light planes will be offered at a cost as low as $1,000. A two-passenger model may cost $1,500 and a five-passenger $3,000. They won't cost much to run, either—seventeen or eighteen miles on a gallon of gas, about fifteen dollars a month for hangar rent, and about 10 per cent of the list price for insurance each year. These planes are expected to offer cruising speeds of one hundred to two hundred miles an hour and will be safe to handle.

And still the immediate picture is pessimistic. Concerning the number of pilots the war has trained, a Civil Aeronautics expert estimates that with all the war-made pilots there'd still be a market for only 39,000 private planes in 1945. You can always learn to fly, but the more important barriers to private flight that existed before the war will not have been removed by the war. The trouble lies in the setup of our communities and airports. The way things have been, a man who owned a plane had to pay a substantial amount for hangar rental and needed a car to get to and from the field. In taking a trip, the private aviator might find himself marooned in an out-of-the-way airport, forced down by the weather.

There are three foreseeable solutions. In the first place, the war has sprinkled airports at a great rate all over the country. The second and third possible answers come in the form of the roadable plane and the helicopter. Planes have already been built and flown with detachable wings so that the pilot can use the fuselage as an automobile. Engineers caution that there are many bugs to be ironed out before the "autocraft" makes a large-scale appearance on the American scene; but they do not hesitate to predict that it will come, and in the not-too-distant future. Many communities are already planning landing strips for planes to run alongside their highways.

Then, of course, there's the widely heralded helicopter, able to go straight up and come straight down, "landing on a dime." The helicopter has proved its practicability beyond all doubt. It can hover like a hummingbird in the air; it can even reverse its direction, something an ordinary plane would find impossible.

The helicopters so far manufactured are not practical for most purposes. They are difficult to handle, vibrate too much (some have actually shaken themselves to pieces when flown), show inefficiency at high altitudes, and are unstable. Engineers are working to eliminate these and other defects, and some think they have the problems licked. However, they cannot prove the worth of their designs until priorities on the necessary materials are loosened and actual tests are made.

The chairman of the Helicopter Committee of the National Advisory Committee for Aeronautics, Grover Loening, flatly declared, in December 1943, that "the true picture today, faced honestly, is that the helicopter for the next few years is limited to usage by professional aviators and professional aviation companies, and is not at all a vehicle to be used by the general public.

"All of this talk that the helicopter is to be flown by everyone from Grandma to the tired businessman right after the war . . . is being so hurtfully overdone that we must call a halt to it."

Faith in the helicopter's future is universal in the aviation industry, but most experts agree with Mr. Loening's reservations.

The first helicopters will be for commercial use—airport taxis, suburban deliveries, bus routes. Their cost will put them out of reach of individuals—anywhere from $7,000 to $15,000. Many experts insist it will be at least ten years before the cost is reasonable enough for widespread use.

In any event, despite the differences in opinion as to the exact year in which the helicopter will make its real public debut, there is complete unanimity that it, like the autocraft, will be a commonplace on the American scene within ten or twenty years. It is then that the full impact of a new way of life for some of you will be felt. There will be many changes in the landscape: airplane service stations, "air camps" along with tourist camps, the opening of resorts in hitherto inaccessible mountains and forests, the development of new suburbs mushrooming around newly built airports, a roof-lifting operation on city buildings to provide landing places for helicopters.

The future of aviation is one of the brightest spots in all the rest of your life. But, precisely because of its appeal to the imagination, too much may be expected of it too soon.

The prospects for the automobile in many ways duplicate the future of the airplane. To start with, advanced designs—the "supercar of tomorrow," built of light metals and new plastics—are certainly coming. But, as with the helicopter, there'll be a longer interval between the end of the war and their appearance than the people have in one way or another been led to expect. If the industry and the country could afford to wait for the new car from one and a half to two years after the end of war contracts, the first models in the showrooms would undoubtedly offer many of the radical improvements about which we've heard. But so long a delay would represent a drastic threat of extended avoidable unemployment. The industry itself has flatly said it would rather come out with 1942 models within four to six months after the end of the war than chance the risks of an eighteen-month delay.

The teardrop dream car will make its appearance gradually over a period of years. The automobile industry foresees no revolutionary changes coming all at once, presenting the American public with a finished "supercar" in any given year. As in the past, each succeeding year's model will incorporate certain improvements and certain changes of design. Perhaps by the fifth, sixth, or tenth year after the war a full-bloom "supercar" will have evolved.

It has been traditional industry policy to hold back on improvements, to parcel out a few with each year's model. In this way the automobile industry helped keep up a continuous demand for new cars. It's an open secret that many an improvement has been kept under wraps until it was deemed advisable from a sales point of view to offer it to the public. Little reason to expect a change. Even if the manufacturers know how and are prepared to build a revolutionary car, they will prefer to have it evolve through a series of yearly models—unless new competition forces the industry to adopt a new policy.

Since market estimates in the industry predict that the country will want some twenty to twenty-five million new automobiles in the first five years after the war, it is reasonable to anticipate a hot race for the plums of this tremendous market. This factor alone may outweigh all the careful reasoning which has led the automobile industry to soft-pedal the "supercar."

Actually it is hard to discover how much of the industry's public statements is intended as a smoke screen and how much reflects the truth. Its specific plans for advance models are shrouded in mystery, and it may have a surprise or two up its sleeve.

Whether it comes within two or ten years after the war, whether it comes suddenly or gradually, whether it is the product of one of the older companies in the industry or of a newcomer, the car you will ride in before the rest of your life has passed will represent a great advance over the prewar automobile.

Here's a composite picture of the "supercar" as it may stand beside your helicopter in the garage of your new prefabricated house. The first thing that will strike your eye will be its smooth lines. It probably won't be streamlined in imitation of the airplane, the way some prewar models were. It's more likely, says one noted engineer, to "resemble the well-designed bus." You'll see one reason for this as soon as you open the door and step inside. There'll be much more room than in the prewar car. Basically, this increased roominess will come from a revolutionary change in motorcar design: the motor will be in the back. Most of the space that's now taken up with the hood and the engine will be saved for the interior. Also, with the motor in the rear, there won't be any need for the transmission assembly that ran an uncomfortable ridge along the floor of the prewar car. Your "supercar" will probably be without a clutch; many models before the war were successfully using automatic transmissions.

You will like the rearrangement of your car's interior. Designers' plans are getting away from the idea of seats arranged in the traditional manner and are moving closer to a kind of club-car or lounge arrangement.

Your "supercar" will probably weigh only half as much as your prewar car. The use of aluminum and other light metals and plastics will reduce the weight without sacrificing strength and safety.

There will be other features, too, such as an air-cooling system to keep the auto's interior cool and dustless. The tires that will be adapted to lightweight cars will insure more comfortable and easier riding. Much lower gas consumption seems to be another certainty. The claim is that as much as fifty miles per gallon will be ticked off on hundred-octane aviation gas. More likely the high-octane gas will be used for "blending." Wider vision and protection against glare through polaroid glass are also certainties. In general, tomorrow's car will be easier to handle, safer at high speeds and on turns, and more comfortable than anything we've known in the past. With mileage on the gallon increased and with improved tires carrying a lighter weight, the cost of upkeep will be substantially cut—but not the cost of the car.

The first ones off the assembly line, old models, are likely to run 20 to 40 per cent higher than in 1941. An eight-cylinder Ford two-door sedan, delivered in New York in 1941, cost $1,126; the same car after the war will probably have a price tag in the neighborhood of $1,400. The price will come down—unfortunately, with unemployment and diminishing material costs. All in all, you may have to wait a while, but you'll get that car; and in the case of automobiles, waiting won't be difficult. Unlike housing, there wasn't much the matter with the 1942 model.

There may be delay for your teardrop car and a little longer wait for the private plane, but there is a certainty that the first years of peace will bring you the FM radio and television. The time needed by the radio industry to get back to peacetime production is short. Standard receivers can be turned out by the factories after eight weeks. The outlook for the new FM and television sets is also favorable. Manufacturers feel confident they'll be able to get into production quickly with television sets costing only $200. Other manufacturers think the price will be closer to $400, but they too see quick production.

The television sets themselves will incorporate the knowledge gained during the war. Images, it is promised, will be sharper, without flicker or distortion. Instead of reflecting the television image in a mirror, there are new designs to project it onto a screen, in much the same way as a motion-picture projector.

Since the television signal is limited to a comparatively restricted area, the question of its commercial feasibility was a constant deterrent before the war. There's little doubt now, however, that network television broadcasting is entirely feasible. One leading company is planning on the assumption that within three or four years after the commercial resumption of television, Washington, D.C., Baltimore, Hartford, Providence, and Boston will have television transmitters. Hooked up with the existing stations in Philadelphia, New York, and Albany-Schenectady, these would represent a television network six hundred miles long, serving more than thirty-three million people.

The plans of this company also envision a linking of a Middle West network with the Atlantic seaboard. Together with secondary networks, this company estimates that within five years after the commercial resumption of television there are likely to be television transmitters in 157 key cities, reaching more than seventy-two million people. Looking ahead to the fifth or sixth year after war, the experts think it will be economically feasible to serve almost every home in the United States with television programs.

There's no doubt that television is technically ready, although we may have to wait several years longer for such advances as color television. But a basic trouble with television is that the receiving sets and the transmitters must be "frozen" together. Technical improvements in the sending apparatus could render receiving sets obsolete. The danger is that standards will be frozen too soon. For instance, if millions of television sets geared to 1944 techniques were sold to the public, there would be a natural enough tendency to go slow on further improvements that might make them useless or would require expensive alterations. This is a problem that is worrying the industry and the Federal Communications Commission. The consensus seems to be that it *won't* prevent a large sale of television sets to the public after the war. But it will prevent as rapid an improvement of television broadcasting and receiving as might otherwise take place.

By and large, though, the airplane, automobile, and television are short-run developments in the technology of tomorrow. Some of the longer range improvements will come from new developments in the light metals and plastics, chemistry, and electronics. To understand the implications, think for a moment of the "ages" through which mankind has passed—"the stone age," "the iron age," and so on. With the discovery of new basic materials out of which he could build his tools and his structures, man has moved from one type of civilization to another. The greatest single change in recent history was the introduction of steel; it's "the steel age" which has given us our railroad-skyscraper-assembly-line civilization.

It now seems likely that we're not far from a new era whose promise is as unlimited as the magic of modern chemistry. More than a million tons of aluminum, instead of the average prewar yield of 100,000 tons, is sufficient to promise sharp change. Magnesium, a commonplace instead of a rarity, is just another of the structure-altering developments. The light weight, strength, and ease of fabrication of the new alloys will have far-reaching effects in many phases of industrial production. You will become aware of them in a wide range of postwar streamlined home appliances, in the new lightweight cars, airplanes, aluminum busses, and streamlined trains. Competition between the old industry metals, such as steel, and the new lightweight metals will be great. The advantage held by steel is its lower cost per pound compared with the lighter metals; but, no matter how uneven the contest, the final result will be cheaper, better products for the consumer than were available before the war.

At the same time all the metal industries will face an increasing challenge from the new plastics. Out of the laboratory has come a whole world of synthetic materials with an incredible range of properties and characteristics. New types of glass will be used in the fabrication of all kinds of things, from new walls for houses to silky fiber that can be woven into fabric.

Typical of the unexpectedness of the new uses to which old materials will be put after the war is "foamglas," which is lighter than cork and can be sawed or drilled as if it were a piece of wood. Since this "foamglas" floats in water, it can be used to replace cork and similar materials. It also offers the advantages of being odorless, fireproof, and verminproof.

Behind the scenes of American industry during the war countless new techniques and advances have been completed and perfected—techniques that will be important in shaping the world of tomorrow. There is, for instance, the electronic "sewing machine," which uses radio current as its needle and thread. It is not for housewives' use, but for industrial processes involving the joining of materials such as plastics more firmly and economically than was possible before. Then there's the electronic tube that acts as an automatic inspector, searching out hidden flaws and offering an invaluable control in certain industrial processes. It would take a many-volumed encyclopedia to list a mere sampling of such new industrial techniques brought to successful application by the war.

Here again a word of caution: Old materials and old techniques will continue. In some cases a great deal of experimentation is still to be done before the new proves its unquestioned superiority to

the old. In still other cases public taste or desire may prefer the old
to the new. But the promise is enormous. With the new reservoir
of materials and techniques which the war will have left us, our
civilization can really move toward greater control of the physical
environment.

The soybean and its thousands of derivatives; synthetic rubber;
the miracle of wood—the new laminated plywoods; coal, air, and
water turned into sheer hosiery—these are likely to prove the
faintest shadows of the magic still to come from the laboratories.

Heat for our houses directly from the sun; energy for our factories directly from the sun; minerals from the ocean; new types
of fuels; new knowledge of vitamins and food—dehydration, freezing; new methods of agriculture; light that can turn a corner . . .

Power from the atom—one ounce of an element like uranium
enough to speed an ocean liner across the Atlantic when the chemists and physicists hit on the final combination. The unforeseeable
consequences of the new discoveries about the nature of magnetism. The electron microscope to explore the microcosm, and
new giant telescopes to explore the heavens. The atom-smashers
which may reshape our world . . .

Many of these are already here. Some are distant. But none are
visionary. They are hardheaded experiments now going on in commercial laboratories. Some may not come for one hundred years;
or they may be announced tomorrow.

And the changes they bring will not be just new comforts and
conveniences for human living. The challenge of new materials, for
instance, will complicate the reconversion problems of many a
company. Can the prewar machinery be used? Will the old products be successful, or will they mean business death as a result of
new rivals in the market? Where a company plans to use new
materials, what happens to the companies—and their employees—
who supplied the old materials before the war?

The old factory machinist who knew every machine in the plant
by heart may suddenly be confronted with rows of strangers. Men
who have handled one type of material all their working days may
be at a loss when the new stuff comes rolling in. All this spells a
big job of labor training and retraining, the painful headaches of

technological unemployment, the death of the old industries and new ones supplanting them, deep-reaching changes in our economy. A mechanical cane chopper on a Southern plantation or an improved cotton picker can mean disaster for hundreds of thousands, can mean economic upheaval in a large area of the country.

More machines and more efficient types of machinery will mean technological unemployment, but new industries will spell new employment opportunities. Prewar television, for instance, provided jobs for only a handful of people. The Federal Communications Commission estimates the potential market for television sets at forty-five million . . . which will make hundreds of thousands of jobs directly and indirectly.

The promise of the new age of science is basic: an economy of abundance and more leisure than the world has ever been able to offer in the past. The promise is that we will be able to turn out enough of everything to give a high standard of living for everybody, with only a few hours of work a day. That's the promise. Many of the heartaches, most of the anguish of modern society, flow from promises that are real enough measured against non-delivery that is equally real.

The war will have catalyzed the power of the machine. It will have exaggerated our expectation from it. The war will have spurred the earth and the elements, the laboratory, the field, factory, and mine, to disgorge more of their treasures. But the war will also have brought us closer to the crucial question of whether man can handle the enormous forces he thus sets into motion.

CHAPTER XIII

Mice, Lice . . .

IT'S NO SCENARIO. The story has already become a classic in medical history. A group of three hundred doctors in Hawaii were listening to a lecture on "Treatment of Wounds, Civil and Military," by Dr. John J. Moorhead. It was Friday evening, December 5, 1941. Dr. Moorhead, authority in his field, had been especially invited by the Honolulu Medical Society to describe the latest methods of treating wounds of violence. The subject was long and complicated. Just as he was starting another lecture on Sunday morning . . . history interrupted. The rest of Dr. Moorhead's course was conducted in the hectic clinic of Pearl Harbor's hospital.

December 7, 1941. Medicine marched into the future. In its march it would stumble over little that was completely new. The sensational, unexpected discoveries would be very few. But it would have the greatest laboratory ever constructed. Much that it knew would be proved or discarded. Much that it had thought or speculated on would have a chance to be applied. The pressure of agony, the needling of time, the desperateness of the hour would catapult your health a generation forward in four years.

December 7, 1941. A grim struggle between life and death. Life won, even on that very day. The results of modern medical care at Pearl Harbor were as dramatic as the shapes of twisted steel that could be seen from the splintered windows of the hospital. The death rate following the emergency operations that day was only 3.8 per cent; no deaths at all from gangrene, scourge of World War I.

The impact on the future is automatic; it's your boy who might not otherwise have come back. And the talents and techniques that saved him may eventually prolong your life. A soldier wounded today has twice as good a chance of recovery as the man who was hit in 1918. But the lesson was learned none too soon. The percentage of men killed outright in action has almost doubled in comparison with World War I. However, of those wounded, only 3½ per cent die from the injuries.

The health hazards of this war dwarf the mud and lice of the Argonne. The mud's still in it, but add the swamps and mosquitoes, the jungle, the crawling slime, the desert, the sun and stinking water.

The aim is better, the ammunition more lethal, and sudden death more certain. But if it doesn't get him on the spot, the chances of the wounded soldier's returning are greater than they have ever been.

Here's a heart-warming score for 1943: Only some 3.5 per cent of the Army's wounded died; the Navy lost only 3.16 per cent; the Marines, 3.15. These figures compare with the following World War I score of fatal wounds: Army, 6 per cent; Navy, 7.35 per cent; Marines, 12 per cent. But we're far from tops. The Red Army, according to official Russian claims, lost only 1.5 per cent of its wounded.

How miraculous this is can never be realized from the cold statistics. Go back to a Yankee doughboy charging amid a blaze of bullets and exploding shells over the pitted earth of Belleau Wood in 1918. A piece of shrapnel gets him; he falls with a wound in the abdomen. His chances of survival—tragically small. More than half of the men so wounded were lost. So serious were abdominal injuries that even as recently as the battle of Dunkirk the recovery rate was only a little higher than 50 per cent. But two years later, after the battle in the Solomon Islands, United States medical records showed that taps blew for only one out of every five, or 20 per cent.

Chest wounds have also been traditionally fatal. During World War I death from this type of wound ran from 24 per cent in the American Army to 40 per cent in the Russian Army. But of almost one thousand men brought to a special hospital during the Russo-

Finnish War, only twenty-nine died. The death rate had been cut to 3 per cent. That figure may drop even lower before all the medical statistics of this war are compiled.

In the last war three out of four wounded men who died were killed by streptococcus, not by injuries inflicted by the Hun. Today medicine is working miracles with the help of the innumerable varieties of the sulfa drugs.

In 1937 the quack "Dr. Massengill's Elixir of Life" left a wake of death in several states before the government got at his polluted sulfanilamide brew. Six years later the dread harvest of war was being impressively reduced by the scientific use of the innumerable varieties of this genuine elixir.

In 1936 a twelve-year-old boy lay in a Washington hospital, seemingly doomed. He was afflicted with a virulent type of meningitis which until that time had condemned to death 99 per cent of its victims. But two days before Christmas of that year the boy was given sulfanilamide, already known but not widely used. It turned out to be a Christmas present, not only for him, but for the world. Two days after Christmas he was getting better. A few weeks later he had completely recovered. Since that time the death rate of the disease has been cut to less than 50 per cent.

Sulfanilamide, sulfapyridine, sulfathiazole, sulfadiazine, and sulfaguanadine give every promise of continuing to expand their "miracle cures" as research discovers more of their secrets. The most striking characteristic of all the work done in sulfa is the speed with which new applications have come out of the laboratories. Although experts caution against considering these drugs as "cure-alls," they don't hesitate to predict new uses for their lifesaving gifts in the years to come.

Doctors point out that the sulfa drugs don't kill the infection bacteria; they merely hold the "bugs" in check until the natural defense mechanisms of the body are able to get their licks in. Of course there are some cases which do not respond to the drugs, and a very few in which their use becomes dangerous, but almost all streptococcus infections have been brought under a considerable measure of control by them.

For life's victories thank these three main reasons: the use of blood plasma in the fight against shock and hemorrhage; the various sulfa drugs; and the mobility and organization of the medical forces.

Plasma, one of the underballyhooed of the war's ballyhoos, is among the best means of treating the shock which previously impeded successful surgical treatment. A head wound in World War I meant about a 60 per cent chance of death. In one of the Egyptian campaigns of this war that fatality figure was reduced to 9 per cent.

It was a gruesome climactic scene in *The Big Parade* when the hero returned without a leg. There'll be returning heroes this time too, but not so many in that condition. The service doctors say: "We lost legs in the last war chiefly from shock, infection, and hemorrhage. Now we administer plasma for shock and loss of blood, and sulfa drugs for infection." Many a man is spared the ghastly stretcher ride to the amputation room. More recently the drug penicillin has joined the defenses against the infection of gas gangrene, one of the chief causes of amputations in the last war. In one hospital during World War I, 47 per cent of the amputations resulted from this cause. That's a page of history gladly turned for good.

Medicine has gone further than merely preserving the heartbeat in a shattered frame. To save the life of a soldier, sailor, or marine who might otherwise die from his wounds is not, in every case, to reduce the tragedy. Some men may be so badly disfigured that they would prefer to die. Burns leave their horrible scars. Twisted bones and torn muscles leave their ugly distortions. But plastic surgery has come forward with its restoration.

To a remote English village during this war a steady stream of crippled men have gone for special plastic surgery. Their experiences offer one of the most brilliant chapters in the story of modern military medicine. An American flier whose nose had been shattered arrived in despair, but left with a better-looking nose than he owned originally. Men whose eyelids had been burned or torn away by the enemy's fire were fitted with brand-new lids, grafted from the skin on the inside of their arms. New hands, new eyebrows, new faces for old. Men who didn't dare to look at themselves in the mirror, men who resigned themselves to a hermit's existence, who had given up all thought of being able to work, live, or love, had been rescued from despair, fitted out with new bodies and new lives.

Even at the front line the latest medical advances in plastic surgery have been applied and have given new quotas of hope. Not only does disfigurement yield to the mastery of the surgical sculptor, but the techniques are also used to prevent certain types of paralysis which would otherwise render the individual a helpless invalid for the rest of his life. By removing skin, fat, muscle, or even bone, from one part of the body and grafting it to another, the plastic surgeon is able in many cases to restore to usefulness hands and feet paralyzed by injury.

Most of these skills and techniques were not learned or improvised in the war itself. But one, at least, had a purely martial origin. Treating certain fracture wounds by simply covering them with plaster of paris was developed in the Spanish Civil War. World War II records amazing recoveries by the use of this new treatment. And none of these is without its meaning for postwar life.

Take the things the war has taught about the treatment of broken bones. A widely used method now is to drive a metal pin through the two parts of a large fracture to keep the bone in place until it knits.

The use of the "radio knife" instead of the traditional scalpel has been hailed as an important preventive of infection and minimizer of bleeding, shock, and pain. Radio waves from the scalpel's blade spread their sterilizing effects to the surrounding tissues as the knife cuts.

A new type of dressing has been developed which quickly and safely controls hemorrhages from wounds, whatever portion of the body is injured. Doctors report that it does away with the old-fashioned tourniquet and promises to save many lives.

When Dr. Moorhead came to Hawaii just before Pearl Harbor he brought with him a little black box which looked like a portable radio set. He expected to demonstrate it at one of his lectures, but, as things turned out, its first showing was in actual use on the Sunday afternoon of December 7. The "little black box" turned out to be an electrical device to signal the presence and position of any bit of metal embedded in the body. In an emergency operation on Sunday afternoon the apparatus revealed the presence of a machine-gun bullet in the spinal canal of a soldier. Moorhead said of this case, "Despite the use of X rays, I would have failed had it not been for the aid afforded by the locator."

The fatigue of the war-weary in America may create enormous barriers against the world. A postwar isolationism designed to insulate America against the problems of a global world may actually succeed in keeping much of that world out. But not the world's bacteria.

Millions of men will return to the United States from all parts of the globe, and some, either as carriers or as patients, will bring diseases that have been uncommon or completely unknown in this country. Global war, sprawled all over the map, has presented many unique medical problems to the nation's doctors. The diseases of the tropics were once of little concern to us. Now malaria, for example, is being studied night and day. And among America's as yet unrevealed secret weapons are the new drugs which Brigadier General Charles Hillman describes as "of inestimable value in the therapy of malaria."

Where military reoccupation and rehabilitation have led, America's medicine and America's doctors have followed. Malnutrition in Sicily; typhus in Italy; bubonic plague in Java; opium addiction in China; tropical fever in Burma; frostbite in Kiska; pneumonia, flu, and syphilis everywhere.

The American Medical Association in 1943 pointed out that the United States is not so immune from "exotic diseases" as we suppose. From the standpoint of contagion, the world is small and the war's effects enduring. For instance, few soldiers on whom the war has stamped the imprint of malaria will ever be sure the attacks won't recur.

Each time the AMA issues a warning bulletin a contemporary John Donne might well counsel against asking "for whom the bell tolls." Listen to the American Medical Association:

. . . Typhus, spread in this country by the rat flea, up by 25 per cent in 1942.

. . . Actual number of cases believed even greater.

. . . Gradually spreading northward along the West Coast and along the granary lines in the Middle West.

. . . Bubonic plague found in the Western states.

. . . Danger! Exotic diseases may invade America by plane and returning troops.

. . . Danger! Filariasis, a disease of the lymph glands transmitted by mosquitoes, and schistosomiasis, an intestinal infection transmitted by snails, must be watched.

None of the preventive action has been spectacular. Preventive measures aren't dramatic, but the work has been good. Field offices for typhus control have been set up, state after state. One field officer carrying out control work reported 231 rats killed by a single fumigation in one small grocery, plus an uncounted number of others gassed in their burrows. Twelve people employed in that store had been infected with typhus in the two previous years.

Six million dollars spent on malaria control alone threw a protected zone around every war industry and military camp in the American malaria belt. It was not surprising, then, that the Army experienced the lowest malaria rate in its history in this country. Rats have been cleaned out of every community in which bubonic plague was reported; mice, mosquitoes, and snails sampled and watched from one end of the country to the other. The enemy is suspect. All planes from foreign ports are fumigated twice. New ocean vessels incorporate the latest rat-proofing specifications.

The war for life continues, and the experience our medical men are gaining in shadowy corners of the world will be of unequaled value in protecting us from the ravages of strange and new diseases that might otherwise afflict this country after the war.

The enemy counted on disease as an ally. So, likely, did we. The Japanese monopoly on anti-malaria drugs looked bad for the health of American men. Wartime necessity spurred research, and atabrine, not fully a match for the Dutch quinine acquired by Japan, helped enormously in the South Pacific fight against malaria. Research continues, and with it news that a still better substitute for quinine is in the offing for your health in the postwar world.

High among wartime drug substitutes is the new synthetic preparation to replace morphine. "Demerol" holds out exciting hope. It is described as having most of the advantages of morphine, with very few of its disadvantages. For instance, Demerol is said to have no effect on respiration, and may therefore be given to asthma sufferers who cannot safely take morphine. Here is a drug in which women may be particularly interested as it becomes more widely available in peacetime. Its use in childbirth promises to relieve pain substantially and to shorten labor considerably.

Long before war's end civilian life was beginning to enjoy this new blessing in thousands of test cases. The reports say that Demerol hasn't morphine's habit-forming character and that its use in childbirth has no effect on the infant. Wider testing and experiments must still validate the claims beyond question before the hope for tomorrow is realized.

For civilians one of the most important results of our wartime medical experience will be better control of epidemics. It has been a military truism that, quite aside from the germs that cause death through infection of wounds, more soldiers have been killed by bugs than by bullets in every war in history. Dr. Hans Zinsser, biographer of the typhus louse, has written, "Soldiers have rarely won wars. They more often mop up after the barrage of epidemics. Typhus, with its brothers and sisters—plague, cholera, typhoid, dysentery—has decided more campaigns than Caesar, Hannibal, Napoleon, and all the inspector generals of history."

We have come a long way from the days when a court trial was frequently more dangerous for the diseases communicated in the courtroom than for the death penalties meted out by the judges. In the "Black Assizes" described by old English writers an ironic, if unpoetic, justice was often done. The prisoners brought into court frequently passed on the typhus lice to the judge and jury, with a fatality that made a mockery of the court's power.

In our own day all too many people can remember the disastrous epidemics that followed in the wake of World War I. Typhus took over three million lives, and influenza brought death to more than twenty-two million. The Boche was a piker compared to his invisible ally. Epidemics have not yet been stopped, but the controls available are miraculous by comparison.

During this war, in the late fall of 1943, an influenza epidemic was reported in the United States. It was of such serious proportions that schools were closed in several areas, but death was at least on a partial holiday. A typhus outbreak in Naples after the Allied occupation was so serious that the city was declared "out of bounds" for the 5th Army troops. Yet America's brush with the grim reaper in Italy remained casual.

Many of the standard draftee jokes which this war has added to the literature of American humor are based on the number of times a new soldier has a needle jabbed into his arm. The jokes may be funny, but the inoculations are in dead earnest. American soldiers have been given comparative immunity against typhoid, smallpox, yellow fever, plague. The experience gained from these mass inoculations will be an important tool in the hands of American doctors in the prevention of epidemics in the United States.

Obviously, every one of the advances made by wartime medicine will be felt directly in the United States, will mean healthier living and better protection against disease for the rest of your life. The new knowledge automatically becomes part of the arsenal of health available for use at home during and after the war.

Another field of wartime medical experience that promises to yield great benefits to the average American family is "anesthesiology"—the use of anesthetics to deaden pain during operations. New anesthetics have been developed which can be used with patients who, for one reason or another, cannot be subjected to the more traditional deadeners like ether and chloroform. The new preparations will be safer and more effective, will make the operations of tomorrow less painful and more successful.

Hardly any kind of human pain has remained immune to the advance. Where burns are concerned, medical progress gives promise not only of relieving suffering and assuring a high percentage of recovery, but also of doing away with the horrible aftermath of scar tissue and disfigurement.

Surgical techniques in brain operations are also making great strides forward under the relentless compulsions of the battlefield. Cases formerly given up as hopeless can now be brought safely to the operating table. Typical of the ingenuity with which medical men are solving the problems presented by the battlefield is the operation performed by a Russian surgeon on a soldier who had a small piece of metal embedded in his brain. Ordinary operating instruments could not safely reach it. Instead an ordinary tenpenny nail was carefully inserted until its point touched the piece of metal in the brain, and then a strong electromagnet was applied to the other end. The magnetism fastened the bit of metal to the nail and made it possible to withdraw it without serious injury to the brain.

Tetanus, once the scourge of the battlefield, was usually fatal when it struck in civilian life. The use of antitoxins had already checked the ravages of tetanus during World War I, but lockjaw was still a serious threat. Search for methods of immunizing people against tetanus continued until final confirmation was given in 1940. Not one of sixteen thousand immunized men at Dunkirk developed the slightest signs of tetanus—although the hell of that battle would ordinarily have taken many lives through such infection.

It's headline stuff when a medical development slashes the mortality rate from wounds by 50 per cent—and it should be. But, less dramatically, there are many fields of medical research, not directly related to the war, which have progressed steadily through the years toward the discovery of new cures for old ailments.

Hailed as an even greater miracle than the sulfa drugs is penicillin, the "drug that comes from bread and cheese mold." Penicillin is described as one hundred times more potent than sulfa, without any toxic aftereffects. It is known to play havoc with the germs that cause bone infection, pneumonia, diphtheria, gas gangrene, and is also effective as a treatment for some of the most noxious forms of blood poisoning. So powerful is penicillin that one drop is said to be able to kill several bathtubfuls of bacteria.

Perhaps the most striking application of penicillin so far is in the treatment of syphilis. Even before penicillin tremendous progress had been made in the treatment of this crippling disease. It was first brought under control by Ehrlich's famous "magic bullet." More recently certain sulfa compounds have been used to make the treatment shorter, less tedious, less painful, and more effective. Still more novel has been the use of an artificial fever method which seems to be particularly helpful in early cases. Now medical men declare that penicillin holds definite promise of being the long-sought, non-poisonous drug which can be used for quick treatment of the disease.

A report in October 1943 announced that in eight days all symptoms of syphilis had disappeared in four cases where penicillin had been prescribed. In reporting this possible landmark in modern medicine, Dr. John F. Mahoney—together with Dr. R. C. Arnold and Dr. Ad Harris, his collaborators—was quick to inject a word of caution. "Since syphilis is a disease which tends to relapse after a longer or shorter period of freedom of symptoms," he said, "a prolonged observation of a large group of patients will be needed to confirm the promise which is held out by the first group." Penicillin has also been found effective in cases of gonorrhea. Scientists have their fingers crossed; this new drug may ultimately prove to be the real "magic bullet" against venereal diseases.

Gramicidin is another germ killer hailed as the equal of penicillin in the treatment of certain diseases.

The steady march continues in the fight against tuberculosis. Within the past generation this disease has been brought under substantial control, but its onslaught still spells tragedy in many cases. In December 1943, from a tuberculosis sanatorium in Illinois, came news of a new anti-tuberculosis drug called diasone, which may still further reduce the seriousness of tuberculosis in the years ahead. Dr. Charles Kenneth Petter, who reported the new drug, was emphatic in his statement that it was not "the final answer to tuberculosis," but declared at the same time that diasone may prove to be a significant step ahead, as important as the introduction of the sanatorium and collapse therapy in t.b. treatment.

New discoveries in the mystery of vitamins have come out, tumbling on each other's heels. Conservative medical opinion is that vitamins will play an increasingly important part in maintaining good health in the postwar years and perhaps in curing some of the diseases which still challenge our doctors. There will continue to be a big difference between the actual progress made and the cure-all vitamin fads that have appeared with monotonous regularity.

Curiously, some of the research proceeds through circuitous scientific channels only to return to medical folklore. One author reports that the Appalachian mountaineers have long had a tradition that eating sand will cure bleeding ulcers. Studies conducted for a number of years at the University of Cincinnati now confirm what seemed to be a mere superstition. Finely powdered silicon may be a healing agent for wounds and ulcers. The conclusion came through an odd relationship of ailments. Consumption used to be called "the stonecutter's disease" because the inhalation of the fine silicon dust caused the lung tissue to become fibrous and therefore useless. The formation of fibrous tissue is exactly what was needed as the remedy for ulcers. The Hollywood coterie may yet avoid its occupational disease, "option stomach," by eating sand at contract-expiration time.

Two of mankind's most burdensome ills have continued to resist all efforts at medical solution. Cancer research goes forward at an unflagging pace, but no responsible scientist will tell you that a general cure is in sight. On the other hand, no responsible scientist would be very much surprised if the answer were to be found next year or next month or tomorrow.

One real advance in cancer research has been greeted by judicious experts with the highest hopes. A new method of treating cancer of the prostate by means of special hormones seems to yield remarkable results. It is important to emphasize that this treatment is limited to the one particular form of the disease—cancer of the prostate. Medical men, however, agree that if this form of cancer is responding well to treatment today, another may be brought under control tomorrow, another the day after tomorrow, until finally the disease is listed as one of life's conquests.

The common cold finds itself in a slightly different situation. Here again no cure is promised, although many scientists think they have promising leads in their investigations of viruses and in the use of the penicillin derivative, patulin. Several important steps forward have been taken in the prevention of the common cold and its dread big sister, influenza. The ultraviolet lamp has proved to be an invaluable new weapon against these diseases. Scientists have shown that it can inactivate or kill most of the air-borne bacteria and viruses in a room conditioned by the lamp. "This sounds simple," says Bruce Bliven, "yet it may prove one of the most remarkable advances in recent medical history."

Use of this simple apparatus, well within the budget of the average family, may rescue your youngsters from most of the children's diseases which, until recently, were patiently borne as inevitable. The traditional childhood cycle of measles, whooping cough, mumps, chicken pox, and even pneumonia may be broken by ultraviolet "sterilization" of the air they breathe. Some experiments indicate that tuberculosis, too, may be checked by ultraviolet radiation.

The effectiveness of sterilizer lamps is demonstrated by what happened in three public schools during the winter of 1940–41, when one of the worst epidemics of measles in our history swept along the Atlantic Coast. Sixty to seventy per cent of the children in some Philadelphia classrooms, for instance, had the measles at one time or another. In three schools, however, the rate was only 12 to 14 per cent. The classrooms in these schools were fitted with ultraviolet lamps.

Science, through the years, has taught us how to protect our drinking water, milk, and foods. Now, as Bruce Bliven concludes, "we are about to cross the last great frontier of sanitary control and purify the air."

No discussion of your health for the rest of your life would be complete without considering the developments that have taken place against the deadly "viruses," which are still a medical question mark. We do not yet understand what they are as we understand the behavior of bacteria. We do know viruses—painfully—through the diseases they cause—smallpox, yellow fever, rabies, and some forms of tumors and cancer. Influenza, measles, sleeping sickness, and the common cold are others on the grim list of virus-borne ills. There is reason to believe that the answer to infantile paralysis may be found through virus research.

If study in this field can give us the cure for even one of these diseases, the characterization of virus research as one of the "great turning points in the history of human thought" will have been justified. A most important advance pointing toward the future took place in 1935, when Dr. W. M. Stanley chemically isolated a virus in its pure form and made it possible to provide specimens for extensive analysis.

While some doors have remained stubbornly shut, others have been opening up vistas which border on the incredible—witches' tales put to shame. As alchemists sought for years to transpose base metals into gold, modern biologists have begun to investigate the tantalizing question of whether life can be restored after death. The famous "automatic heart" developed by Dr. Alexis Carrel and Charles A. Lindbergh made the headlines in 1935. Before that, in 1912, Dr. Carrel had discovered a way of keeping animal tissue alive long after the rest of the body was dead. The piece of chicken heart which he set aside at that time is still living in its carefully controlled solution at the Rockefeller Institute. Both experiments, however, resulted only in methods of keeping *living* tissue alive.

In November 1943 an audience of one thousand people, including leading scientists and medical men, gathered in New York to see a motion picture of the restoration of life in an animal that had been dead for fifteen minutes. Reporting this pioneer work, the New York *Times* said: "The experiments were hailed by biologists as promising a new epoch in medical science, bringing closer the day when operations now incompatible with life will be possible. These may include repair to a damaged heart or brain and the restoration of persons who died of shock and hemorrhage. The procedure suggested vast new horizons in surgery and physiology."

These hopes of a future "cure for death" rest on an interesting apparatus called the "autojector," developed by Professor Bryukonenko and his staff in the Soviet Institute of Experimental Biology at Moscow after many years of experimentation. The device is designed to perform the physiological functions of the heart and lungs.

At the New York showing the picture of a dead dog appeared on the screen. One part of the autojector was connected to an artery and a second part to a vein. Serving as an artificial lung and heart, the autojector supplied the animal's blood with oxygen, pumping it into the dog and circulating it through the arterial system. A second pump, connected to the vein, drew the oxygenless blood through the venous system back into the autojector, where it was again recharged with oxygen and returned into the arteries. Thus mechanical means provided the system of blood circulation required by life.

Almost unbelievably, after a short while the dog's head moved slightly. When light was flashed before the closed eyes, they responded. The dog's heart began to beat, and the slow, rhythmic breathing of a living animal became apparent. The spark of life had been rekindled in a corpse. When the heartbeat and the breathing became normal, the autojector was disconnected. The blood and respiratory systems continued their functioning. The screen then showed pictures of the animal three days later—frisking around and gulping a hearty meal.

Three such animals have been brought back from the dead in these experiments, and have enjoyed normal health since 1939. Alive more than four years after they had died!

The same apparatus has been used to revitalize and keep alive individual organs of an animal, such as the lung and the heart. One of the scenes that brought gasps from the audience showed a dead animal's head—severed from the rest of the body—coming to life, responding to the stimuli of light and sound, and even licking its lips when acid was placed on its mouth.

One of the most fascinating speculations of the future involves the use of this knowledge in restoring life to those who might otherwise be on their way to the mortuary. The principles discovered by the Russians are applicable only where death occurs without the impairment of vital organs. In the past the greatest obstacle to resuscitation has been the disintegration of the brain tissues very soon after death. This new method would preserve the brain tissue. Although the war interrupted scheduled experiments with humans, we may not be too far from the day when perhaps——!

These Russian experiments are interesting for another reason. They underscore the internationalism of the language of science. America will profit even from the medical discoveries that the Germans have made in their attempt to prolong the fighting power of their military force. It is difficult to appraise the relative or comparative weight of national contributions which have been made to your health. We know that the recent advances in sulfa drugs have been notably American in origin. The Russians, with typical

Dostoievskian mysticism, have tackled some of the broader, semi-metaphysical questions of life and death. They have taken the lead, for example, in "transplanting" experiments—using the blood and various tissues of cadavers in the treatment of wounded soldiers. Even nerve tissues have been transplanted. The possibilities are limitless.

Professor Bryukonenko, of autojector fame, is already experimenting on many uses of the apparatus which may mean a normal, healthy life for persons otherwise doomed to chronic disease. There are certain blood ailments, for instance, that have resisted all efforts of treatment. The irrepressible Professor Bryukonenko has the idea that the autojector may eventually be used to drain off diseased blood and—using blood plasma—to fill the patient's body with new, healthy life.

Yes, the mice and the lice, the bugs and viruses, are taking a beating. Yours is the profit. Even in the vault of death the faintest rattling may be heard.

Every step forward in medicine is a contribution of longer life to you and your family. Even before most of the recent discoveries the chief statistician of the Metropolitan Life Insurance Company believed that a life expectancy, at birth, of seventy years was at hand. In 1936 Professor C. C. Furnas, of Yale University, also asserted that with the biological equipment and knowledge that already existed, ten years could be added to the normal sixty-year life span. That doesn't necessarily mean you'll live another ten years. The mortality rate takes a beating from the hazards which afflict the young child. Five per cent of our babies still die in the first year. But the medical profession insists this could be cut in half quickly, and that alone would lengthen the average life by two years. Elimination of tuberculosis among children would add another year. And Dr. Furnas concludes:

An indefinite amount could be added by lessening the toll of the degenerative diseases of middle age, such as diabetes. Sensible hygiene, decent food, and a reasonable standard of living seem to be all that will be required to bring our expectations up to threescore and ten. It seems reasonable to expect this within the next generation . . . unless too many wars or too many hilarious periods of prosperity upset our trends.

The chances now for a long life and a healthy one are better than they have ever been. Man has progressively been learning how to acquire a longer life, even if he hasn't always known what to do with it.

Russian medicine has approached this problem with little respect for traditional achievement and conservative appraisal. Professor Alexander A. Bogomolets was given the reward of Hero of Socialist Labor for the discovery of a potentially life-lengthening serum. It has already proved valuable in the treatment of arthritis and war injuries. Once again the Russians are using the leftovers of death to make life. Obtained from horses after repeated injections of the cell elements of the spleen and bone marrow from human corpses, the serum has hastened the healing of wounds and the knitting of fractures in thousands of cases.

But, more important, Bogomolets insists that the perfection of his serum, combined with the existing success already achieved in the improved functioning of digestion, blood circulation, and the nervous system, could increase the normal span of human life to 125 or 150 years. Hail, Bogomolets!

It's not only from Russia that heartening predictions come. Dr. Katherine Bain, at a meeting of the American Dietetical Association, said: "Knowledge of the facts of nutrition is changing so rapidly that one's imagination is unequal to coping with the future. But if only the present knowledge of nutrition is put to use in the generation yet unborn, that generation will be made up of healthy, well-nourished, intelligent, adaptable, well-adjusted individuals."

Unfortunately, Dr. Bain's "if" is a very serious one. Some ugly statistics indicate just how serious. The truth is that we are not using the resources of medicine. That's why between 45 to 50 per cent of the young men who reported for Army induction examinations had to be rejected. President Roosevelt said this record was "an indictment of America." General Lewis B. Hershey, director of the Selective Service System, characterized it as a "condition of which we, nationally, should be thoroughly ashamed."

It is true that since 1900 our annual death rate went down from fifteen per thousand to less than eleven per thousand. It is true that in that same time the average length of life of our population was extended from about forty-eight years to almost sixty-two years; but the percentage of rejections at Army physicals shows clearly that though we may be living longer, we have not been living too well. The list of our major and most common deficiencies includes bad eyes, decayed teeth, diseased tonsils, incipient tuberculosis, syphilis, flat feet, and malnutrition.

Here is an unusually graphic illustration of how bad things have been. Army standards in 1941 required a man to have at least six upper and six lower teeth which met—hardly too rigorous a test. Yet as many as one out of every five failed to meet even this limited requirement. The chairman of the American Medical Association's Economics Committee has estimated that if everybody over fifteen years of age had his teeth fixed, the total cost would be $3,860,000,-000. Another dental expert explained, "People spend $1,600,000,000 a year on tobacco . . . $200,000,000 more than they spend on all medical care, including surgery and dentistry."

Michael M. Davis, chairman of the Committee on Research in Medical Economics, has put it this way: "Only the American people themselves, individually or through organized action, can bring down the obstacles of ignorance and cost, and can supply the medical facilities that are absent or insufficient in some parts of the country."

The draining off of doctors by the armed forces didn't help any. Many a city and town was left inadequately equipped with medical service. In many cases the large increase of population brought about by war-job migration made the doctor shortage even more critical. We have just been plain lucky to come through the war period without national disaster on the health front. It is possible that the lack of doctors at home during the war will be felt several years after peace comes, when minor ailments that were perforce left untreated may develop into serious sickness.

On the credit side of the ledger, the war has brought about a new understanding of the problems of industrial health which may have real significance for the future. The establishment of hospitals in factories, for instance, has offered medical attention to many thousands who never before received proper care. In some cases the treatment has meant better health for a great number of people who would otherwise have suffered for the rest of their lives. For instance, many who came out of the hills of the South for war jobs were found to have hookworm, for which they were treated and cured.

In general, the factory hospitals have been well staffed and equipped. The emphasis has been as much on preventive medicine as on treatment after accidents or illnesses. At a factory in Cleveland eight cases of mumps were detected in one department. The medical staff went to work at once, and a potential epidemic was checked. In one city where the drinking water was contaminated by a flood, a large company administered anti-typhoid shots to thirty-five hundred employees. Not one worker came down with the disease. Similarly, frequent factory checkups and examinations help to nip in the bud such diseases as tuberculosis, syphilis, and occupational illnesses.

The work which some large companies have been doing in nutrition will also be reflected in postwar health. Many people have learned for the first time what a balanced diet really means. That knowledge will endure as a permanent guarantee of better health.

If this type of industrial health activity were to continue and expand in the years ahead, we would have an important ally in the fight to raise the national health level. Unfortunately, however, even under the pressures of wartime conditions, such industrial health plans have been the exception rather than the rule. After the war, when labor shortage no longer necessitates the fullest use of all available manpower, many companies may decide that the expense of a factory hospital is not warranted. Even if all these progressive companies continue their health policy, there is very little reason to suppose that any substantial number of other firms will follow suit. Widespread change in American medical practice will come only from public pressure, and not from the generosity or enlightened self-interest of a handful of industrial establishments.

But the profession is in for stormy days. The contrast between war and peace will stoke the fires that have been smoldering under the medical societies. So far the challenging developments have all been in the techniques, the talents, the instruments, the discoveries of medicine. There has been little change in the methods by which those benefits can be made available to the average civilian. For the Army it's been a different story. There was no fee to be paid by the South Pacific soldier to whom medicine gave not just one nose, but three of different colors, shades, and interchangeable to match the altered skin color in the various seasons. In war over 10 per cent of the American population will have gotten medical services without doctor's bills. The surgeon in an army base hospital has no schedule of fees, no overhead to meet, no economic standard to protect. But in 1946 he will have.

The economic difficulties involved in making the benefits of medicine available to you will not be as great as those in housing, refrigeration, and air conditioning. Income and cost, of course, are hurdles, but it is not too unusual for doctors to work without fee or for small compensation. The big difference, though, between medicine and other kinds of activity is the fact that innovations spread more quickly in the healing profession. New discoveries move rapidly into the clinics, the wards, the country doctors' offices. The speed with which up-to-date methods are disseminated among practitioners will even be increased. The war has taken the side-street and country doctors out of their little offices and brought them into close contact with the best in their science. Yes, the former ten-year gap between the medical discovery and its public use will be whittled down.

Yet cost will continue to be a problem affecting your health. Disease will not reel under the blows of medical progress as soon as you might hope. Before the war you could always stir up a hornets' nest of discussion by throwing the phrase "socialized medicine" into the controversial ring. Voices would be raised immediately to argue that the money, time, effort, and sheer dedication expended on medical training give a doctor the right to make as comfortable a living as his talents, skill, and popularity warrant. In reply would come the argument that medicine is in the nature of a public trust, a community responsibility not properly discharged when financial considerations stand between a sick person and the medical care he needs.

Even if compulsory health insurance comes, as is probable, the private practice of medicine will continue and the doctor will still be free in great part to determine his own fee structure. This, of course, would be contingent on the patients' willingness to pay. For those in the lower income brackets, medical service would be provided by private practitioners but at specific fee schedules. To the extent that such a fee schedule exists for some patients, the charges of independent doctors will undoubtedly be affected—just as a municipal power project serves as a yardstick to reduce the rates of the private utility.

Socialized medicine, involving government payment of medical fees, will yet come. But long before it does there will be a tremendous growth of group health insurance, all too often confused with socialized medicine.

By the winter of 1943 group hospital insurance could boast of thirteen million members, paying one hundred million dollars a year for protection against hospital costs. The impetus of wartime conditions jacked the membership up even further. During December 1943 fifty thousand people a week were joining, partly because of increased activity along these lines by business firms. At the start of 1944 over three hundred thousand companies were sponsoring, in one way or another, group hospital insurance for their employees.

Not quite so popular, but gaining momentum, are the companion group health plans which are designed to lift the weight of doctor's bills from the patient's shoulders. In some places, such as San Francisco, employees of the city and county are compelled by law to participate in a medical care plan. With both hospitalization and health insurance, the patient doesn't have to worry about finances—just the lice, mice, bugs, and bacteria. And Tovarich Bogomolets and Company are trying to lift even that burden from the human race.

But the road ahead isn't without its ruts. Although there is little, if any, opposition to the hospitalization plans, group health plans are encountering hostility. Nevertheless, they are here to stay. The last critical barrier was removed in January 1943, when the Supreme Court upheld the conviction of the American Medical Association and the District of Columbia Medical Society as trusts conspiring to obstruct the activities of a co-operative medical association. Significantly, the decision was unanimous.

There won't be such unanimity among members of the medical profession, but the direction of the future is unmistakable: group health plans will enlarge the area of medical service, provide better care for low-income groups, and present new opportunities for the profession. Within a generation the current debates will be considered odd, like the charges of "anarchy" and "socialism" once leveled at workmen's compensation.

In one curious way the war will affect professional attitudes toward group health. Hundreds of thousands of doctors who have entered the Army have lost their practices. When they come back to civilian medicine they will no longer have a vested interest in an existing group of patients. The returning medicos will be more likely to accept co-operative medicine, particularly in the large metropolitan centers where doctors have always concentrated in large numbers.

As for the extent of medical service over the country, no sharp change will be apparent after the war. The centralized Procurement and Assignment Service, set up to distribute America's doctors for military purposes, is unlikely to continue after the war, though a more equal allocation of medical personnel is a desperate necessity for the nation. During the war there were many charges that the PAS was doing much less than a successful job of proper distribution. The pressures working against a sound geographic distribution of our medical force in wartime will certainly operate more strongly in peacetime.

The controversy over group health plans pales into insignificance compared with the stormy opposition to "federalized" medicine. The fuse of this explosive issue will be the Wagner-Murray-Dingell Bill in Congress. Part of this new social-security bill—sometimes called the "American Beveridge Plan"—would provide for compulsory medical and hospital insurance for "all persons covered by the old-age and survivors' provisions of the Social Security Act, for their dependents, and for about fifteen million others now excluded from those provisions."

Under this program just about anyone who needed medical attention or hospitalization could get it without worrying about whether he could afford to be sick. Out of its social-security funds the gov-

ernment would pay three dollars to six dollars a day for as many
as thirty days a year toward hospital expenses, and if you had to stay
in a hospital longer, a lower allowance would continue for another
thirty days. People who suffer from chronic diseases and require
constant institutional care would receive one dollar and fifty cents
to three dollars a day.

There are several methods by which the doctor would be reim-
bursed. Among the arrangements suggested are the following: A
medical group in a given area would set fees for the treatment of
the various conditions; or there might be a flat per capita payment
spread over the list of patients covered by the particular group;
or doctors might work under a whole- or part-time salary arrangement.

The organization of this federalized medicine structure would
be under the administration of the Surgeon General of the United
States, assisted by a National Advisory Medical and Hospital
Council.

There are hot arguments on both sides. Many groups, both inside
and outside the profession, contend that physicians must be free
of control. They argue that federalized medicine would seriously
impede medical initiative, lead to unwarranted interference and
abuse by government bureaucracy. The National Physicians Committee is the leading spokesman for the opposition and has been
conducting a vigorous campaign with the co-operation of such
publishers as Frank Gannett and such interests as the United Cigar-
Whelan Stores Corporation. Dr. Morris Fishbein, editor of the
Journal of the American Medical Association, summarizes the ob-
jections of organized medicine when he says, "The American
Medical Association has accepted the principle of insurance against
. . . cost of sickness (and) has heartily approved the provision (by
government) for medical care of the indigent and the medically
needy . . . But use of federal funds for care of the indigent is
far different from . . . a federal mechanism involving the expenditure of four billion dollars annually, as proposed by the Wagner
bill."

The basic argument on the other side is simply that the right to
medical treatment should not depend on ability to pay for it. It is

interesting that the conservative New York *Herald Tribune* declared editorially that despite the flaws in the Wagner bill, the "spread the cost" principle is needed by the American middle class. The *Herald Tribune* urged that the medical profession's opposition to the Wagner bill would solve no problems, and suggested that doctors work out "some better program for attaining the same objective."

As in the case of private group health plans, compulsory federal insurance is inevitable, but only after a fight that will last many years. The long-time trend in medicine moves almost without deviation in the direction of greater social availability. The Public Health Services in the United States, for example, have, within the limits of their authority and appropriations, reached an increasing number of people. In 1943 the Public Health Services brought medical care to 511,023 patients, mostly in rural communities, an increase of 17 per cent over 1942.

In many ways medicine stands on the brink of the private-enterprise glacier. It is the first segment that is likely to break away or melt away quickly under the heat of the state. Enterprise will be in the saddle at war's end, but the war itself will already have done much to shake medicine loose from the hardier areas of the profit system. The dean of Columbia University's Medical School, Dr. Willard C. Rappleye, predicts important changes.

"It seems reasonable to assume," he says, "that the profound social and economic conditions that are likely to follow the war will necessitate significant changes in medical practice. The close relationships between income and sickness, both as cause and effect, suggest that the problem of medical care cannot be divorced from those of unemployment, old age, income, living conditions, and other features of social security.

"For large elements of society the problems of illness can be met only through collective provisions for medical care which aim to distribute the costs over a large group of the population and over a long period of time."

The opportunities for service and personal success in the medical profession will nevertheless be unlimited in the decades ahead. One important consequence of wartime living will be a greater public awareness of health and its problems. The educational campaigns conducted by government and industry, in the effort to reduce absenteeism, will bring the nation closer to the old Chinese idea of preventive medicine, of using doctors to keep people healthy rather than to cure them after they get sick.

In addition, the tasks of medicine will be greater. The strain of wartime living brought about a 6 per cent increase in tuberculosis in Great Britain, and Dr. Alexander Miller, of the New York Academy of Medicine, has pointed out the possibility of a similar increase after two or three years of war here. The wholesale migrations of large parts of the population, increased hours of work, and inadequate housing facilities may leave us for many years with a legacy of lowered resistance to disease.

Two factors make difficult the lot of the would-be recorder of medical progress. So much is being accomplished that no one chapter can tell the whole story, and the advance is so rapid that much that is said here may already be superseded by the time you read it.

The pattern of medical progress, though, emerges quite clearly. The first aim of modern medicine was the struggle against the individual's diseases. From this, medicine proceeded, in an ever-widening, organized struggle, to learn and fight the causes of diseases. Most recently the third stage of the profession's functioning has attained prominence—the conscious struggle for the prolongation of human life itself. The studies of Steinach, Schmidt, and Voronoff may have had very little success as yet. They do, however, clearly indicate the new aim: forward to Methuselah. Medicine may go further and accept Gershwin's challenge in *Porgy and Bess:* "But who calls that livin' when no gal will give in to no man what's nine hundred years?" The ultimate aim may well be not the mere prolongation of life but the prolongation of active life.

CHAPTER XIV

... and Madmen

IF ONLY the same rate of progress that we have made in dealing with the ailments of the body had been achieved in the treatment of the mind. If only penicillin could eat away at the shadow of the Oedipus, or sulfa hold in check the suicide compulsion while the will to live regains ascendancy. If only a metal pin could be driven through the fractured personality of the schizophrenic. If only the tedious months and the restless years on the psychiatrist's couch could be cut in half by war-taught knowledge. Then for many of the mentally anguished the price of war would be well paid.

But psychiatry and its treatment of the various mental ills enter the future with no such dramatic legacy. And the contrast is all the more pathetic when compared with the progress made in World War I.

Psychiatry became an accepted profession in World War I. There was psychiatry before then, of course. Freud had already given the world his revolutionary theories, and even before him substantial psychiatric research and discovery had already enriched medicine. The importance of mental health and personality was appreciated a long time before scientific psychiatric research was opened up. Most high-school students, in their required reading, unwittingly pass over the prophetic wisdom in Hawthorne's *The Scarlet Letter*, published in 1850:

So Roger Chillingworth—the man of skill, the kind and friendly physician—strove to go deep into his patient's bosom, delving among his principles, prying into his recollections, and probing everything with a cautious touch, like a treasure-seeker in a dark cavern. Few secrets escape an investigator, who has opportunity and license to undertake such a quest, and the skill to follow it up.

If the physician possesses native sagacity, and a nameless something more—let us call it intuition; if he show no intrusive egotism, nor disagreeably prominent characteristics of his own; if he have the power, which must be born with him, to bring his mind into such affinity with his patient's, that this last shall unawares have spoken what he imagines himself only to have thought; if such revelations be received without tumult, and acknowledged not so often by an uttered sympathy as by silence, an articulate breath, and here and there a word, to indicate that all is understood, if to these qualifications of a confidant be joined the advantages afforded by his recognized character as a physician—then, at some inevitable moment, will the soul of the sufferer be dissolved, and flow forth in a dark, but transparent stream, bringing all its mysteries into the daylight.

But it was not until World War I gave psychiatrists and psychologists the innumerable experimental situations, the literally hundreds of thousands of cases, that the infant science was able to grow with real vigor. Psychiatry's growth from a weak sister of the medical sciences to a full partner came none too soon. The figures on psychiatric cases between 1920 and 1940 show a rising graph of tragedy—admissions to mental hospitals growing steadily year after year. These increases do not necessarily mean that our society is breeding a greater incidence of insanity, though there is other evidence to support such a conclusion. Only in recent years have we been able to recognize mental ailments that formerly went unnoticed. Perhaps even more important, the old-fashioned stigma attached to insanity is beginning to disappear. Between the two wars we have learned that it is not always best to keep the family closet tightly sealed.

Interest in the healing power of psychiatry will grow because of World War II. Psychiatric screening before induction will have given almost twenty million men contact with a psychiatrist under the direct auspices of the United States Government. That will do much to dissipate the impression that the mental medico is a cross between Svengali and a hand-holding Park Avenue smoothie.

A significant indication of the serious need for psychiatric treatment is the official recognition of that need. The Office of War Information, in December 1943, reported: "In the last war the rate of admissions for neuropsychiatric diseases in Army hospitals averaged about thirty per thousand per year in the continental United States and slightly less than twenty per thousand per year in the AEF. . . . In this war the admission rate for neuropsychiatric diseases is about fifty per thousand men in the continental United States and slightly higher in some overseas theaters."

One out of every twenty found "normal" on induction develops sufficient psychiatric difficulty to require hospital attention.

Psychiatric screening at the induction centers will not be an unmixed blessing to its practitioners. Psychiatry will take a beating for the many unfit who have been permitted to slip into the Army. Some experts predict a sizable psychiatric problem for the country at war's end because not all of the unfit were kept out. The cost to the government will be substantial. Breakdown on military duty is a permanent social and financial liability of the Army or Navy. Unquestionably, much of the criticism will be justified and should improve the quality of psychiatric service in the event of a third World War. The screening hasn't been uniform; in examination centers it can hardly be said to have existed. There isn't enough psychiatric talent throughout the United States, nor is it always well trained. Urban centers may not necessarily have more dirt, accidents, or mental ills, but they do have more bathtubs, doctors, and psychiatrists. Where mental tests *are* given they are not always thorough, if only because of the pressure of waiting lines. A cursory psychiatric interview cannot do as well in discovering a repressed mental disorder as a quick aural examination in the case of a punctured eardrum. Psychiatry will have acquired, and in the years after the war will benefit from, the knowledge of how to look into the soul more quickly and accurately. But this is no substantial accomplishment. There doesn't appear to have been too much to learn in this direction before the war began. Looking in is easy. It's the reaching in and taking out that's hard.

The teapot tempest about the muddy and uneven results of the screening will tend to obscure the more substantial problems which concern the psychiatrists. They are worried, not about the small number of homosexuals who may have slipped into the Army, but about the larger number of mentally disturbed who had to be rejected. The big problem has been kept at home. One of the most disastrous effects of war is that it not only removes from the community the most desirable men but it thrusts the physical and mental leftovers back on the community. Wisely, the psychiatrist refrains from publicly emphasizing this fact. It would destroy the sympathy and understanding which the psychiatrist must use in his treatment. Privately he expresses his anxiety over the increasing proportion at home of weaklings, drunkards, irresponsibles, as well as mentally disturbed.

As a matter of fact, all of us at home are suspect. War is always a time of psychological dislocation. Many of us in normal times manage to maintain our mental equilibrium by only a narrow margin of balance. The upsets of wartime living can push us over the brink, some into insanity. Many times that number may not become psychiatric cases, but they present significant neurotic problems for the community in the days ahead.

Tomorrow's social heritage will flow from the inevitable effects of war. The fabric of ordinary social relations is easily ripped, values are turned upside down, traditional rules of conduct are discarded. Imminence of death, news of death, tensions, abnormal fears, indecision, hasty and ill-considered action, confusion, instability, result in many definite symptoms of social and personal unrest. The entire phenomenon of postwar escape is a problem that faces both the community and the psychiatrist in the years to come. The tremendous increase in juvenile delinquency—an increase breaking all social thermometers, jumping 50, 100, 200 per cent above past levels—is another danger signal for the future.

The psychiatrist is concerned, of course, about the procession of young girls—twelve- and thirteen-year-olds—passing through the police courts on prostitution charges. He is concerned, of course, about the gangs of youngsters, like the "Pachuco" kids, who run in packs, stealing, committing arson, cutting a swath through just about all the crimes in the statute books. But the psychiatrist is even more concerned about the portents for the future. Can these boys and girls who are juvenile delinquents primarily because their home lives have been disrupted by the war ever be brought back into the fold? Is there hope that a fourteen-year-old girl who has been soliciting, stealing, drinking, and smoking marijuana can ever become adjusted to the kind of life she might have lived if her mother and father had exerted normal parental discipline and authority?

The men returning from the battlefields will present similar challenges. It won't be easy for a pilot who has been living at a speed of four hundred miles an hour to return to the pedestrian tempo of Main Street. It won't be easy for many men who have learned to hate and to kill to take up ordinary civilian pursuits. For every lesson taught by our Army officers to "harden" their men for battle, we shall need a lesson to "soften" them for peace. Men who have killed others, men who have known the fear of being killed themselves, men who have seen their buddies ripped apart by bullets and shells, can't wipe these memories off the slate when the bells ring out an Armistice.

The thing that worries the psychiatrist is that in their effort to take up normal lives many of these men will try to repress their memories and their reactions. The psychiatrist knows that it is precisely in this direction that the danger of neurosis or psychosis lies. In short, in every area of our wartime activity, from the home front to the battle front, we have been sowing the seeds of what may prove to be an epidemic of mental disease that may burst out years after the war. The resilience and adjustability of the individual is remarkable. The comparative ease with which he can be made to meet the peculiar requirements of war illustrates this effectively. But he was trained, guided, and shaped to do so. Unfortunately the road back will be one of individual improvisation. Therein will the danger lie.

Psychiatry will have learned no new methods to cope with the increased number of cases. Fortunately the nature of the scars left on the mind by the military or civilian aspects of war hardly differs from the traditional mental difficulties encountered in peacetime. Fortunately, too, the world's psychiatrists have had another laboratory of immense size in which to re-evaluate, refine, and sharpen the existing tools. Although no spectacular discoveries have occurred or appear to be imminent, progress has been made in certain types of treatments. "Shell shock," for instance, is being handled more successfully in this war. Doctors were comparatively helpless in handling it during World War I, and there are still many wrecked men in hospitals all over the United States who are tragic examples of the seriousness of what the doctors of this war call "traumatic war neurosis." During World War I only a small percentage of such casualties was able to go back into the fighting lines.

The common practice then was to remove a shell-shocked man as soon as possible and as far as possible from the front. Now the practice has been reversed. If a soldier seems to be losing his grip, an Army psychiatrist talks to him. He is immediately disabused of any idea that he may be sent back of the lines for a rest. A typical case, reported in *Time* magazine, "was a technical sergeant who went berserk after the body of his commander, decapitated by a shell, fell in his lap. The sergeant shrieked, jumped out of the tank, ran wildly in circles, with shells falling around him. His comrades got him back into the tank and to a first-aid station." After only three days of treatment by a psychiatrist he was able to rejoin his unit.

The proof of the treatment: In the African campaign, when the Medical Corps was still treating shell shock with hospitalization, long rest, etc., only 2 per cent of the patients recovered sufficiently to get back in the fight. With the new method, 60 per cent of the men are returned to active duty, and a substantial number of the remaining 40 per cent are made fit enough to be used for duty behind the lines.

As in many branches of science, little more was involved here than the experimental rediscovery of a traditional truth. Fear is frequently conquered by subjecting the victim as soon as possible to the force that produced it.

Unfortunately there is no backlog of development antedating the war that promises sensational results in the years ahead. On some levels of research into mental ailments there have been advances. Shock therapy, for instance, is better understood and is being more widely used. In the period from 1935 up to America's entry into the war some seventy-five thousand mental patients received such treatment with considerable success. The various techniques of shock therapy, such as use of insulin, metrazol, cardiazol, and electric shock, have yielded heartening results, though still considered by some psychiatrists of doubtful value. In the first place, the doctor is not ready to minimize the dangers involved in the fact that the shock treatments operate by causing violent convulsions. Psychoanalysts, in particular, caution that while the shock may "seem to cure" in some few cases, they cannot be sure that it doesn't leave a deep residue of potential danger in the subconscious. Secondly, the cases that yield are, at least thus far, both limited and selected.

Psychiatry, like other branches of medicine, has found it wise to review discarded methods. The therapeutic values of Mesmer's manipulations are being resurveyed and reapplied. Hypnosis and hypnotic techniques, which dominated the study of the mind even before Freud, are proving useful.

The greatest advance in the future is not likely to be in the quality of psychiatric service but rather in the extent to which it is used. Unfortunately, both the expense and the tedium of thorough psychoanalysis are likely to continue high for many years. A near minimum cost of $1000 a year for one, two, or three years will be an insuperable barrier for many. For those who can afford to jump the financial hurdle, the three, four, or five hours a week involved may be a major deterrent. Yet the benefits of mental medicine will inevitably come within reach of an ever-increasing portion of the population. The trend has already started with the wider use of psychologists and psychiatrists in schools, clinics, welfare agencies, child bureaus, and courts. It will undoubtedly quicken after the war.

The most important single key to the future of psychiatry lies in the fact that in the five years preceding the war the subject was given an increasingly prominent position in the curriculum of almost every important medical school. The days when a doctor had a smattering of ignorance in the field of mental ills are pretty well over. Nowadays almost every young M.D. comes out of school with a general background in psychiatry and its problems, and the opportunities for specialized studies in this field have increased immeasurably within the short span of a decade. There has been some progress.

Yet the vast majority of Americans who need treatment will remain untouched, until the bridge of time can be crossed and mental peace can be achieved with something approximating the speed of the dentist or physician. "What's the chance of hurrying it up?" is probably the most common question asked of psychiatrists. There is a slight chance, but it's little more than that.

The faint breach in a long and otherwise unbroken horizon is the possibility that psychiatry, coupled with biochemistry, may yet produce the key to a more rapid alteration or adjustment of personality. Research along these lines starts with the fact that the average individual's personality changes after the consumption of some hard liquor. A purely chemical effect is produced, a genuine psychic change for a short period of time. Will the exploration of the chemical effects on personality yet yield the formulae that will alter an individual's usual behavior? Will the laboratory technician be able to insulate the child against the trauma which in some cases initiates the growth of neuroses? The scientist knows that the same influences will affect two children differently. He's able partially to pattern the physical reasons and partially to alter them. The exact course of the mental pattern and its intensity are not predictable. When neurotic deviations occur they are at present susceptible to effective treatment only through almost purely intellectual processes. Psycho-biochemical discoveries will be important to the more than half million mentally sick now in institutions throughout the United States. For the nation the benefits of such research will be even more significant because of the health they would bring to the millions who are sane and capable but suffer distortions of personality. Chemistry may yet lift the veil on the manifold mysteries that becloud the mind. But it hasn't yet.

Dr. Edward Strecker reports his experience with a patient, a young woman, who was left with a serious emotional conflict after a disastrous love affair. Included in her many symptoms was a great inability to reach decisions and cope with the problems that confronted her. "A moderate dose of benzedrine sulphate masks the symptoms, and for a few hours there is a resumption of former decision and capacity to manage her problems satisfactorily." In another case a young female schizophrenic heard voices and "felt" them over the skin surface of her entire body. The young lady was subjected to a severe course of metrazol therapy. On conclusion of the chemical treatment she readily and voluntarily stated that the voices she heard were imaginary and demonstrated other indications, though by no means complete, of an ability to accept reality.

Unfortunately, in such cases, and there are many, the "exactly how" and "why" of the responses to the various chemical substances is not clearly understood. Almost as important is the fact that those are selected cases. Even there the results are not startling nor more than temporary. When the answers and methods are found, really fundamental changes in the behavior of the individual may be accomplished. And for this it would not be too long to wait the rest of your life.

But one group of potential patients seems to be eluding the therapy of mental medicine. The unsuccessful chase will probably continue for generations beyond ours. Psychiatry will have learned increasingly how to heal and comfort the sick, but it is with one type of madman that it will have its most difficult challenge. When Dr. Strecker was a young physician in a mental hospital he was given to simple questions such as, "What is sanity?" He tells how his superintendent patiently explained that sanity was the capacity for being dextrous in the matter of keeping out of insane asylums. The madmen with whom we are here concerned are those who have been extremely dextrous—the crowd-men, the mob. It is of them that Ortega y Gasset warned, "If that human type, the mass-man, continues to be master in Europe, thirty years will suffice to send our continent back to barbarism."

Dr. Edward Strecker's *Beyond Clinical Frontiers*, a study of the challenge presented to psychiatry by the crowd-man, is a brilliant summation of an overshadowing phenomenon that beclouds much of the future.

Dr. Strecker's measure of the mob-man provides an invaluable guide with which to gauge the ebb and flow of human conduct in the years ahead. "The mass-man of our day is a combination of Neanderthal man and robot, seemingly differing from the former in that there is little, if any, promise of evolution; from the latter in that he has learned to gather en masse and use the impact of violence. The crowd-man need not be observed in mobs. There are many facets to the crowd-man, and some of them may be examined in a single specimen: 'He is happy to feel as one with everybody else.' He is not only commonplace, but he makes a gospel of being commonplace. Although the crowd-man en masse has the enormous physical stature of a brute, yet he has only the mind of a child."

The psychiatrist is aware of the *individual's* retreat from reality in the search for succor, and he knows what to do about it. But he stands helpless before a *mass* retreat from reality. Profound books are written calling one group "paranoiac," a nation "schizophrenic," an organization "deluded." But the techniques of science are helpless to prevent or change the devastating flow of such mass action. Nietzsche warned of the "flood tide of Nihilism rising." He caustically described the mob as "a Procrustean bed on which every spiritual superiority may be lopped off to the common measure and every little ego consciousness may be stretched to the stature of full manhood." Philosophers before and after him moaned and groaned, but the mob advanced anyway.

The mob will dominate substantial sections of the generation after war. The essential purpose of these men who feed their madness by assembling in groups will be a flight from difficulty, pressure, and reality. The retreats and escapes take many forms. Most basic will be the effort to win a sense of security, to dissipate the clouds of confusion, by the artificial assurance and comfort gained from group association. The insecurities and frustrations will be hidden by the pomp and pretense of the various little knots of men parading their collective strength. The individual inferiority will be camouflaged by the many little wars against other "inferior" people.

War and depression spawn the crowd-men and their elaborately organized attempts to escape the real problems which confront them. Modern propaganda owes its success not to the ingenuity of the fabricator but to the susceptibility of the recipient. If there are large groups who need "answers," the inventor of the simple tall story that explains everything has a ready audience. Particularly in the years immediately after the war there will be an abundant variety of "answers." The panaceas, the recriminations and proofs, the programs and prejudices, will dwarf "thirty dollars every Thursday," "every man a king," "the money-changers" of yester-year. Once more the rest of your life runs into the inevitable consequences of the fact that the war will have solved few problems and complicated most. Every group manifestation of escape already in existence before Hitler crossed the Polish border will be magnified by the added pressure on unresisting minds that the war will have released.

Some will march backward with an anxiety born of nostalgia and find the door closed. Some will march forward with neither road map nor signpost only to have the door slammed in their faces. Some will seek to sit where they now stand and find that the chair has been removed.

Nor will all of the marching and massing and association be limited to economic questions or confined to specific social levels. The inability to accept reality and the need to escape it cross all lines. You can see it on the street corner, at a lynching bee, and in the parlor car. As the pressure from outside increases on each of the groups, cohesiveness grows from within, and the clash of irresistible force and immovable object ultimately produces disaster. The riot, the plot, the group hatred, the hanging are varying expressions of these madmen beyond clinical reach. The diagnosis "mad" becomes incontrovertible with the outbreak of violence.

The range of narcissistic, self-pitying, problem-escaping, navel-gazing groups is once again best caught in the words of Strecker. "From one perspective, some of the groups that gather in clubs and drawing rooms are not unlike the massing of the clans for a lynching bee. Both are disregarding the realities of life. The one ignores the plain fact that the economic and social setup has changed and it is inevitable that it will be changed more. The other refuses to believe that chaotic conditions no longer exist and flagrantly sets aside law and order, which are the safeguards upon which every member of the lynching mob depends for his own security."

Many of the forces which produce both the unity of the mob and the pressures creating it have ironically been provided by the refinements of our civilization. The plane has been hailed as an instrument that will bring the world together. It may just as likely spread the bacteria and insanities of the world more rapidly. The newspaper, the motion picture, the radio are instruments which speed ideas. The ideas may represent approaches to problems or methods of escape from them.

All ages of man have been crowd-minded—survival has, in fact, depended on it. But psychiatrists are certain that this age, more than others, is dominated by the mass reaction. Students of the problem throw out the gloomy warning that the trend is so great and so powerful that unless some unanticipated compulsion forces us to face the problems of the world and reorient ourselves to reality, there will be very few people beyond the influence of the crowd.

The war will have made the realities of your everyday life less bearable. It will have worn thin your nerves, weakened the social fabric that has rooted and sustained you, presented you with a vast cost, material and spiritual; meanwhile, technology will have sharpened the mechanisms and the devices by which you can run away.

Physical medicine has long ago marched beyond the treatment of the individual, the relief of existing illness. Preventive medicine has already shrunk the shadow of smallpox, typhoid, tuberculosis, and the multitude of plagues that you're never likely to experience. But psychiatry has found no way to spread oil over the swamp and kill the infection known to exist and threatening to spread. Yes, the mice and the lice are retreating. Life is winning; the hand of death seems to be losing its cunning. But in the distance is the unmistakable rumble of the approaching mob. Science, which has been conquering the invisible germ, stands impotent before the forces it can merely identify and catalog. In the hour of urgency for the forces of sanity and courage, the forces of fear and insecurity and the will to retreat will assert themselves with a new strength born of desperation.

It's a long bloody road from cave man to mob-man. Perhaps the great historic irony of the future is that, in the tug of war with reality, the people will yet be called on to protect themselves against the people. What will be the proportionate strength as between awareness and escape, between reality and retreat? Who will be the victor in the war of intellect with violence?

V. F. Calverton anticipated this struggle for the mastery of to-morrow when he wrote:

The hope of the race, as you can readily see, is dependent more upon psychological factors than physical. The tragedy of the world today is psychological and not physical. What man, by virtue of his mind, has done to the physical world is phenomenal. Machinery alone represents a form of control over the outside world that is far more miraculous than any of the fictitious miracles recorded in the Bible and the Koran by the ecclesiastical gossips of ancient days. The trouble is that man has been so successful in controlling the outside world that he has almost come to believe that that is the only thing he needs or can control. As a result he has lost all sight of *the man inside* whose mind alone made all those things possible. . . . Already, however, his mind is creating things, in the form of machinery, that he is rapidly losing his ability to control. At the very time that he creates new antitoxins to save people's lives, he invents new and more deadly instruments to destroy their lives. His mind today is, in consequence, at the breaking point. . . .

Not until man learns to control *the man inside* will he be able to control *the man outside*.

Calverton concluded that all the world needs "is another World War for it to go mad as a whole instead of just going mad in parts as it is doing now in the case of separate individuals." That was 1936. The world has had that war. The validity of the prophecy will be in your hands—and in your minds!

CHAPTER XV

The Real Enemy

AMERICA WANTS PEACE. Nothing fancy or special, nothing new or modern, no dressings, trimmings, wrinkles, or gingerbread—just peace. This is the fundamental attitude of millions. Along with it, each little group has its own demands on the future.

Deep down, you want to be let alone. You'd like not to be bothered by wars and enemies, unemployment and international currency, labor or capital, inflation or ration points, OPA, WPB, FEPC, WMC, or FDR. You want to sleep late one morning.

Amy Greif had you in mind when she wrote this ditty for the *Saturday Evening Post*:

> *Professor A. wants a postwar world*
> *Where "nations will be polite,"*
>
> *Architect B. wants a postwar world*
> *Where "buildings attain new height,"*
>
> *Doctor C. wants a postwar world*
> *Where "knowledge has conquered disease,"*
>
> *Diplomat D. wants a postwar world*
> *Where "everyone aims to please,"*
>
> *Senator X. wants a postwar world*
> *Where "Labor and Capital kiss,"*
>
> *Minister Y. wants a postwar world*
> *Where "nothing will go amiss,"*

Lecturer Z. wants a postwar world
Where "battle banners are furled."

THEY MAKE ME SICK!

*WHAT I WANT—QUICK * * **

IS SIMPLY A POSTWAR WORLD!!!

Here's one aspiration on which G.I. Joe and his civilian brother agree. Buried under it is a hope and a conflict. The *clash* has already been mentioned a number of times—it comes from the gap between attitude and action. The more you want to be let alone and the less *your* action makes it possible, the greater will be your frustration and your agony. The more intense your desire to be left at peace, the more exaggerated will be your concomitant action that leaves no one at peace.

The *hope* is that things will take care of themselves. The normal tendency is not to stir ourselves any more than necessary, to trust that somehow or other problems will solve themselves. With considerable pain we established our rapport with the present and the past. But the future is always more disturbing because it implies new adjustments, unanticipated change. The future always demands some stirring or movement.

At no time is this hope more acute than when we are tired. If only the telephone wouldn't ring; if we could bolt the front door and pretend we're not in!

Psychiatrists insist there is only a certain amount of grim fact that the mind can take, or at least is willing to take without real compulsion. "No one need face the unrelieved actualities of his surroundings. Indeed it is doubtful if anyone could face them, even if he so desired." The truth will make you free? It may make you mad. Perhaps that explains why periods of greatest difficulty are marked by the most exaggerated and anxiously sought methods of escape. All groups, all levels of intelligence are affected, though differently.

An important European diplomat recently came to this country on a brief confidential trip. His object was to learn the American outlook on the world after war. At a private dinner he met the most astute journalists, educators, political leaders, industrialists, international lawyers, and a representative of one of the world's most influential banking houses. Some rather unpleasant probabilities were suggested around that dinner table. The most fervent protest came from the sophisticated international banker. "Surely we must have learned. It just can't happen!" And he meant it. Will he be able to face it if it does? Or will the desperation with which he clings to pure hope shatter him on the reefs of actuality?

Sociologists use the label "cultural lag" to describe this gap between reality and its acceptance. It's a shame the gap was not labeled more strikingly. It's the basic key to the period immediately after the war and an important determinant for the years beyond. In many respects the most dangerous problem America will face after the defeat of her enemies will be her inability to anticipate, accept, and act on the realities that will then exist.

Along with the reliance on hope, the trust in luck, will come a revival of old aspirations and attitudes. It will be a sort of going home to old principles. Many fight for old things and old habits.

The slogans that appealed to us in former years will gain new vigor. We fight to preserve our way of life. The traditional philosophy of the independent spirit of America, of free enterprise, self-reliance, and political self-determination will be expressed with new intensity.

The National Association of Manufacturers and the United States Chamber of Commerce are not alone in championing the role and promise of free enterprise. Such doughty warriors of reform as Vice-President Wallace and Stuart Chase drop their despair and put their money on expanding private competitive business. Predictions that postwar America will be the scene of ever-greater production by individual enterprise and ever-greater capitalistic opportunity are uttered by labor-union officials, by scientific and professional groups, and by almost every publication in the country, regardless of its old subscribers and previous condition of servitude to the Left.

Marxism will be at its lowest ebb in America at the end of World War II. The Young Communist League was shrewd to hole in under a new name, anticipating the ringing endorsement of the profit system by its parent Communist party. The theme songs of capitalism ring out in the halls where the "Internationale" once was heard.

The nation as a whole will make an enormous effort to forget or repudiate recent history. We will go back to what we call the "pioneer spirit," but not to the economic and social conditions which once created it. When that environment passed, the pioneer reality went with it to the heaven of outmoded aspirations. Such an effort could be successful only if the characteristics of the period after the war were in tune with the attitudes. But if the economic and political complexities of tomorrow do not dovetail with rugged and traditional American individualism, then individualism is in for a beating. It will be uncomfortable, frustrating, and dangerous—like the paratrooper jumping from the plane only to discover he left his chute behind.

There's a word that covers the inevitable and historic reaction to war—escape. The nature of our participation in World War II will magnify that historic aftermath. World War II caught us before our cynicism about World War I had worn itself out. Pearl Harbor found America still saying it couldn't happen, it shouldn't happen, it needn't happen. When the impossible, the undesirable, the unnecessary does happen, the ensuing embarrassment produces very uncomfortable results. When unreality kicks back on us we do not become disciples of reality but look for new illusions to give us comfort. More than ever scapegoats must be found to carry the responsibility. We have no other alternative; to admit we were wrong in the first place is to exhibit a human strength rarely present, particularly after catastrophe.

The war will have given this country an enormous shaking-up. Few aspects of American life will emerge untouched. Few of the relationships between people and between groups will remain unaltered. Methods of production, the birth rate, the geographic distribution of the nation's population, the strength and influence of government—all these will have been caught up and whirled around in the cyclone.

But your attitudes will not have changed greatly; your conduct, yes, but not your attitudes. This has been a total war technologically, but not psychologically, not in the minds of the people of the United States. We will not have suffered shock or the prolonged pain from which escape is impossible.

It takes a stunning blow or prolonged suffering. But America will have suffered no such experience. American cities will not have been bombed. American homes and children were safe. We didn't even experience the shock of strong belief in a virtuous cause. Less than in World War I did America fight for a positive aim. In many minds this was no war *for something*. It was a war *against somebody*—and part of the time we argued over who that somebody was. Victory was the one chance we had to solve the problems from which the war originated. But even those who saw that will find it difficult to face the problems still waiting for solution. Resentment against the inconclusiveness of war (inconclusive except in the strictly military sense) is unavoidable.

When the war is finally won, tradition will seem the safest haven in the uncertainties around us. Traditional attitudes will be strengthened: they must have been good, since we won the war with them. More important, though, they had better be good because we're used to them.

It's ironic that only defeated nations look forward. This is one of the few principles that run like a consistent thread through human history. John Stuart Mill said it a long time ago: "Nothing is more certain than that improvement in human affairs is wholly the work of the uncontented characters."

Our pride in the achievement of victory will make us look back. So it was with the Allied military chiefs after World War I who clung to the traditions of nineteenth-century warfare which had proved successful. Security could best be assured by putting the clock back, or at any rate by keeping the hands from moving. General Billy Mitchell learned the futility of bucking the victor psychology when he pointed his finger to the sky as a major theater of twentieth-century warfare.

Politically, too, a change in attitude was shown only by the dissatisfied or defeated powers. The attraction of Bolshevism, Fascism, and National Socialism lay not in their obscure, elastic, and frequently incoherent doctrines, but in the fact that they seemed to offer something new, a "wave of the future." The past is no prize to the vanquished; it didn't pay off. Revolution is for the conquered, nostalgia for the conqueror.

The tenacity with which we focus on the past was illustrated in the interim between the World Wars by the economic watchwords that began with the prefix *re*. Successively we were concerned with *re*construction, *re*trenchment, *re*parations, *re*payment of war debts, *re*valuation of currency, *re*storation of the gold standard, and *re*covery.

*Re*peace will be so nice! And the only obstacles to our insistent demand for a return to the old will be the facts themselves.

So the first basic aspect of your mental life at war's end will be your thinking back. You can expect a wave of motion-picture epics once again dealing with yesteryear—the empire-building, the laying of the railroads, the gold rush. *Cimarron* may be dusted off and refurbished for your pleasure. New versions of the old spectacles— *The King of Kings, The Ten Commandments*—with 17,000 characters, filmed in technicolor, and recorded for fantasound by 94 cameras, supported by an orchestra of 430 pieces conducted by Stokowski sitting on Toscanini's shoulders.

Our aspirations will be those of an America eager to relive the age of expanding frontiers. But that frontier frame of mind will have no home in the changed economic structure of America's industrial society. The ideal of the self-made man with a self-contained enterprise functioning in full freedom will hit head on against the wall of an industrial community that doesn't fit those aspirations.

A man standing beside an assembly line doing a one-operation job is out of harmony with his environment if in his daydreams he's chasing Indians across the Kansas plains. If he either daydreams too much or begins to reject the notion that he's standing at an assembly line, that fellow's in trouble. He's suffering from mental heartburn. So, by and large, will the nation. We'll worship the covered wagon and forget that we're paying dues to the American Automobile Association.

But the difficulty will be further complicated. Not only will unrealizable aspirations clash with the tough realities, but aspiration will clash with aspiration—all in the same man. He will want the ideals of a pioneer life—freedom, opportunity, competition, and enterprise; he will also want the more recently acquired ideals —peace, order, and security. These last he picked up since the homesteading days. And both sets of aims will have been made more desirable by the experiences of war.

But the conflict between security and freedom is not easily resolved. Among the major obstacles which the radicals have failed to overcome is the need for harmonizing the economic security provided by the state with your individual liberty.

The encroachment of security on freedom occurs not only in the citizen's relation with the state but in every social group organized to protect individual security. Man has not yet learned how to safeguard his liberty against the instruments of his own making. We see it in the trade associations, passing resolutions in favor of free competitive enterprise and then fixing a fair price which only "a chiseler" would break. The worker joins his union to protect himself against the boss. The farmer joins his grange or league to buttress his position against the middleman or the railroads. The oboe player combines with other oboe players to block the manufacture of a machine that can turn out sounds just like those made by an oboe. The giant corporation, chilled by the hostility of the world and its ruthless competition, joins with three other giant corporations so that no two of them will be at the same place with the same merchandise at the same time. After all, it's friendlier that way, and so much more secure. The state joins with other states and the statesmen lay their guns on the green table and pledge each other inviolable security, bolstered by covenants written in indelible ink on vanishing paper. And all the individuals in the group spend half their time chafing under the rules, the bylaws, the constitution, and the covenant.

The importance of the contradictions is not in what you think. After all, who cares what you think? The contradictions are serious only when your thoughts are so incompatible with your surroundings that they may lead you to do violence to yourself or your neighbor. Why else would we lock up a poor fellow just because he thinks he's Napoleon?

Trapped by the inconsistencies of belief and fact, you will seek escape. You will contrive a rope ladder to flee from the painful prison. It will be woven of many threads—not all of the same strength or texture, nor all of colors that blend. Only after you've left the window you may discover that your improvisation can't carry your weight or doesn't reach to the ground.

Not all will be torn by the contradictions and the desire to escape from war, disillusion, cynicism, guilty conscience, frustration, boredom, unreason, spiritual emptiness. Nor will those things be present in each of us in the same proportion. But they will be so much in evidence in the nation at large as to alter the course of its history, to encumber its adjustments to new situations, and to threaten it with otherwise unnecessary confusion, dislocation, even violence.

Such is the inventory of new nervous responses or the responses that have been given added sharpness by the events peculiar to this day. Among the earliest to crop out will be the sense of guilt—if for no other reason than that the world after war will not look much prettier than the old one for which so many lives were spent. The guilt will have been magnified by the many promises we made to ourselves and to each other.

Every patriotic program consists of two parts: the appeal to destroy the enemy and the assurance that in the process many things will be "preserved." Some of the things that were to be "preserved" weren't with us in very sharp focus before. The freedoms America hoped to extend to the world were in some cases neglected at home. Not every soldier left the blueberry pie and ivy-covered cottage of the advertisements, and the simple fact of war and victory won't make them available on his return. The slum you pass on the way to work will still be there in 1947, only you'll feel a little differently about it. In a generous moment you promised yourself it wouldn't be; perhaps that time you drove by and saw the star-studded service flag strung between the tenements. . . .

Nor will the guilt be lessened by the accident of geography that brought civilian America unscathed through war. Even our wealth in resources and industrial capacity, which provided victory and a high standard of living at the same time, will hurt conscience.

It isn't right for you not to have suffered—and you will suffer plenty as a consequence.

Another of the mental currents that will flow more quickly was with us before the war and will be enormously heightened by the war. Boredom is one of the great problems of today. Technology has yet to provide an adequate antidote to the ailment it spreads. The technological impetus of war brought disinterest in increased doses. The split operation of quickly trained and diluted skills at the wartime assembly line left the worker with no appreciation of the job next to his, no perspective as to his own function, and little identification with the entire process. Detachment is deadly.

The radio and movies are only partial answers. Television will be another. Yet boredom will persist. Mechanical ennui has been best described in a movie. Do you remember the memorable scene in *Modern Times* when Charlie Chaplin, with a wrench in each hand, simultaneously tightened two protruding bolts over and over again? Chaplin caught the temper of the machine. Boredom was one of the causes of absenteeism for which no answer was found in wartime. It will be more serious when there's no longer the psychic lift that war itself gives. It will be more dangerous because the human being will look for something, anything, to fill the void.

Retreat in many forms will dominate the mental motion of the years after war. There'll be no logic to it. It will be retreat from war, from the problems which preceded and produced war and the problems which will follow war. In addition to being a retreat from self it will be a retreat from organized government.

Government has intervened in the lives of Americans for so long a stretch now, and in such unpalatable forms during war, that many will pretend to themselves that things would go a lot smoother if there were no government.

Since the effort to escape is futile, retreat from reality often brings us into the arms of a more virulent reality. A retreat from governmental intervention may prove to be a retreat into full governmental domination, into a completely predigested way of life. There is good reason to fear this outcome. Government has an unavoidable role to perform in a community; it is a reality which cannot be escaped. Denial of that reality by itself multiplies the problems which, with each day's delay, compel more aggressive action by government. The effort to shake off government is often a symptom of individual or group insecurity, conditions which make the victim an easy customer for the cure-all. The complete remedy frequently turns out to be complete government—a government which governs more. The search of the discontented in modern society for an environment compatible with full individualism may land them within the walls of the most oppressive control.

People within government will be no more immune to the government antipathy than their critics. One industrialist, unembarrassed by his own prominence in government activity, recently lashed out at the "meddlesome mediocrities whom we have permitted to guide our affairs." In the course of his remarks he gave an excellent illustration of the typical rebellion against supervision and restraint on enterprise. He told of the fifteen-year-old Vermont boy who was asked how much he would charge to cut the lawn. The young Yankee replied: "Thirty-five cents if I do it my way. Forty cents if I'm bossed."

Private business will enter the postwar period with its greatest mass support in almost a generation—a backing enlarged by the public antipathy to government. But that fact is not without its portent of strife—strident, acute, unavoidable struggle. The enthusiasm with which people talk of free enterprise when they mean private enterprise will lead to embarrassing disappointments. If business is no more competitive after the war, if monopoly doesn't diminish in strength, if small business has fewer opportunities, if the trend toward the concentration of wealth goes on, then free enterprise is not so free, and many will feel that the team's been wearing the wrong jerseys.

Enterprise will be so largely unopposed that the responsibility for meeting the problems of the nation will rest much more squarely on its own shoulders than would have been strictly necessary. Having assumed the burden, enterprise must harmonize the conflicts, be all things to all men, create both the frontier and security, provide employment without government. If it doesn't, someone's going to be mad. Having permitted the impression that government activity and private enterprise are incompatible, that Uncle Sam's heavy hand impedes industry and employment, business will have to carry the load that might otherwise have been palmed off on government. And if it drops the package, folks will blame enterprise and find a new whipping boy to replace the bureaucrats.

The contest between business and government has worried many observers who are concerned about the implications for the future. C. Hartley Grattan, in a study of "What the Businessman Thinks," had this to say:

As a rule business spokesmen fail to take a rational view of the scope of government activities. This inspires disquiet in many quarters not necessarily hostile to business. Business is, in this country, a system of power of major importance, but by its very nature it is incapable of meeting the needs of the American people as the sole system of power. Government is also a system of power, but there are very good reasons for opposing any movement to make it solely responsible for all the needs of the people. If either of these two major powers on the American scene appears to want to destroy the other by plan, then the neutral citizen has genuine cause for alarm.

A number of those a good deal closer to the business scene are even more disturbed. Charles E. Wilson, former president of General Electric and executive vice-chairman of the War Production Board, used language a lot less temperate than Grattan's in addressing a meeting of the National Association of Manufacturers: "I don't want to be an alarmist, but I tell you frankly that I am deeply alarmed today over the possibility that a right-wing reaction may draw some sections of capital so far away from our traditions as to imperil the entire structure of American life as we know it."

Even if they wanted to, they couldn't draw it away if there weren't a substantial section of the American public already amenable. The attitude of a Grattan or a Wilson is by no means universally shared by others in and out of the business community. But those who disagree with them express equal concern about the future. Former Congressman Samuel Pettengill, now a widely quoted critic of government in business circles, says:

Two facts stand out. The American system is being torn down and national socialism erected in its place. The second fact is this. The job is not being done in the open, but largely in the dark.

At one end of the stage we have the smoke screen of war; at the other, the public's gaze is diverted by tossing into the air the bright balls of moonshine prosperity. In the middle, cunning men are at work.

Consider, as one device among many, the government corporation. An ingenious tool. We have some fifty-one such corporations—as much a Chinese maze as the public-utility empires.

Talk about the spider webs of Wall Street. They are puny compared with this Darkest Africa of Federal Finance.

In the staid *Saturday Review of Literature*, David L. Cohn, a sincere advocate of enterprise, satirized the more extreme position taken by some businessmen by putting this speech in the mouth of a fictitious J. Wilbur Snavely, sales engineer of the Aseptic Feather Pillow Manufacturing Company:

After we've sent every yellow-bellied Jap to kingdom come and our boys return to their jobs and loving families, this country will be run by sound men along sound economic lines employing the basic fundamentals that have never failed us and the common sense of our forefathers, like the time, for example, when they wrested Manhattan Island, where the great city of New York now stands in her commercial majesty, from the Indians for twenty-four dollars. That's what made us a great nation and that's how we ran it from the days of George Washington until we turned it over to a lot of socialists with foreign ideas that are opposed to the American Way. You know the men I mean. (Laughter.) But now we're fighting for the American Way again and for Free Enterprise, the system that made us what we were in 1929, when we reached the highest pinnacle of prosperity ever known to man, and where we would be today if we had not listened to a lot of lunatics and communists but had let the law of supply and demand operate like God intended it to, because, as that great man President Coolidge told the country, "When men are out of work, unemployment results!"

The conflict that is growing between this concept of free enterprise and the role of government is not exaggerated in Cohn's piece. Dr. Alfred P. Haake, managing director of the National Association of Furniture Manufacturers, approaching the same subject in an address before a group of lumber manufacturers, made the following comment: "You ought to make about a million dog-

houses—and then I would like to take those doghouses and merchandise them, and with each doghouse furnish without charge a
full-grown, live bureaucrat. If we got about a million of those boys
out of Washington the rest of them would have room to work and
get something done."

Not only the average businessman, but the community at large,
wants: free competition, the free operation of the law of supply
and demand, the destruction of monopoly, opportunity for the
small businessman, high employment provided by business undomi-
nated by government. But the prospects, as we have seen in preceding chapters, fit almost none of these concepts.

Business is far from unanimous in echoing either David Cohn's
satiric conception or Dr. Haake's real one. The dissenting forces,
however prominently placed, are not representative. It will be some
time before they are heeded. Take the words, for example, of Eric
Johnston, president of the United States Chamber of Commerce:
"We must understand that the rank and file of people might be
willing to relinquish freedom and the democratic form of government if that is the only way to obtain security." A similar approach
is the intensive research activity of the Committee for Economic
Development, in an effort to solve the complex economic problems
of tomorrow by a method other than harangue. Unfortunately the
period ahead will not place a premium on temperance and ob-
jectivity. Without them the intricate, balanced solutions of intricate, interrelated problems cannot be achieved. Without them we
cannot reconcile security and freedom.

The conflict was summed up by Wendell Willkie when he
warned the farmer that "the urge—the temptation—is to go back
to a completely free and independent economy where all relationships with the government are abandoned. A bright and rosy dream,
that is; too bright and rosy to be true. Don't be suckers for the
good-old-days theory that it no longer is necessary to depend on
supported prices, soil conservation plans and federal guarantees
of stable market conditions . . . If we could go back to the good
old days we'd find when we got back there we'd have ten-cent corn
and twenty-cent wheat . . . Let's leave that dream for the little
crew of reactionaries whose longing for the good old days is a sort

of childish homesickness." But the will to go back will not be denied, nor the demand at the same time for two-dollar wheat and dollar-fifty corn—freedom *and* security.

In 1941 a survey was taken in a London working-class district to determine what people considered most necessary for their own happiness. Here are the results as published in *Mass Observation:*

Security	129	
Knowledge	118	
Religion	104	(personal or organized)
Humor	80	
Equality	79	
Beauty	34	
Action	23	
Pleasure	10	
Leadership	8	
Politics	2	

An American poll on the expansion of social security showed that 76 per cent approved a plan under which "the government would pay higher social-security payments to everybody, young or old, who is in want because of unemployment or illness or disability after the war."

Yet those who emphasize the importance of their financial security frequently show how little they understand themselves. For there are other securities that are at least equally important: the security that comes from having a place in the community, the security that comes from being in tune with the times, the security that comes from having a faith that sustains, the security that comes only in the absence of conflict, when reality can be faced without fear. But the dislocations of war and its aftermath challenge all of them.

The center for the enjoyment of these securities is the family, the basic social unit in our civilization. Anything that threatens the stability of the family exaggerates the demand for security or the neurotic rebellion against it. War enlarges the dream of the home. For many a long month there will have been practically no fireside without an empty chair. Both the boys and the folks at home yearn to restore the unity of the broken circle.

Home is taken for granted in normal times. The family is accepted like eating or laughter, or very quietly, like sleep. Until it's interrupted. Then all the need, the longing, the tears, the empty ache, turn to what was or could be.

In many places and in many ways war has ripped this portion of the social fabric beyond repair. People have grown apart. New friends, new ways of living, new and separate needs will take the place of the old. The child camp followers, the youngsters wandering the streets of Times Square and downtown Los Angeles, the rising level on the barometer of juvenile delinquency, are evidence of a destroyed security.

More marriages have been made by the war, many more than would otherwise have occurred. Yet the net gain in genuine marriage, in lasting relationships, may prove lower, the sociologist warns.

On the other hand, thousands of relationships will have gained real meaning because of the war. The personal ties usually taken for granted will, in some cases, under the impact of separation, develop a shading and a depth that might otherwise never have existed. The parent whose child has been desperately sick knows that the lonesome hours have changed something permanently and quite wonderfully.

Just as war itself has opened up a new sense of appreciation to some of the boys in uniform, some families will actually be helped by the dislocations of war. But they will weigh small in the balance.

The increasing skill and employability of women, the removal of hundreds of thousands of young men from the "eligible" group, the cross-country migrations of families or pieces of families, are changes which will tug and tear at a fragile entity. The estimated millions of American women for whom, by unavoidable arithmetic, marriage will not be available are another of the social strains under which we shall live for many a year.

Mere mathematics can frequently alter the course of history. The demand for security will be greater if only because America is becoming a nation of older people. In the short span of a decade, from 1930 to 1940, the average age rose two and a half years, and the tempo of that trend is increasing. Astute politicians will expect an increase in political conservatism. Psychologists will expect a greater demand for security. Naturally the stronghold of Townsend's old-age-pension scheme was in one of the two states that had the highest proportion of the aged.

There is, however, something much deeper and more likely to bring fundamental change in the United States than the disruption of family life or the increase of the aged. It existed before the war and has been enlarged by what the nation is passing through. There is a spiritual ache in America. The machine has made the difference. We have not yet learned to live with it even though we have learned to work with it.

Psychologists assigned to the fighting forces have noticed challenging phenomenon. Neurotic hysteria in war is actually least prevalent where you might expect it to be most prominent—in the air forces. The psychiatrist's thesis is that the morale and spirit of these men is higher because they have a greater sense of individual responsibility. The more mechanical and automatonlike the human being becomes, the greater is his "resort to primitive or at least socially inadequate reactions."

Dr. R. D. Gillespie, world-famous British psychiatrist, concludes that "the individual identifies himself with his job, which becomes a pivotal value for him. Psychoneurotic reactions to an occupation are likely only when the job or employer has come to be regarded as an enemy. Where a man can say 'I'm a doctor' or a carpenter or a solicitor, rather than 'I work in a bank' or in an office or in factory, psychoneurosis on occupational grounds is less likely." But one of the unavoidable characteristics of the rest of your life is the march toward the more impersonal employer, the more personal job, the less skilled occupation.

Much of the meaning of living has already escaped us. The practice of group murder by the dictators has developed in us a callousness to mass tragedy. Arthur Koestler pleads vainly that the world believe and be moved by the unparalleled barbarism and atrocities that occur in front of its unimpassioned face. More than elsewhere the people in America are untouched and impassive, for the war has struck no real emotional response. Max Lerner says: "I don't find among Americans the living sense of being a Pole, Russian,

Jew, Croat, or Serb in Europe today. Even after the Detroit riots I find little understanding of what it means to be a Negro in America today."

This absence of the larger feeling might seem to indicate that search for "meaning" or spiritual security is less pronounced than usual. Again the psychiatrist steps in and points out that he who can't love makes the most intensive, exaggerated, and least satisfactory search for affection; or, failing that, will expend his emotion in bitter denials of its existence.

This spiritual ache will grow more acute as unemployment rises, as the boom towns of war become the ghost towns of peace, and as the move to a less certain future begins. And for the jobless themselves, unemployment itself has a direct impact on psychic security. In family life the unemployment of the father seems to have a more disturbing effect upon the children than the actual death of a parent. Unemployment will involve more pain because many of the idle will have skills they never had before.

In more pious days dogma took care of the inevitable "search for meaning in human misfortune." *God's will* was once an adequate explanation for many who no longer accept it. *Human weakness* or *original sin* may satisfy some. But others will demand a theory more in keeping with the materialist and scientific temper of the times.

There is an inarticulate revolt against the pragmatic character of the day, but it will not contribute to a spiritual revival, for the instruments of organized religion have themselves been caught up in the whirlpool of "practicalism."

Men will band together to hide from themselves. To compensate for their spiritual hunger they will seek sustenance in groups.

But there will be a group loneliness in America, and separate blocs will increasingly ask, "Who represents us?" Even now the farmer feels neglected by his fellow citizens, deserted by his government, betrayed or forgotten by his President. Cityfolk are more provincial than ever. Labor is sensitive to public criticism and quick to say, "Slander!" The Midwest complains that it is under attack from every other section of the country. The South has recaptured its post-Civil War spirit of injured innocence, it is certain that it is misunderstood and maligned.

The National Opinion Research Center polled the public with this question: "In general, do you feel that the people in this country are taking the war seriously enough?" Fifty-four per cent said no. In other words, most Americans thought that most Americans didn't take the war seriously enough. Or, in still other words, many of that 54 per cent are actually saying, "Lonesome me. I'm the only one taking the war seriously."

Everybody is concerned about everybody else's morale, and Washington is apparently not satisfied with anybody's. The New York *Times* editorializes, "Perhaps even the majority of us feel superior to the majority of us."

It's funny, but it's also deadly serious. The group cohesions have become solid and promise to become more so. Eliot Janeway, in *Life* magazine, observed that "the farmers are hating labor with a perfectly unmatched ferocity. The farmers have made up their minds that they can't and won't live with labor. It will take another depression to shake their tragic stubbornness and show them they can't live without labor." They will have that depression, and the bitterness against labor will reach its peak before better years begin to cancel out the antagonisms. But not before the animosities will have left deep furrows in American culture.

Labor, too, has been developing a defensive group cohesiveness that increasingly threatens its own peace of mind and the welfare of the nation. A John L. Lewis leads the parade of those waving banners exalting group isolationism. Industry, in the meanwhile, is preparing to teach the boys a lesson or two—a lesson that will bring new violence into the arena of industrial relations.

Everybody's accusing everybody else of making money. Each group charges that the other is getting fat and is milking the nation.

In the interplay of economic and social relationships in America, hate will begin to displace the normal rivalry and contest as the driving force.

As the tensions grow and the resulting bitterness takes root, new disorders, of which we've had a foretaste in war, will disfigure the American scene. One of the contributions that Nazi Germany has made to the art of politics is the lesson that anti-Semitism pays. It is folly to pretend that Hitler has not driven home the point to the American demagogue, the ambitious leader, the local politician, the street-corner rabble-rouser, the editor of self-styled semi-religious journals. The scattered examples of public revulsion were hardly numerous enough to cancel out the increase in adherents to the groups selling their new Protocols of Zion.

Even when the war still provided some outlet for the frustrated emotions there were growing evidences of this retreat from reason. Prize-fighting Sergeant Barney Ross, a hero of the battle of Guadalcanal, appeared at a patriotic rally in Boston. Ross is a Jew, and was booed for that offense against the community. He rose and said, "I have learned to take the boos with the cheers. I have accepted my share of both of them. Tonight is no time to change." The crowd responded with cheers. Sportsmanship won out in Boston in 1944, but will it in 1945, 1946, 1947?

Minority religious sects, particularly the more active kind like Jehovah's Witnesses, are also in for a growing storm of resistance, some of it violent. Almost any community can find a minority whose life can be made miserable for the crime of deviation from the norm: the Poles on the North Side, the Mexicans across the tracks, the handful of Italians in the Slovene neighborhood, the Puerto Ricans down by the river. It's nothing new—only the passion and the violence will seem novel.

But the baiting of all other minorities will be overshadowed when we confront the most vulnerable target for violence in America—the Negro. The frayed temper which emerges from war, the will to retreat, the need for escape, the inquisitor's comfort in finding a scapegoat, will provide the fagots, but economic conflict will light the fire. The war has done more than the Emancipation Proclamation to give the Negro an economic place in America. But a nation which was reluctant to harness the Negro's energy at the workbench even in its manpower crisis will certainly press for a surrender of his new status when his presence becomes competitive. If we resented the Negro when we needed him, how will we feel when we don't need him?

"Watch out for the first symptoms of a shrinking economy,"

Dr. Louis Wirth, professor of sociology at the University of Chicago, warned the National Urban League. "Race tensions today are as nothing compared to what we may expect when the sirens blow and bells ring and peace comes again."

The problem will rack the nation and bring confusion even to those who seek to attain full citizenship for the Negro. The conflict between the "all-or-nothing" group and those who seek "one step at a time," the issue of gradualism or revolution, may, on its own level, develop a violence that will merely feed the larger social problem.

During World War I one and a half million Negroes came North and never went back. During World War II, in an atmosphere hardly as sanguine, that number is almost certain to be exceeded. One of the surprising developments has been a narrowing of the gap between Northern and Southern attitudes toward the Negro. A survey made by the United States Employment Service in January 1942, six months after the President's executive order prohibiting discrimination in war industries, indicated that 51 per cent of American industrialists did not and would not employ Negroes and that only a minor difference in percentages distinguished the employers of the North and South.

The relations between whites and Negroes in the United States will not remain a purely domestic matter. Hemispheric unity may be involved. In 1941 the then President of Haiti visited this country. After official receptions in Washington the Marine Band was asked to give him a farewell salute at the railway station when he left. The Southern leader of the band refused to be present but instructed the band as to what they were to play. He probably assumed that the "ignorant islander" wouldn't know the difference, and the President of Haiti, entering his train to the tune of "Bye, Bye, Blackbird," gave no sign that he did. But throughout the countries of the Caribbean and South America the story is mentioned whenever relations with the United States are discussed.

Here at home the antagonism will at first lead to accidental outbreaks, appearing in some localities as naturally as weeds in an untended garden. It will not be long, however, before the organizer appears. The local propaganda will be channelized, exploited, and fed by an ambitious group here and there, by the deliberate agitator, or by a corrupt municipal machine. Before they have spent themselves the disorders will become more widespread, more ambitious. National organizations will provide the literature, direct the drives for membership, systematically feed the furnaces of antagonism. The independent groups will then join hands in a "coordinating committee."

The Klan may prove small fry compared to some Exalted Order of the Hooded Knights of the White Camellia. Certainly there is reason to anticipate organizations of real magnitude. The prejudice and vehemence of the antagonisms will outstrip those which existed after 1919.

Many of our uprooted and delinquent youngsters will live in a daydream world of the old Wild West or seek to emulate the more recent jungle fighting of the Solomons. In the absence of Redskins or Japanese, they will find their own neighbors more accessible to attack.

The restrictions and repressions imposed by the war need outlets. Because hatred of the enemy was not so strong in this war as in the last, a larger amount of the criticism and grumbling was directed toward the political party in power. This deflection of aggression away from the government to the political party in power is a safety valve normally adequate in democracies. But the years ahead won't be times of normal pressure, and when the steam continues to rise, scapegoatism will be the next step. Scapegoatism is merely diverted aggression. It allows you to place the blame conveniently and safely.

Entire communities may be taken over by a localized fascism using the newly sharpened techniques that grew out of Europe's experience. It will not be called fascism, of course, except by its critics.

On a national scale, we are moving into a period of hectic activity by blocs, made more feasible by the split within both political parties, the possibility of a Republican majority in the House of Representatives and a Democratic majority in the Senate, with both majorities indecisive. Pressure groups will be able to dominate policy. Since the bloc is a combination of minority groups, the individual unit wields a disproportionate power in the community. Each, in respect to its major immediate demands, becomes the government, replacing the people as the source of authority. Government by bloc is the method by which minorities unite with other minorities to defeat the will of the majority.

A national fascism, however, reflected in a federal administration, seems unlikely in the foreseeable future. The federal government will not accept the philosophy expressed in these local manifestations. More likely it will resist these local manifestations—but not without difficulty.

America's heterogeneity may yet prove to be its best protection. The scapegoats will be diverse. The antipathies will not be nationally uniform, so that a permanent common ground will not exist. Antagonisms between the groups may cancel each other out. America, as a matter of fact, has a curious record of local intolerance and monolithic municipal government coincident with expanding democratic practice in federal government. Able builders of the democratic ideal have been placed in the White House on numerous occasions by little power-hungry bosses.

The extent and duration of the local and regional retreats are unpredictable. They will be determined by the depth of the people's need for escape. But the battle of retreat will start directly after war's end, and the forces of escape will have the advantages of the terrain.

Before war's end 30 per cent of America has already indicated its disapproval of the principle of the freedom of press. Three out of every ten of you believed that even in peacetime newspapers should not be allowed to criticize our form of government. But at that same moment when the passion for democratic expression becomes dull in some of you it will become brighter in others. The wind that blows out the fire may also serve to fan a brighter flame. From a passive, middle-of-the-road acceptance we move to both extremes. Liberty for all will be what it has always been—a passion felt by a very few. Will that passion be great enough? Will it obsess a sufficient number of you? There is tomorrow's largest and most ominous question mark.

The nation will come close to the brink of disaster. Only the threat of imminent ruin will be able to turn us back; only the grave peril will serve as the cathartic that can purge the social system.

And all because people want to "belong." For fear of the blackball, they blackball their neighbors. Self-protection is the shield of insecurity; it is also the sharp edge of the knife. Dr. Franz Alexander describes the self-protective mechanism as follows: "In order to justify internally one's own hostile aggressions, there is the tendency to attribute these aggressions to others: It is not that I hate *him*, it is not that I want to attack *him*, but he hates *me* and *he* wants to harm *me*. This projection necessarily leads to fear and mistrust of others, and eventually to hate and supposedly self-protective aggressions."

In the national ego, too, will be the same search for security to be effected by the same devices. True, America will no longer be a nation of isolationists; it will be a nation of ex-isolationists. The doctrine of 1784, George Washington's admonition on foreign policy so frequently re-echoed before Pearl Harbor, will not be heard so often at war's end. But it will take more than this war to make America internationally minded.

If you are asked, "Should we take an active part in world affairs?" at least 70 per cent of you will answer yes. "Do you want world peace?" An affirmative answer will be hurled back unanimously. Once again, though, it will be one thing to want and another to do. In the midst of the war that blasted the fallacy of isolation, almost as many people who favored participation in world affairs answered yes to the question, "Should we keep out foreign goods?"

When the passion for world collaboration was at its peak and a United Nations was a desperately necessary mechanism, 47 per cent of the public said that "America should become economically self-sufficient." The gap between idealistic attitudes and the specific measures to implement them was large during war and will become larger when the issues concern immediate, practical action.

The confusion between aspiration and reality is well illustrated by a Massachusetts referendum offered to the public during one of the war election years. It read, "Shall the representatives in the general court from this district be instructed to vote to request the

President and Congress to call at the earliest possible moment the convention of representatives of all free peoples to frame a constitution under which they may unite in a democratic world government?" The Massachusetts candidates for the Senate that year were Henry Cabot Lodge, isolationist, and Joseph Casey, supporter of the Administration's foreign policy. In one district the percentage who voted for Lodge was more than 85 per cent; the percentage in the same district who voted for the resolution was 75 per cent.

Attitude and action. At the end of World War I newspaper polls showed that the people were three to one for joining the League of Nations. We didn't join.

The ex-isolationism of America seems likely to find expression in a new form of American nationalism. The demands for permanent military bases are nationalistic. The demands for an alliance with Great Britain or with Great Britain and Russia, as an alternative to world association, are nationalist. Here's a mid-war reading on the gauge of nationalist pressure: 66 per cent of the people favored keeping out of foreign affairs and protecting our own interests with a large Army and Navy. Only 27 per cent of the people wanted international union with an international police force—the United States to be policed also. Twenty per cent of the people approved complete disarmament and equal sharing of resources. Twenty-eight per cent of the people were for admitting foreign goods without tariff, and the same number of people were willing to forget reparations from our enemies. This was mid-war. As peace becomes real and war more remote the motivations for unity and co-operation among the United Nations will weaken or disappear entirely.

Not least among America's international problems will be this country's position as an industrial power in a world which, both during and after the war, will be going through rapid and intensive industrialization. World competition, however, will actually prove less dangerous to the American economy than the emotional exploitation of our understandable fear. The position taken by Hugh Comer, president of the American Cotton Manufacturers Association, will be significant in the evolving fears of tomorrow: "We in the South are not in favor of giving machinery to lend-lease countries and then competing with it later on. In other words, we are

willing to share our milk with those who need milk, but we don't
believe we should be asked to give away the cow." To emphasize
his fear of the postwar perils that will result from retooling countries in need of American machinery, he exhibited two bolts of
chambray fabric, both identical in outward appearance. One, he
said, was made in a Southern cotton mill and the other in Japan just
before Pearl Harbor. The low price of the Japanese copy, said Mr.
Comer, had forced the American textile mill to shut down. How
immune will you be to economic nationalism of this kind when
employment levels fall? The will for national survival will burn
strong indeed in those early years to come.

The growing wartime respect for both Churchill and Stalin was
itself odd evidence of America's future nationalism. Those leaders
captured American imagination because they were speaking frankly
for national interest. A fantastic number of Midwesterners learned
to quote one sentence from Churchill: "I did not become the King's
first minister in order to preside over the liquidation of the British
Empire." Those few words spread across the American plains like
a prairie fire. And with each new move for the strengthening of
Soviet nationalism, Russia's Uncle Joe found new warmth and
acceptance in the American parlor.

In a world of Russia first, Empire first, Americans will want
America first. Dr. Haake invited a genuine American response
when he said, "Mr. Wallace suggested, a while ago, that every man,
woman, and child in the world ought to have a quart of milk every
day. Of course it wouldn't work in China, because to them milk is
poison. The only way we could get those guys to get milk is to use
a stomach pump on the reverse angle. Henry Wallace is a glorious
fellow, honest, sincere. Of course he didn't make a very great go
of it out of his own business." And Dr. Haake hit the climax in his
world exploration when he concluded: "Now Adolph Berle thinks
he's going to make the Arabs eat with knives and forks. He has another guess coming. Those guys are going to continue to stick their
arms in up to the elbows when they have a feast. That is the way
they like it and that is the way they're going to do it."

The response will be by no means unanimous. In the course of
the war America will have learned about the world in which it

lives. Teheran, Makin, Stalingrad, Chungking will be real places for many who couldn't pronounce them before. There will still be cynical laughter when someone talks about the Chinese drinking milk, but hundreds of thousands of American boys will bring home the profound discovery that the Chinese actually do drink milk. They will know that Hottentots, Arabs, and Zulus are more than names. The war has taught us to accept our Allies, to respect and admire some of their ways and all of their fortitude. But insecurity has led us to suspicions too. And when it's all over, will we have found that whole world so much of a headache, so great a problem, so much of a danger, that we shall seek to make a planet of our own with a twenty-foot wall around us?

War does make us think of causes, and we do want to change them. From our own uneasy consciences come some of the largest promises, and then war is over and few of the things we said would happen actually do—at least by themselves. There will be two alternatives: either to make them happen or to become disillusioned. Will the idealism engendered by this war actually survive it? Or will the postwar literature again be filled with the language of disgust and self-deprecation?

We are brought back sharply to the wish to be let alone, the trust that things will work themselves out. We fall again into the human failing, particularly in periods of stress, that looks for the easy way out and is disappointed when it doesn't find it. One of the Army chaplains became quite disturbed by the effect of those startling instances of men in battle zones who in an hour of desperate agony prayed for deliverance and were miraculously saved, the shipwrecked men on rafts whose prayers to God were answered. His concern was for the many whose anxious pleas bring no awe-inspiring solution, and so he appointed himself the shepherd of those who pray and are not saved.

More than the wish will be necessary to unravel some of the problems ahead. Those who just drop a coin into the wishing well should not be surprised if the only reward is a splash in the face. But they *will* be surprised. War is the tortured patient who promises before the operation that he will pay the surgeon any fee for survival. "Money's no object, Doctor"—until recovery. How difficult then to recapture the desperation and the sincerity of the promise!

Those who have relied on the wish will feel that the war has let them down.

The realities at home will begin to crowd in. The injustices inevitable in mass demobilization, the complex confusion of reconversion, the impenetrable difficulties which flow from the government-owned property, the tussle between inflationary and deflationary forces, the struggle against the rising wave of unemployment, the heartbreak that follows shrinking production, the agony of unused plants, the aimless march back to forgotten communities, the bitter look in the Negro's eyes, the multitude of "down-with" soapboxes, the split in government, and the pressure by self-seeking blocs.

These and a thousand others will be there begging to be faced foursquare. So will the returning veterans. Large groups of them will remain in the big cities, some because they are restless, some attracted to city lights and craving excitement after the strain of their war experiences. Others will hope to better themselves by obtaining jobs at higher wages in the urban industrial centers. Occasionally you will see them in strikes and riots.

The first wave of civic welcomes, parades, and banquets will be over. The newly set up employment offices, particularly at first, will grind slowly. The return to the old job or the search for a new one will be harried by many difficulties. Editorials will remind the public more stridently that returning soldiers expect something more substantial than a cordial welcome and empty promises. The contest between men and women for the place at the workbench will draw heat in isolated places. Salary levels will begin to drop. An occasional soldier will be found on a street corner selling a "Welcome Home" sign. Others will start house-to-house canvassing in their uniforms.

And the world will still be with us. The instances were few during war in which the individual nations refused to subordinate their less acceptable aspirations. Of course there was occasional recrimination, a little undercover feeling each other out to see whether anyone would make a separate peace. But compared to what will follow the war, the big boys really were one happy family. Almost with the very hour of war's end the wrangling will start.

The Russians' march across the face of Europe was of military advantage to us during war. But will they be able to move another inch without re-exciting the prewar American suspicions?

The repressed Chinese antagonism toward the British will burst forth with fresh vehemence when the war is terminated. Stories that were suppressed during the war will not improve their feelings toward each other or our feelings toward them.

The dying embers of collective security will be replaced by the blaze of a new venture into power politics. Idealism is never nourished by power politics, even when it successfully keeps the peace. Many will have been made so dizzy by the shifting diplomatic angles and the variants brought on by military expediency that they just won't try to make sense of it any more. Darlan and Badoglio will have been only the first. It's upsetting to have your nation's press lavish articles on a General Mihailovich only to follow with the revelation that he was really little better than the enemy and that General Tito is the genuine Yugoslav ally.

The bubbling volcano that will be Europe for many years following World War II will make many in America wonder what the shooting was for or about and how we ever got into it.

The congressional investigations, with their disclosures of war profits, industrial chicanery, administrative fumbling, bungling, and just plain fraud, will eat away the spirit and distract the mind and the will from the larger causes and problems.

Our good neighbors will seem no more democratic than they ever were. England's march to the left and Russia's march toward Asia will disturb and worry us. The drum beaters will play up both for all they're worth. The confidence in peace itself will ultimately decline. And then, in sharp contrast with the mood that followed World War I, America will start preparing for the next war.

All of these realities will be like so many hammers hitting against your head the morning after. And in a hang-over despair we will begin to dose ourselves with mental nostrums. Disillusion, apathy, and "make hay" will take over. We will then face one of the saddest effects of war and of all such periods of strain. In applying our own strength for victory, so great an effort did we make, so much of our energy and our heart and our resources did we use, that we will long to relax. We will look forward eagerly to a spiritual, physical, and emotional vacation. We will want to run away.

War is a heart attack. The shock, the pain, and the fear of death may be so great that the patient, on his survival, may rush to enjoy all the pleasures of the life that was threatened, to enjoy them quickly and irresponsibly. When that happens to the individual he can expect another attack. If it happens to an entire nation, it can expect another war.

The "make-hay" psychology will be both the most immediate cultural impact of the war and the greatest threat to our ever winning it. To really "make hay" the war must be cast aside, the blame must be placed elsewhere. The problems must be shunted and the buck passed. There will be no time for illusions. Illusions got us into the whole mess. It will take years to learn that disillusion is a dread disease second to war itself. And postwar disillusion will be next to impossible to detect; it will masquerade in the garments of "brutal reality," "blunt, cold truth," "hard-boiled fact."

No matter what action is taken, it will appear that America has bungled the peace. No matter what victory will be accomplished, it will be incomplete. No matter how small the unfulfilled promise, fulfillment will seem even smaller. The new youth will turn away not only from the settlement of the war, but from the values of a world that permitted it to happen.

It won't be hard to poke fun at the speeches, the movies, the plays, the radio programs that followed Pearl Harbor. And the sophists won't find it hard to minimize the menace that confronted the nation before and after Pearl Harbor, even to argue that it was folly to defend ourselves.

The disillusion that followed World War I is frequently attributed to the inept and fruitless handling of the peace. The incompetence of national leadership only aggravated the disillusion that had already begun to eat into the people. Even before the Senate's rejection of the Versailles Treaty, F. Scott Fitzgerald's *This Side of Paradise* had captured the spirit of the twenties and won the lavish praise of the critics. Sinclair Lewis also was recording it in the manuscript of *Main Street* before the "wilful men" had completed their work.

Maxwell Anderson may well revise *What Price Glory*. He will have a ready audience and he'll come closer to the spirit of 1948 with his 1924 play than he did to the spirit of 1944 with his 1944 play.

Prepare for a multitude of "Utopias" to be offered to those who can't take the blood and guts of some new Hemingway. The same person is often a customer for both. A dash of Hemingway to cancel out the illusions of the past and a dash of Blank with his easy, irrefutable pattern for a perfect future. Both are refugees from present reality.

So, too, will be the multitude of lodges, clubs, societies, orders, movements. Some will serve a useful function—charitable, civic, political. Others will have value if only because they will let you, and many others like you, work out your frustration in a gaudy costume as you parade in splendor on the Atlantic City boardwalk. Still others will be the instruments of the revolt against reason itself.

Restrictions and deprivations will not end with the war, and there will then be no *external* foe to hate. The result: greater political dissension, more pressure groups, more government by bloc. Feelings lifted to a high emotional pitch will seek new objects for hate—enemies within. Sharp cleavages will begin to appear between men and women, ex-servicemen and civilians, older workers and younger workers, native born and foreign born, white and black, Jew and Gentile, business and labor.

The rigidity of each of these alignments will depend primarily on one question: How much employment? Increased tension, discrimination, and intolerance are inevitable. Their magnitude and violence are in the lap of the economic gods.

The more complex, the more acute, the less comfortable the economic environment becomes, the more strident will be the witchhunters in America. Each little group with its own little ax will hunt its own private little victim. And the chase will not only mean street fights. When a staid professional group like the New York Medical Society distributes a leaflet attacking the extension of medical insurance and government sponsorship of medical care, we see a traditional economic conflict in operation. But when in the course of that conflict the author of the legislation is called the "German-born Senator Wagner," medicos are using the hatchet, not the scalpel. Reason is replaced by venom—argument by force.

The struggle between frustration and intelligence will fill the rest of your life. Before your span is ended it will have boiled over violently more than once. War itself will be difficult to prevent for more than a generation. In some forms and in some places this war will not really have come to an end.

The world is approaching a series of revolutionary struggles between freedom and security. Perhaps out of them will yet come the amalgam combining both precious metals and providing the flexible, permanent base on which peace and a just reality can rest.

America approaches the future with a physical and material strength unmatched by any country. It enters tomorrow with the resources of mind and science ready to be harnessed to the demands of an expanding life.

America proceeds into the future with more than a measure of respect and friendship from the world's great and exhausted powers.

America will hit the shoals of unemployment and free itself. It will rub along the reefs of depression and then reach new levels of production. It will run afoul of the weeds of native fascism, spawned in the morass of retreat, frustration, and fear.

"That we are in conflict is to the good," says philosopher Charles Morris, "for tension is necessary to the greatest achievement. Stalemated tension, however, engenders frustration and anxiety, while integrated tension unlocks creative achievement. A frustrated, anxious, and neurotic America is one possibility; a liberated, expansive, confident America is the other. To prevent the former and to achieve the latter is our responsibility."

You start the rest of your life with no real enemies—except you!

Index

Index